Rescue Archeology

Rescue Archeology

Proceedings of the Second New World Conference on Rescue Archeology

Edited by Rex L. Wilson

Organization of American States
Southern Methodist University

Southern Methodist University Press

First edition, 1987
Requests for permission to reproduce material from this work
should be sent to:
>   Permissions
>   Southern Methodist University Press
>   Box 415
>   Dallas, Texas 75275

Library of Congress Cataloging-in-Publication Data

New World Conference on Rescue Archeology (2nd :
  1984 : Dallas, Tex.)
  Rescue archeology.

  "Held in Dallas, Texas from November 15–17, 1984"—Pref.

  1. Salvage archeology—America—Congresses.
I. Wilson, Rex L.   II. Organization of American
States.   III. Southern Methodist University.
IV. Title.
CC77.S36N48   1984   930.1'028   87-4530
ISBN 0-87074-220-5

Designed by Whitehead & Whitehead

61,715

Contents

Preface

As explained in *Rescue Archeology*, the Organization of American States, the National Trust for Historic Preservation, and the organizers of the First New World Conference on Rescue Archeology expected that the week-long meeting in Quito would positively influence national and international attitudes and policies affecting the world's archeological resources. We know that a well conceived, funded, and publicly supported rescue archeology program is especially important to the developing nations of the Western Hemisphere and the island nations of the Caribbean. The First New World Conference on Rescue Archeology ended with the adoption of the following recommendations:

1. THAT each government through its normal process for planning governmental projects or reviewing privately funded developments should insure that, at the very earliest planning stage, it be determined whether and to what degree each project will affect archeological resources.

If it is determined that archeological resources may be affected, consideration will be given to avoiding and otherwise protecting them.

If the archeological resources cannot be preserved *in situ*, their significance shall be determined in the broadest possible scientific context. If it is deemed that the information which may be lost is important, then funding for appropriate recovery, analysis, and publication and other public presentation of that information will be provided as an integral part of the project funding and scheduled at the earliest practical stage in the development of the project.

2. THAT the importance of our cultural heritage be responsibly and assiduously communicated to the public by every means available.

3. THAT concern for and understanding of our cultural heritage be incorporated into education at all levels through formal courses, exhibitions, and extra-curricular activities.

4. THAT university courses in archeology be expanded to include practical training in the objectives and techniques of rescue archeology and cultural resource management.

5. THAT an understanding of the methods, objectives, and techniques of archeology be introduced into the training of architects, engineers, planners, and others whose professional activities may have a direct or indirect effect upon our cultural heritage.

6. THAT archeological museums organize exhibitions which encourage the preservation of our cultural heritage as an urgent necessity and establish education programs designed to inform the public about the objectives and results of rescue archeology.

7. THAT American nations enact laws to protect archeological remains, where necessary, or consider the issuance of regulations, decrees, or specific provisions on rescue archeology.

8. THAT the governments of those countries with specific agencies responsible for the development of scientific research take into account the need for rescue archeology and propose and coordinate rescue archeology plans with institutions qualified to carry out rescue archeology projects.

9. THAT the Organization of American States include in the agenda for the next meeting of the Interamerican Council for Education, Science and Culture a topic on development planning and cultural preservation and insure that experts in the preservation field participate in the meeting.

10. THAT closer international cooperation in the rescue archeology field be established.

11. THAT all governments cooperate closely to combat illicit traffic in cultural property by concluding bilateral agreements that cover artifacts as well as monumental antiquities; by ratifying the UNESCO Convention (adopted by the General Conference of UNESCO on 14 November 1971) and the San Salvador Convention (adopted under the auspices of the OAS in 1976) as a means of prohibiting and preventing the illicit import, export, and transfer of ownership of cultural property.

12. Finally, given the positive achievements of this First New World Conference on Rescue Archeology, it is recommended to the institutions concerned with the problems of rescue archeology, especially the Organization of American States, to cooperate in organizing a second conference which will emphasize those specific aspects that could not be dealt with at this first meeting because of its general nature.

Much positive activity was carried out by Western Hemisphere governments following the conference, but much remained to be done. Some of the unfinished business from the Quito meeting was addressed during the Second New World Conference on Rescue Archeology, which was organized to pursue the principal objectives relative to archeology and historic preservation in the Western Hemisphere. One objective was to identify and attack the nagging and long-standing deficiencies in archeological programs being carried out in large public works projects. The second was to stimulate a higher level of consciousness and feeling of public responsibility for threatened cultural resources in North, Central, and South America and in the Caribbean Islands.

Sponsored by the Organization of American States and the National Science Foundation, the second meeting was held in Dallas, Texas, from November 15–17, 1984. Co-hosts were Southern Methodist University and the Southwestern Division, U.S. Army Corps of Engineers. Participants included business leaders, international financiers, and government administrators; construction engineers, designers, and builders; environmentalists, archeologists, and historic preservationists. Major decision makers participated in the several round table discussions. The program was designed to promote frank and open discussion, which can lead to cooperation and mutual understanding of the peculiar problems presented when a nation undertakes to protect and preserve the cultural heritage of its people.

In designing the first conference held in Ecuador, the organizers took care to identify the general archeological situation in the Caribbean and Central and South America, recognizing that most Western Hemisphere nations are currently in a rescue mode with regard to archeological investigations in large public works projects. The organizers considered the fact that most archeological work being conducted in the New World today, as it was thirty years ago, is in direct response to such projects undertaken at public expense. As true now as in the immediate postwar years, the alternative to "rescue" or "salvage" archeology is loss of the data base without study. Although the United States, for example, has legislated recognition, significance, and protection, and has provided more funding, work continues in a rescue mode—archeologists have no real choice other than to react to situations in which others decide where and when archeological work will take place and how much will be done.

The Second New World Conference on Rescue Archeology also recognized that most nations of Central and South America are several years behind the United States and Canada in the development of national archeological programs. Given the economic and social problems that exist in the greater part of the hemisphere, it can be assumed that many years will pass before many of those nations progress beyond "rescue archeology." The substantial costs of holding the Second New World Conference on Rescue Archeology were underwritten by the Organi-

zation of American States; the National Science Foundation; Southern
Methodist University; the U.S. Army Corps of Engineers; the U.S. Bureau of Reclamation; the U.S. Department of Transportation (Federal
Highway Administration); the U.S. National Park Service; the Smithsonian Institution; the Owens Foundation; Woodward-Clyde Consultants; the Gilmore Foundation; the Advisory Council on Historic
Preservation; and the National Trust for Historic Preservation. Without their support, the conference would not have been held.

We are pleased to acknowledge the very good help of the Dallas
Archeological Society; they played a major role and contributed in many
ways to the success of the meeting. Financial and logistical assistance
was given by the Dallas Chapter of the Archaeological Institute of
America, the Texas Archeological Society, and the Council of Texas Archeologists.

There were 171 registered participants, about 70 of whom were archeologists or historic preservationists; more than 40 registrants were
engineers, planners, or administrators. Approximately 30 attendees
represented countries other than the United States: Mexico, the United
Kingdom, Guatemala, Peru, Ecuador, Brazil, Argentina, Venezuela,
Costa Rica, Australia, Canada, the Federal Republic of Germany,
Panama, Jamaica, Honduras, Colombia, Chile, and Puerto Rico.

At the close of the Friday morning session, a special ceremony was
held to honor nine distinguished scholars who have made outstanding contributions to the cause of rescue archeology in the Western Hemisphere. Those receiving awards were Ignacio Bernal, J. O. Brew, Carl
Chapman, Alberto Rex González, Emil W. Haury, Fred Johnson, José
Luis Lorenzo, Charles R. McGimsey III, and Waldo Wedel.

The final session, moderated by José Luis Lorenzo, consisted of a
summary of the major results of the meeting. Participants were those
who had moderated the several discussion groups. The session concluded with the adoption of a series of formal resolutions, which are
presented in part six of this volume.

No system of measurement can quantify the work that went into
holding the conference and ensuring its success. As co-chairmen, Gloria
Loyola-Black and I are indebted to Fred Wendorf and Larry Banks for
their magnificent efforts in Dallas. Many others were personally involved
and to all of them we say thank you very much.

Carlos Baied, an Argentine attending the University of Colorado,
transcribed and translated much of the Spanish discussion into English. We are pleased to acknowledge his authoritative help.

Editing the proceedings was a monumental task; the most pains-taking, laborious, and generally difficult part was handled by Susan Wilson. She transcribed the entire conference as recorded on the cassettes and prepared a first draft for preliminary editing. She identified speakers and committed to writing every utterance, making no distinction between the profound and the inane. We are deeply indebted to her for her exacting work.

Where do we go from here? By its nature, archeology—and rescue archeology in particular—is an evolving process. We can adopt a policy of triage, saving only the most significant sites and monuments that are in the most urgent danger and that can be immediately funded. We can continue to stimulate governments to identify, protect, and preserve elements of their national patrimony and to provide all possible assistance. Or we can simply give up, sit back, and allow development to continue with no real consideration for the preservation and protection of our cultural heritage.

The latter option is not ours to choose; we cannot and will not do nothing. To this end, we are planning the Third New World Conference on Rescue Archeology to be held in Venezuela in 1987. In our view, rescue archeology represents, in a broader view, the thought of Lester Brown when he said, "We have not inherited the earth from our fathers; we are borrowing it from our children."

Rex L. Wilson
Editor

Rescue Archeology

Opening Remarks

Fred Wendorf, General Chairman
  Department of Anthropology, Southern Methodist University

Donald Shields
  President, Southern Methodist University

Robert J. Dacey
  Brigadier General, U.S. Army Corps of Engineers

Ray Barnhart
  Administrator, Federal Highway Administration

Gloria Loyola-Black
  Department of Cultural Affairs, Organization of American
  States

Ann Guthrie
  Executive Director, Cultural Property Advisory Committee to
  the President of the United States

FRED WENDORF
I wish to bring the Second New World Conference on Rescue Archeology to order.

DONALD SHIELDS
Ladies and gentlemen, it is indeed a great pleasure this morning to welcome you to the Second New World Conference on Rescue Archeology and to bring you greetings from Southern Methodist University, the host and cosponsor for this important conference. SMU is very proud to be your host for these meetings. We are most appreciative, as I'm sure you can all understand, of the work of our faculty members: Fred Wendorf, Richard Rubottom, and Michael Collins, of the organizing committee. We are also deeply gratified with the caliber of cosponsors and

supporters for this conference, including, among others, the Organization of American States, the National Science Foundation, several United States Government agencies, and the Smithsonian Institution, as well as a number of private firms and foundations. We are also very pleased with the number and quality of visitors the conference has attracted. Particularly, we would like to welcome those representatives from other nations. We invite you to enjoy not only the hospitality of our University but also that of our dynamic and vibrant City of Dallas.

The response the conference has received from sponsors as well as from participants—at least from my perspective as a scientist, not an archeologist, not an anthropologist, but a chemist, interested very much in archeology—underscores the importance of the issues that will be addressed over these three days. It underscores the dual commitment, if you like, that all of us share: a commitment to the further development of all our nations for the benefit of our peoples, to the preservation of our cultural heritage, and to the enhancement of our understanding of those who preceded us. These concerns transcend purely disciplinary boundaries; that is very clear from the representation in this room. They involve not only the archeologist but also the developer, the builder, the legislator, the government official, the planner, and the informed citizenry. And as I understand it, this conference is the first international meeting in which representatives from all these different areas have been brought together for the exchange, for the dynamic exchange, of ideas concerning the recovery of scientific data from endangered prehistoric and historic sites throughout the Western Hemisphere.

So, on behalf of the University, let me wish you a most productive and enjoyable conference. And let me invite you, if your schedules permit, to spend some time visiting our campus. We are proud of it and of the work we do at SMU, and we'd be more than happy to share our enthusiasm for the University with you.

ROBERT J. DACEY

It's a rare privilege to have an opportunity to address the group gathered here this morning, one that represents such a diversity of interests. And although we have had a diversity of interest in the past, I think we now have a common focus and a common interest in what we are going to talk about in this conference: rescue archeology.

First, on behalf of the U.S. Army Corps of Engineers and General Heiberg, the Chief of Army Engineers, and particularly on behalf of the Southwestern Division, which I represent here in the southwestern part of the United States, we welcome all of the attendees to Dallas, and particularly our distinguished colleagues who are visiting from other nations.

The term *rescue archeology* is relatively new. It seems to have evolved from the old terms of *salvage* or *emergency archeology*, which we used several years ago. In simple terms, rescue archeology can be summarized as an attempt to bring engineers, planners, policy makers, and archeologists together to deal with issues of protecting, preserving, and if necessary, rescuing the sites and monuments of our past during the planning, design, and construction of public works.

Now that might have been a neat statement written by somebody to present this morning. But in actuality, I was quoting from J. O. Brew's statement of objectives, written for the Interagency Archeological Salvage Program in the United States when it was formed immediately after World War II. Since the program began in the forties it has undergone the typical evolution of a relatively new discipline in the planning process. The first step, of course, was to make the professionals who represent that discipline part of the planning team.

During the fifties and sixties we included archeologists as part of the planning team. But they didn't have any clout. They did not have the statutory authority to step in and demand equal consideration for the archeological and historical values while we were considering the economic and engineering aspects. Consequently, we did not reach the level of professionalism that all of us would have liked.

You could ask the question, "Why is a soldier addressing this group here this morning?" Well, the study of the profession of arms is the study of history. Every soldier must continually review history because, as in the trite phrase, "if you don't study history, you're doomed to repeat it." We study history because the more we can learn about what exactly happened in some particular event, the better we can lead men in the profession of arms should that day ever come.

We have reached a level of professionalism, I think, on the archeological and historical side today in which the archeologist, as part of our planning team, is a full professional member, with his aspect of that planning given the same weight and consideration as any other. By identifying the archeological aspects early on, including them in all our engineering considerations, and assuring that adequate resources are programmed to meet our archeological and historical responsibilities during the initial phases of projects, we have begun to achieve some of the goals that Brew envisioned. Legislation has helped. But I think the maturing of the professional side of archeology is more the determining cause.

We have not reached the ultimate level. I guess we'll have reached full maturity when every engineer, as part of his engineering curriculum, is required to take courses in archeology, and when every engineer fully understands the responsibilities of the engineer and the architect to archeological values and to the profession of archeology. We now require engineers and architects to take courses in geology because in addressing the geotechnical aspect of a project, one needs at least a working knowledge of geology. We've got to push to get that same level of recognition for archeology; the well-rounded, well-grounded engineer and architect must also have a working knowledge of the field and the resource. That is not to say that the engineer should expect to do the professional job that archeologists do, but rather that he can participate more fully with archeologists as part of a planning team.

Although we've learned some things here in the United States, we don't offer what we've learned as a model because we've made a lot of mistakes. We don't need to repeat those mistakes nor do you. During the next few days we will explain how we got to where we are and where we want to go. We hope you will borrow from us anything you think could be useful to you. We hope also that you'll critique where we think we are and where we think we're going, and give us the benefit of your expertise to improve our programs in the future.

RAY BARNHART

We do support your efforts today. We have a true sensitivity to archeological preservation and data recovery, and a sensitivity to the quality of the environment. We became involved in archeology some thirty years ago. In New Mexico, Fred Wendorf took the lead in involving the Federal Highway Administration in archeology. Because of the joint efforts of the then Bureau of Public Roads (now the Federal Highway Administration) and the state of New Mexico, we now have legislation that permits other states to become involved in archeological data recovery. In the sixties and seventies the program was sort of catch-as-catch-can. During those years, we were at the eleventh hour when encountering something of significance and attempting to deal with it. But we have progressed; we have become a more enlightened society. Our efforts today are part of an orderly planning process in which we look at where roads and public works shall be, we try to anticipate the presence of prehistoric and historic data of scientific value that should be recovered, and we make plans to preserve cultural resources, to circumvent them, or at least to record them so that we can retain as much as possible of the rich heritage that is ours.

We have permitted the states great latitude in establishing their own efforts. Here in Texas, for example, we have eleven archeologists involved in our cultural resources program. Although they are doing an excellent job, our archeological work is not consistently excellent across the country. For we do have highs and lows in involvement with and sensitivity to this area among our many states. We are hopeful that a new awareness and a new sensitivity to that which is important will permeate the engineering field such that other states will emulate the efforts of New Mexico, Ohio, West Virginia, and Texas. We have made great strides in many states; we are especially proud of the bridge study effort in Ohio and the recording of those bridges. The work of the Corps has been outstanding in historic preservation, and those efforts will be eligible for federal participation through the Federal Aid Highway Program.

The purpose of this conference is not only to examine the successes but also to look at the ongoing program—to review the goals we should have and to examine the shortcomings of our current efforts, where they can be improved and how we might improve them. While we are making great strides in identifying and conserving our cultural heritage, some of our preservation efforts do not appear to be as productive or as honest as most of us would like them to be. Some of the laws that were designed to protect our environmental heritage are being used and abused by a handful of people; they are not being used to preserve the finest part of our heritage but simply are being used to obstruct and to deny, on selected bases, necessary projects. In many cases there has been a totally callous disregard for the value of what we have discovered and protected and a disregard for the total cost involved. And when we have a callous disregard for cost effectiveness and worthwhileness of that which we would preserve, we alienate public opinion and undermine the cause we seek to serve.

Very seldom in the work archeologists do is there a mention of cost. Cost has not seemed to be a great factor among many people. But I am terribly concerned about cost. When I look at conditions around this country today, I look at some 280,000 bridges that are structurally and functionally deficient—facilities that are needed in order to maintain our commerce and our quality and way of life—and I am concerned about cost. At the same time, I am concerned that we do in fact pre-

xxii / OPENING REMARKS

serve the finest of our cultural heritage. But I plead that we should be able to define more clearly what is good and desirable, what should be preserved, and what someone simply desires to preserve not because it has long-term meaning or value, but simply because it is something that is as old as you or I might be.

The thing that concerns me most is that the legitimacy of what you want to accomplish is diminished, is challenged, because so often when we encounter something that people believe should be preserved, we find that professional archeologists, professional preservationists, place no true value on that particular thing. And so those critics who would deny a legitimate historic preservation program will seize upon those exceptions to discredit the entire preservation movement. This is one of the real challenges we face, not just in the area of archeology but in the area of all our environment.

In Washington, money has no value. It is only a commodity to be used to accomplish things. So let us more clearly define our goals. We in the Federal Highway Administration will most sincerely work with you to support your goals and to make a more meaningful program a reality.

Thank you for inviting me here. I am most anxious to find out what you professionals will arrive at, what kind of counsel you will give us, what standards you will establish in order to gauge the merit of that which we would preserve. I look forward to seeing the results of your discussions.

FRED WENDORF
Thank you very much, Mr. Barnhart. Yours was precisely the type of address and consideration that we hope will be forthcoming during this conference.

This conference is going to be a little different from the traditional meetings of archeologists and those of other professionals. We have attempted to bring together people who are directly affected by rescue archeology and cultural preservation programs throughout the New World—the administrators, the managers, and the engineers, together with the archeologists—to discuss, on an equal and free exchange basis, the problems we face in trying to preserve our cultural heritage, to discuss not in a confrontational setting but in an environment in which each of us is seeking an appropriate solution.

GLORIA LOYOLA-BLACK
I am happy to bring you this message from the Secretary General of the Organization of American States, Joao Clemente Baena Soares, to the Second New World Conference on Rescue Archeology:

I take particular pleasure in addressing this message to those who organized the Second New World Conference on Rescue Archeology, and to those attending the conference. I regret that I am unable to be with you in person in Dallas, but I can assure you that in spirit, I share your concerns.

It was an honor for the General Secretariat of the Organization of American States to have sponsored the First Conference in Quito, Ecuador, in 1981. The success of this significant professional and institutional exchange at the hemisphere-wide level was unprecedented in the field of archeology.

Since then, we have been and continue to be eager to promote as many activities as we can to strengthen and safeguard our historical past. The protection of our common heritage is but a reaffirmation of the principle set forth in Article 3 of the Charter of the Organization of American States, which notes that "the spiritual unity of the Continent is based on respect for the cultural values of the American countries and requires their close cooperation for the high purposes of civilization." We give life to this mandate when we point out that development inevitably produces physical changes that affect our heritage, and that that impact must be understood at the highest policy-making levels.

By inviting to this meeting the government sectors that are most directly involved in the planning, financing, and execution of development projects, we are seeking to produce the interaction that is so essential to rescue archeology. We therefore have a vital interest in the outcome of this new dialogue, looking to the possibility of future action in this new dimension that we are just beginning to explore.

May I wish you every success in your deliberations, and express the hope that they will bear fruit in concrete and forward-looking actions.

ANN GUTHRIE
I am proud to share with you an important development in the United States that has occurred since the First New World Conference on Rescue Archeology in 1981. During the last year and a half, the United States Congress has passed, and President Reagan has signed, legislation implementing the 1970 UNESCO Convention on a means of prohibiting and preventing the illicit import, export, and transfer of ownership of cultural properties. With this act, the United States joins fifty-two other countries in an international effort to protect endangered cultural treasures. It has pledged to take steps to combat illicit trade of such materials in international commerce. The United States is the first major art-importing country to implement this convention. And the United States

has pledged to meet its obligations under this convention regardless of the status of its membership in UNESCO.

The United States is concerned with assisting other signatory countries in the protection of their archeological and ethnological materials that are part of their cultural patrimony and that are in danger from pillage. Also, the new statute denies entry into the United States of any inventoried item of cultural property that has been stolen from a museum, monument, or related institution in a signatory country. To obtain United States protection for endangered archeological or ethnological materials, a country is required to request assistance and to enter a specific bilateral or multilateral agreement with the United States. If it is an emergency, the United States may provide unilateral assistance upon request. Under such agreements or in an emergency, the United States will impose import controls on designated items or categories of items. To be able to provide such assistance, the President must make foredetermination. To assist the President in assessing the need and urgency of a request, a Cultural Property Advisory Committee was established. It is housed at the United States Information Agency for Administration and Technical Support. The committee consists of eleven private citizens who represent the interests of archeology, anthropology, ethnology, the museum community, commercial dealers in art, and members of the general public. There are three archeologists on the committee: Fred Wendorf of SMU, Clemency Coggins of Harvard University and the Peabody Museum, and Leslie Wildeson, who is now the Colorado State Archeologist and Vice President of the Colorado Historical Society.

It is the committee's responsibility to review each request for assistance and to prepare a report for the President, setting forth recommendations as to whether the United States should impose import restrictions on designated archeological or ethnological materials. If the committee recommends U.S. action and the President agrees, the United States then enters negotiations for an agreement with the requesting country. The U.S. Customs Service is involved in the negotiations. Such agreements run five years and can be extended for five years.

The United States took a different approach with regard to stolen cultural property. Since 1983, any item of cultural property that has been documented as belonging to a museum, etc., located in one of the signatory countries, has been prohibited entry into the United States. The United States has pledged to assist in the return of stolen cultural property. Enforcement of the law is the responsibility of the U.S. Customs Service.

Passage of this law and the establishment of the Cultural Property Advisory Committee is a noteworthy accomplishment for the United States. We look forward to seeing that the United States plays an active role in preserving cultural treasures that are of importance not only to the countries from which they originate but also to all of us in our understanding of mankind's common heritage.

Keynote Address

Galo Plaza
   Former President of Ecuador and Former Secretary General of
   the Organization of American States

GALO PLAZA
I want to thank President Donald Shields for inviting me to give the keynote address at the Second New World Conference on Rescue Archeology. It is a high honor indeed.

I am not an archeologist; therefore, there is not much of a contribution I can make from a scientific point of view. But I have always been interested in and fascinated with the discoveries of the mysteries of the past through archeological investigation, and I have been actively connected with the "Programa de Antropología para el Ecuador."

The reason I accepted this responsibility is because I sincerely believe I am in a position to focus attention, beyond scientific circles, on the negative impact that large-scale economic development has on prehistoric and historic remains and particularly to enhance the awareness of this problem among those responsible for administering these projects in Latin America. We must take some bold steps now to find a way to preserve more of our past, because the next few years are certain to witness an enormous and irreversible loss of our cultural heritage.

The First New World Conference that took place in Quito in May 1981 reported that almost nothing is being done in most of Latin America to preserve our prehistoric heritage. This situation must be corrected.

The First New World Conference made twelve concrete recommendations to promote international communication and cooperation among planners, developers, and those primarily concerned with the preservation of the historic and prehistoric cultural heritage of the Americas. The conference concluded by recommending a second meeting to continue what had been so successfully launched in Quito. This is now being inaugurated under the best of auspices here on the campus of Southern Methodist University.

We are fortunate to have assembled at this conference not only an impressive number of the outstanding scholars involved in rescue and conservation of archeological resources throughout the hemisphere, but also a good representation of concerned planners and managers from the public and private sectors. I am optimistic that from this meeting of minds, clear guidelines may emerge for solving some of the monumental problems that face us.

While essentially political, the action that must be taken on the results of this and the preceding New World Conference also has administrative and technical components. How do the administrators of housing, highway, pipeline, or reservoir construction projects fit rescue archeology into their programs with minimum inconvenience and delay? Who decides how much archeology is enough and at what cost? Who pays? In many Latin American countries there are only a few properly trained archeologists, and they generally have full-time academic and administrative commitments. Where are we to find trained personnel to fill the gaps?

In approaching the problems of rescue archeology and of the preservation of important prehistoric and historic sites and values on a hemispheric scale, it seems to me that one overriding reality looms over all other considerations. While the resources, expertise, and technology are overwhelmingly concentrated in English-speaking North America, the greatest percentage by far of endangered archeological sites, from monumental masonry complexes to remote paleolithic campsites, are located throughout Latin America.

In North America, the need for rescue archeology and site preservation was recognized several decades ago. Awareness of the problem has increased steadily, not steadily enough, but steadily at all levels, and a multitude of diverse resources have been brought to bear on the problem. The question in North America is essentially reduced to: how can we do it better?

In sharp contrast, in Latin America public awareness of the importance of our archeological heritage and of the devastation that is taking place is practically nonexistent. The stark reality is that in the Southern Hemisphere there are practically no resources at our disposal for rescue archeology and historic preservation, no programs to speak of, and a severe shortage of trained archeologists and specialized technicians to carry out the job.

Because we are dealing with the national patrimony of individual American states and with a universal cultural heritage, we must not forget that each individual country faces a different set of research and preservation problems. If we are to succeed in halting the destruction, we must respond realistically to these problems by defining our priorities at hemispheric, continental, regional, and national levels.

To cite a specific example of what could be done, the foundation with which I am involved in Ecuador plans to launch an archeological field school. If the lack of trained personnel for archeological fieldwork in tropical South America is a limiting factor, the establishment of a permanent international field school within the region is a necessity.

The latest research indicates that the earliest known ceramic cultures in Latin America were located on the central Ecuadorian coast. Dating from the middle of the fourth millennium B.C., they are considerably older than those of the earliest known ceramic cultures of Peru and Mesoamerica.

Excavations and surveys carried out by a permanent research team on the coast of central Ecuador have revealed sites with chronological sequences spanning five thousand years of prehistory, from 3800 B.C. to 1500 A.D. The population of this area evolved from primitive agriculturalists to a sophisticated sea-trading state centered in a district known in the Spanish chronicles as Salangame. The major stimuli for the development of such societies came from the trade of *Spondylus* shell, from a favorable geographical location, and from the use of indigenous balsa wood to construct large oceangoing sailing craft.

A research center sponsored by the Programa de Antropología is already in existence on the coast of Ecuador at Salango, in Manabí Province. It is engaged in a long-term, problem-oriented archeological program. The basic infrastructure of staff, accommodation, field equipment, and laboratory facilities required for an international field school is already established at the center. The abundance, variety, complexity, and time depth of the archeological material in the vicinity make the Salango Research Center an ideal base for a field school.

We plan that the Salango Research Center will run comprehensive training programs in all aspects of archeological field methodology, techniques, and logistics appropriate to tropical prehistory. The program will train archeologists to tackle the practical problems of excavation and preservation in South America. Because the school will be open to students from throughout the hemisphere, we hope that the support required for its implementation will be forthcoming from sympathetic bodies in North, Central, and South America.

As a contribution to an overall rescue archeology effort, our proposed field training program is relatively modest. But it is a start. If this conference generates support for similar endeavors, plus concrete guidelines for planners, managers, and archeologists, the time we spend here in Dallas will not have been wasted, and future generations of Americans will know a bit more about their past.

Rescue Archeology

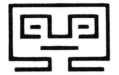

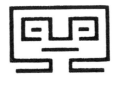

PART I

Rescue Archeology in the Western Hemisphere Today

Carl Chapman, Moderator

CARL CHAPMAN
This session's purpose is to establish very briefly the historical background of the Second New World Conference on Rescue Archeology and to review the status of rescue archeology in the Western Hemisphere at the time of the first conference in Quito, Ecuador, in May of 1981. Second, the panel will present information on various parts of the Western Hemisphere where notable progress has been made and will identify problems that have developed since the last conference.

BENNIE C. KEEL—Panelist
Anyone reading the volume on the proceedings from the First New World Conference on Rescue Archeology must surely come away with the impression that there were marked differences in the concerns of the participants. Most Latin Americans focused on issues of national identity, while most North Americans seemed to concentrate on the institutionalization of a cultural resource management process. To the former group the emphasis was obviously on the end result, whereas the latter group concentrated on the means without any formal or explicit formulation of ultimate goals other than the "preservation of the past heritage for future generations." This dichotomy on one level expresses the difference between the traditional empirical and positivist attitudes that characterize the American approach and the more ideo-

logical approach that characterizes the Latin approach. In Latin America, archeology has been used as the mediator between science, culture, and identity, whereas in the United States the uses to which archeology has been put are symbolic of the displacement with which, culturally, the United States as a people tends to deal with its colonial past and subsequent relations with native populations.

I raise this issue as an introduction because in order to understand where rescue archeology in the United States is today and where it is going, it is important to have an appreciation of this dichotomy. We must constantly respond to calls to justify our archeological endeavors, and it is only in this truly national context, and in the explicit formulation of national goals and priorities that relate cultural resource management as a process in the service of these ideals, goals, and objectives, that we can really justify what we are doing. The need for a definition of these priorities has recently been underscored by the Society of American Archaeology's recent attempts to lobby Congress in support of a National Research Council study devoted to defining and setting national archeological priorities. In the following paragraphs, I will bring you up to date on recent developments in cultural resource management in the United States, then return to the major issues I have raised by indicating the convergence of various interests and directions.

James Fitting, in his status report at the first meeting in Quito, identified three major problems, which he characterized as administrative, sociological, and intellectual. By way of review, I shall discuss the progress that has been made in each of these areas. On the administrative front, criticism continues to be leveled at the federal archeological establishment as a whole, and at the Department of the Interior in particular, for the lack of a comprehensive and coordinated approach to the federal archeological program. In particular the General Accounting Office, in a report issued in May 1984 entitled *Federal Government's Progress in Implementing a National Archeological and Historic Preservation Program*, still finds faults with the Department's approach.

It should be emphasized that considerable strides have been made in the area of program administration. The position of Assistant Director for Archeology was created within the National Park Service to give prominence to the Service's and to the Department's commitment to archeology. In a Departmental context, it should also be mentioned that the Assistant Director for Archeology is also the Departmental Consulting Archeologist and, as such, serves as the leading Departmental authority on archeological matters.

Another organizational step that was taken in the last year was the creation of the Archeological Assistance Division. This Division provides staff support to the Departmental Consulting Archeologist and provides technical assistance to other federal agencies on matters relating to archeological resources. The Division is also responsible for monitoring federal archeological activities to ensure uniform actions and efforts throughout the government and to provide the necessary technical guidance to agencies and to the professional community on archeological matters. Day-to-day liaison with field operations is carried out by archeological services units in regional offices in Philadelphia, Denver, Atlanta, San Francisco, and Anchorage.

Another major development was the institutionalization of anthropological and ethnographic concerns within the National Park Service's cultural resource management program. For too long, anthropology within the National Park system has been the sole purview of archeologists, and it is only recently that anthropological and ethnographic concerns have attained a valid role within the program. This institutionalization has recently received strong impetus and assertive validation by the NPS sponsorship of the First World Conference on Cultural Parks, which brought together representatives of thirty-seven nations and in which native relations and concerns were a major focus. The National Park Service has also recently signed a Memorandum of Agreement with the American Folklife Center of the Library of Congress designed to follow up on the recommendations in the Center's Cultural Conservation report.

The above are essentially organizational steps that have been taken to improve the management aspects of the cultural resource management process. Major steps have also been taken in trying to deal with the problems faced by managers in implementing the process itself. Fitting, writing in 1981, identified seven major problem areas: (1) dearth of overviews, and their importance in comprehensive planning; (2) lack of regional research designs, and their role in determining resource significance and ultimate treatment; (3) level of survey required for various kinds of projects; (4) failure to discriminate in evaluating significance; (5) extent of data recovery that should be undertaken; (6) lack of reintegration of survey and data recovery data; and (7) information dissemination.

The National Park Service has made comprehensive planning the keystone of the cultural resource management process. It is only in the context of rational planning that many of the seven problem areas highlighted above can have any reasonable chance of being resolved. At the meeting in Quito, Lawrence Aten presented the outline of the Resource Protection Planning Process, which the Service is promoting as a model planning effort. The institutionalization of this planning model is embodied in the publication of the Secretary of the Interior's Standards for Archeology and Historic Preservation, which was published in 1983 and is the keystone for historic preservation projects in the United States. The purposes of the standards are (1) to organize the information gathered about preservation activities; (2) to describe results to be achieved by federal agencies, states, and others when planning for the identification, evaluation, registration, and treatment of historic properties; and (3) to integrate the diverse efforts of the many entities performing historic preservation into a systematic effort to preserve our nation's cultural heritage.

The standards are essentially constructed in three parts: (1) the standard itself, which is a broad statement of policy, followed by (2) a series of guidelines that link the standards with (3) the more specific guidance and technical information available. Standards and guidelines are provided for preservation planning, identification, evaluation, registration, documentation, and professional qualifications.

In this context a number of agencies, such as the Corps of Engineers, have taken the initiative to implement the RP3 process and build the requisite regional planning structure that will allow them to carry out their responsibilities at the district level within the framework of comprehensive planning. In other areas, the Corps has undertaken the initial step in the process by commissioning comprehensive overviews and literature searches at the division level.

The profession itself, through the Society for American Archaeology, is sponsoring a major initiative in regional planning by organizing a series of regional conferences devoted to evaluating the state of the resource and to charting future directions.

It seems obvious that once a comprehensive planning process is in place, many of the issues that are perceived as problems become more readily manageable, since the planning process itself defines the criteria that are to be used for establishing research priorities, defining adequate levels of surveys, discriminating among various levels of significance relating to research priorities, and defining the extent of adequate data recovery or alternative treatments. The process of reintegration of survey and data recovery results into the planning activities, currently the weakest link in the chain, then becomes an automatic requirement.

Other federal agencies are also attempting to grapple with specific aspects of the overall cultural resource management process. For example, the Bureau of Land Management, the largest land-managing agency in the United States, is looking into the applicability of predictive modeling techniques as resource management tools. One of the conclusions of the original GAO report was that it would be prohibitively expensive for the federal government to undertake a one hundred percent survey of all the lands under its jurisdiction and control, and that more efficient ways would have to be found to deal with the survey and the identification requirement. The current emphasis on predictive modeling is one potential solution to this problem. However, as several recent examples have demonstrated, the use of such a technique has to be judicious and must have the support of all the parties involved in the process in order to properly serve the interest of the resource that we are mandated to protect.

The area of information dissemination is perhaps one of the most sensitive. On the one hand, we are criticized by our academic colleagues who say that much of the cultural resource management literature is sterile, while at the same time they castigate cultural resource management practitioners because not enough of the information from projects is broadly available (the academics thus having their cake and eating it too). The fact of the matter, as Colin Renfrew pointed out in his plenary session address to the SAA several years ago, is that it is imperative that we find a means to make available all the results from all research activities undertaken as part of the resource management process. If we have failed anywhere, as bureaucrats, as professionals, and as academics, it is in this regard. Cultural resource management practitioners have accepted this inferior status attributed to them by the academic elitists (a problem Fitting included in his "intellectual" category) and as a consequence have used the reasoning that their results are not significant enough to merit publication as an excuse to not follow up on professional responsibilities to publish. A related problem is the lack of actual publication avenues for cultural resource management results that do not fall into the "best," "earliest," or "greatest" category.

The Society for American Archaeology has accepted the challenge and has successfully lobbied Congress for the development of a nationwide computerized archeological data base. For the last two years Congress has provided funds to the National Park Service for the development and implementation of this project. The data base is designed to accomplish three purposes: to improve planning, to avoid duplication, and to aid the Service in overseeing and coordinating the national program and in reporting to the President and Congress annually on its scope and effectiveness.

The data base will track information on federal archeological projects, on reports emanating from those projects, and on data bases where people can get more detailed information should they so desire. For the first time, the national computerized archeological data base will provide a central repository for federal land managers, private contractors or academic professionals to get the most up-to-date and complete listing of archeological research activities in a particular area. It is hoped that the data base can form the nucleus for a larger management information system in archeology as well as set the tone for a standardization of information collection effort, at least at the regional level. In this way, we can begin to share data more effectively across state and regional boundaries, and we can make the larger-scale regional plans more readily attainable.

As you can see, some rather significant steps have been taken to consolidate the gains that cultural resource management has made over the last ten years. The process as a whole has been under recent attack. Too much has happened too soon, with not enough significant results to demonstrate that the effort has been worthwhile. Over the last two years, we have had the opportunity to pause and evaluate where we have been and where we intend to go. This, it seems to me, is a healthy, questioning state of affairs.

Archeology for antiquarianism is no longer a viable commodity, especially with the public footing the bill. As in the Latin context, cultural resource management practitioners need to come to grips with the public purposes of archeology in the federal establishment. A number of rather sensitive issues in the relationships between archeology and native peoples have been lurking in the background. The role of native peoples and communities in the overall cultural resource management process—either as a result of the provisions of the American Indian Religious Freedom Act of 1979 or of the requirement to consult with Indian groups specified in the Archeological Resources Protection Act of 1979—the crucial issue of the disposition of human remains, and finally the overall professional and academic relationship between native peoples and the archeological establishment are all of immediate concern and all have tremendous potential for a long-lasting impact on the practice of archeology. As the major stewards of the cultural heritage for the whole nation, we can no longer continue to skirt these issues.

As National Park Service Director Russell Dickenson stated in his opening speech to the First World Conference on Cultural Parks:

To further National conservation and preservation goals that affect native resources, then, it seems to me that we must seek innovative forms of rapproachment among native communities, government land managing agencies and groups who share that concern. This clearly would require: First, recognizing and respecting the unique qualities of native cultures and the directions that native peoples wish their cultures should take; developing permanent working partnerships with native communities to effectively incorporate them as allies and partners in planning a future that will significantly affect the lives of their children and their children's children; thirdly, it is time for those of us concerned with cultural resources to recognize the value of cultural differences and different cultures in ensuring the growth and development of the world's heritage; . . . finally, land managers and professionals must acknowledge their roles in a world system that includes native and other localized groups, each of whom depends upon the others to create and protect the resources that all value, each in their own way.

Surely we must accept the director's admonishment as a call to action, and to some extent as an accounting of our public purpose. Already I have met with a group called American Indians Against Desecration (AID) to hear firsthand their concerns and their demands, specifically their demand to have their ancestors, along with the sacred objects that originally accompanied their ancestors, reinterred. Clearly, AID's goals are contrary to those of many, if not the majority of, archeologists and physical anthropologists. Resolution of the value conflict between these two systems will not be quick and easy, but I am committed to searching for the most reasonable rapproachment possible. This is an issue that will occupy much of my time in the immediate future. It is by our future actions on issues relating to native peoples that we can to some extent continue to validate archeology's legitimate public role. I hope to be able to share our progress in resolving this issue at the Third New World Conference on Rescue Archeology.

LAUTARO NUÑEZ—Panelist
Chile's situation appears similar to that of other South American countries searching for means of development. These countries must reconcile the use of resources for both survival and cultural purposes. These two situations do not always lend themselves to orderly development.

At this meeting I would like to point out that, despite the survival problems in Chile and in other South American countries with similar situations, cultural strategies related to rescue archeology have overcome the most dramatic problems that characterize the last decade.

It is best to cite some data, since numerical indicators will help us to understand the real situation. During the last ten years in Chile, 140 sites have been rescued under normal academic procedures, that is to say, rescued by means of what the university is able to contribute through investigation and teaching. Despite this, through personal communications, obviously not published, we have registered 120 sites that have been irreversibly lost. There is no possibility of culturally documenting these sites. Of those 120 sites, 80 percent were cemeteries, 7 percent were settlements, 3 percent were different types of work places, and the remaining 10 percent were sites related to rock paintings.

What do these data tell us? We learn that during the last decade attention has been focused on the excavation of Indian cemeteries for various historical reasons. First, archeology in Chile has a museographic orientation, where funerary findings have been so spectacular as to justify the building of several new archeological museums. Second, it is of fundamental importance to place the archeology of Chile in relation to our problems of cultural identity, that is, in relation to the investigation and definition of our roots in a land of continuity between a pre- and post-European tradition. Perhaps one of the most efficient cultural mechanisms has been the exhibition of these funerary materials. Their directly didactic nature reflects the nature of Chilean roots.

Nonetheless, this funerary emphasis has been modified in the last four years, because the new anthropological/archeological criteria have shown, through a holistic approach, that the reconstruction of the society ought to consider the totality of the cultural remains: settlements, ideological aspects, dump sites, and among these, cemeteries. Half of Chile is desert, and represents, along with southern Peru, one of the few places in the world where archeological collections are well preserved. The loss of 50 percent of the unrescued sites gives us the exact dimensions of the problem, because no organic traces have disappeared due to the desert conditions. It is almost a sociology of the past.

Thus, a high percentage of loss of organic material is prevented because the desert has preserved the material. On the other hand, the situation involves a challenge that we should accept as an ethical rather than an educational obligation. We don't have the daily news of the sites that are lost due to various reasons throughout the country. With these losses, we lose not only our identity but also the unique possibility of testing scientific models. If the past gives us the totality of the human answers, it is obvious that the models with which we investigate our past will find here the best scholarly possibilities.

When we observe causes that, during this decade, have prompted the rescue of archeological materials, we can isolate at least thirteen. It is important to indicate that the top priority, which involves 40 percent of the causes of rescue, is linked to the building and maintenance of roads. The second priority, up to 30 percent, is linked to urban expansion. It is noteworthy that a highway is a more decisive element than urban expansion. A third priority, industrial growth, agrees with the industrial status of our countries in the process of development. A fourth priority is linked to agrarian expansion, which involves little that relates to rural construction. Looking at the situation in these terms, we ask what academic, juridical, or institutional structures have we achieved in our country to deal with rescue archeology?

As an academic, I am aware that the applicable law, the National Monuments Council law, is more than sixty years old. When this legislation was enacted, the situation was very different. But the law has never been modified. Even more dramatic is the fact that six years ago, legislation dealing with details, duties, and rights and sanctions was created. Yet since this law isn't written, it is not enforced. Therefore, works that disturb the surface of Chilean land are not supported by ad hoc regulations. Thus, the situation is somewhat unrealistic.

How? Since the Council is in the capital, there are no regional or state councils that can control what is happening if an archeological site is registered through the construction of a road five hundred kilometers from the capital. There are only two site inspectors, on the average, per region. Each region in Chile can be compared to a European country. Two site inspectors simply cannot control what happens regarding the destruction of our patrimony.

Second, although the legislation specifies illegal situations that may be controlled by the police, the demography is so extended, and our territory so vast, that archeological sites are very isolated. And their destruction is much more likely than their protection. On the other hand, federal institutions such as the Ministry of Public Works or the Ministry of Mining are the ones that expose the sites as they disturb the land surface. It would seem obvious that each ministry ought to have legal norms or attitudes regarding its own federal apparatus when it disturbs the earth's surface. But since the Council is supposed to regulate the norms, a cycle of avoiding the responsibility is produced. Basically, the problem is that the Ministry of the Treasury has not allocated sufficient funds to implement the National Monuments Council law. We academics maintain not only that site destruction is a matter of conscience but also that our national patrimony will be saved in proportion to the conscience of the Chilean people.

One of the most needed practical measures we academics and the Council have agreed on is that whenever the land surface is modified, regional councils will be created under the main Council that can determine what rescue measures are needed as the land surface is modified. If these measures, which have a jurisdictional and economic nature, could be enforced toward the end of this year (1984), we academics could develop rescue programs with great efficiency.

Our country is traditionally a cultured one; it has always been so. We have great sensitivity reinforced with common sense. Our engineers know what an archeological site is. All the rural police know an archeological site when they see one. Everyone helps in the restoration. I have personally seen engineers and policemen work together with shovels, because they take pride in their Chilean roots. But we do need a legal body for institutional support, so that the university can make plans and thus end, in Chile, a period of individual and spontaneous initiatives relating to rescue archeology.

We cannot continue to count too heavily on our sensitivity. In Chile, we need to establish a rescue archeology program in which the National Monuments Council, along with the affected ministries, the universities, and above all, the regional organisms can have a long-term program on both the regional and national levels. The program's aim would be to reduce the causes of site destruction, if not to eliminate site destruction altogether.

I will not tire you by reading the material I have synthesized, but I do have one more thing to say. I have traveled many miles to be at this meeting, and I want to take advantage of this opportunity to learn your ideas on the best course of action for the southern cone of South America, where conditions are similar to what I have described in Chile. We are asking this conference for specific recommendations, so that our countries can refine their legislation, regiment their legal actions relating to rescue archeology, and stimulate the creation of specific restoration and protection programs. Once national bodies have proved that they can establish and carry out such programs, they can seek international support through international conferences so that the programs can last longer and be more effective.

MARIO SANOJA—Panelist

I will start with some problems that were stated by my colleague, Lautaro Núñez, and will summarize our problems with the preservation of our cultural heritage in Venezuela. I should say that the problems of rescue archeology are not exactly as I described them at our first conference in Quito, i.e., they cannot be separated from the historical problems or from the educational problems of our country. Rescue archeology cannot be thought of as nothing but archeology, nor can it be regarded simply as a late answer to the problem of the destruction of our cultural patrimony. Instead, as Dr. Núñez mentioned, it must be part of a complete global policy that includes the legal and educational aspects as well as the cultural ones.

Regarding the legal aspects, we have, like Chile, a law covering our artistic and cultural patrimony that was enacted in 1945. It addressed the problems we had at that time but did not anticipate many of the serious problems that have attended our development over the past forty years. The oil boom of the fifties made possible the expansion of public works such as roads and irrigation projects and, in general, caused a slow transformation of the country due to construction programs. The 1945 law posed a particular problem for archeologists; we found that although the statute discussed the protection and preservation of our cultural patrimony, it was still too vague, too general, to afford much protection. One of the very important things we have to take into consideration, as in many other countries in Latin America, is that everything below the ground surface is state property. This derives from laws passed during the colonial period, which made the Spanish Empire the owner of all riches found underground. Of course, these laws applied particularly to precious metals, thus ensuring that all gold and silver became the property of the Spanish Crown. This concept of property was passed on to the republican form of government, such that logically, by extension, all archeological riches found underground are state property.

But the authorities in the law have not been carried out. In only a very few cases has the protection of our cultural patrimony actually been guaranteed. No regulations exist to provide the structure for such protection to be carried on effectively. On the other hand, there is a very important element having to do with the historical and cultural aspects that has greatly influenced the preservation of our cultural patrimony. The way in which this has been conceived in other countries has come to set an example.

Before the sixteenth century, i.e., before Christopher Columbus arrived and the colonization of this territory by the Spanish was begun, there was practically no "culture" or "civilization." These came with the Europeans. Accordingly, Venezuelan culture has long been character- ized by a degrading attitude toward anything that has to do with pre- Hispanic Indian culture. This is because in the teaching of history in the elementary and high schools, this period of almost fifteen thousand years of history is simply not represented. Only a very vague concept of pre-Columbian culture is presented. This narrow interpretation of history not only has affected education, but also continues to support the notion among the general public, including our political leaders, that Venezuelan history begins with the arrival of the Spanish in the sixteenth century.

Therefore, the protection of all that existed before the Spanish ar- rival is seen to be not very important. This is why, with few exceptions, we have been unable to organize any real cultural preservation programs. Instead, we have generally made only a technical response to the ur- gent problem presented by the destruction of archeological sites.

On the other hand, due to the political and cultural aspects, the idea has developed that "cultural" is the culture that has to do with public education. This means that the educational policies of Venezuela have been directed to the arts: sculpture, music, literature, and so forth. This is why we have several art museums, but practically no anthropological museums where we can exhibit, in organic form, the history of Venezue- lan culture and society. Evidently, this is not an isolated fact but represents the view of our whole national history. Therefore, in our case, the cultural preservation problem involves not only the physical preser- vation of something important to our people but also the preservation of our cultural identity, our national identity, our heritage as a nation.

So one problem that presents itself before ethnographic and historic preservation or rescue archeology is the need for a program that ad- dresses all the educational and cultural aspects necessary to identify what needs to be rescued or preserved. In this sense we have started a program at the university in which we attempt to design a strategy to carry out these programs. We are working in northeastern Venezuela, which has been particularly affected by the development of industry. It is an area that has a very long history, archeologically speaking, which started perhaps around 9 B.C. with the possible presence of hunters as- sociated with the paleofauna and which continued down to the sixteenth century when, through a system of continuous development, societies of some complexity appeared that can be identified as Indian tribes.

We have tried not only to excavate the archeological sites but also to propose a work model that complies with what I have been discussing.

In our opinion, the results of a rescue archeology program should be an educational program, a program to make our people aware of their cultural heritage. It is especially important that the residents of the archeological zones being studied participate in the rescue of the vestiges of their history. We have added this to our work project and are reaching farmers and students who live in neighboring regions, teaching them proper exploration methods and techniques.

We believe that in this way local citizens can be a very important factor in the investigation of archeological sites by serving as helpers to the professional archeologists. Because participants in these excavation programs become familiar with the significance of their cultural heritage, they will stimulate the development of cultural centers and will encourage the preservation of cultural forms peculiar to their communities. Another element we want to work on is the construction of a museum using materials, techniques, and designs that can be elaborated by the community. In one area, making clay and walls of packed clay uses techniques which do not require any other material than what we can find in nature—clay, sand, stones, wood, and straw and which can be accomplished industrially with the help of the architects in the university. We hope to plan a museum that will function as a pivot for cultural action in the community. These cultural projects, based on research promotion and cultural exhortment, are directed by professional archeologists and are coordinated with the programs of the regional museum.

In this way we are trying to develop a strategy that will promote the rescue of archeological objects and will stimulate local inhabitants to participate in cultural programs that will benefit their community. We hope to realize a higher level of awareness and to encourage participation in the rescue and preservation of our cultural patrimony both regionally and nationally.

Recovering archeological materials in sites that represent our ethnic roots permits us to reconstruct the sites and gives us an idea of how the process of occupation took place. The preliminary results of the analysis of data and excavated specimens have been translated to a graph that can be reproduced in a museum. In this way the results of the data recovery and analysis will be taken directly to the public via graphics. We are also planning to publish the results of our research not only as conventional scientific reports but also in a form that is visually accessible to the community. This way the excavation results that are usually only shared among scientists can also be shared among those who are not archeologists, especially teachers who can use them to explain our cultural identity.

In addition to serving as an educational device to illustrate the characteristics of the way of life of our indigenous people, the published excavation results will also explain to the public, to the owners of these lands, and to the farmers, that those objects they consider rare or commercially valuable are really the remnants of the people who once lived in the area, some of which are being destroyed by industrial expansion. In carrying out our ethnographic and rescue archeology programs, we try to demonstrate that archeology is not an attempt to take anything from our people but an attempt to save an important element of regional identity.

MARIA JOSE CON—Panelist

I will present a very general overview of rescue archeology in Mexico over the last two hundred years. I have chosen this topic because the Quito conference covered theory and practice as well as legal aspects. Since that conference in 1981, there have been political and economic changes in Mexico, changes that have changed perspectives and activities regarding the protection of the nation's cultural patrimony.

The interest in conserving, understanding, and disseminating information about the ancient peoples of Mexico originates in the liberal ideology that began at the end of the eighteenth century. Two relevant incidents characterize this historical moment. The first is the discovery of two important monoliths: Coatlicue and the Piedra del Sol. The second is a sermon that Fray Servando Teresa de Mier delivered on December 12, 1794, when he dedicated the catechization of the Indians, not to the Spaniards but to St. Thomas in the figure of Quetzalcóatl.

In 1790, due to extensive floods, a series of public repair works were begun in Mexico City, and a number of archeological remains were discovered. Their discovery is not as important as the fact that, for the first time since the conquest, the Viceroy Count of Revillagigedo ordered that the pieces found be studied and exhibited. Thus ended the tradition of the destruction of anything related to the ancient inhabitants of Mexico. In essence, this was the beginning of the recovery of our national patrimony. (Later, however, when Alexander von Humboldt visited Mexico and tried to see these pieces, he found that they had been buried again. But he managed to recover and re-exhibit them.)

It is not until 1900 that we can actually speak of rescue archeology in Mexico. This is the result of the construction of a large city channel that ran the length of Targua and Guatemala streets in downtown Mexico City. These works were under the direction of Leopoldo Batres, who was the Inspector of Archaeological Monuments of Mexico. However, even though Batres spoke of the archeological and historical importance these excavations would have, he waited to act until the excavations reached the main temple, which he erroneously located beneath the cathedral. This lack of vigilance in the excavations in Santa Teresa Street caused the loss of important dates and information about the different eras of the main temple; in addition, this first rescue emphasized exclusively the findings of major relevance.

In 1901 there was a resumption of salvage operations that provided new data. These new materials were published by Antonio Peñafiel in 1901 in a book entitled *La Destrucción del Templo Mayor en México*. Not until 1913, however, were rescue and exploration work done, by Manuel Gamio during the demoliton of several buildings on the corners of Seminario and Guatemala Streets in downtown Mexico City. Peñafiel was the first person to accomplish integrated work in rescue archeology. But it wasn't until 1930 that another important rescue archeology task, the Falcón Dam, was undertaken. The work was performed in cooperation with the United States government since the dam and reservoir were located on the border between the two countries.

It would be a long and tedious task to name all the projects that have since been completed. It is, however, important to mention that in 1963 a section specifically dedicated to rescue archeology was created by Professor José Luis Lorenzo within the Department of Prehistory. Since 1963, rescue archeology in Mexico has been carried on continuously and in a methodological way.

A crucial step in Mexican anthropology was taken in 1972 when the legislature passed a federal law regarding artistic, historic, and archeological monuments and zones. This law brought radical changes, because since that time our national patrimony has been protected by law. The law requires both public and private institutions to pay for any destruction or partial deterioration caused to archeological remains. The law limits the actions of institutions and sanctions violators, providing a new direction in Mexican archeology. It creates new responsibilities, not only for rescue archeology, but also for archeology in general.

Because there are currently many rescue archeology programs and other projects underway in Mexico, I brought some books to share with you. One is a bulletin from the Consejo de Arqueología, edited in 1984. It summarizes all the archeology projects currently being developed in Mexico.

Against that historical background, I will now evaluate the current stage of development of Mexican archeology. At present, the number of projects underway in the country immensely surpasses our capacity to dedicate time to them. We are at a point where we don't produce the specialists in proportion to the number of projects that need to be done. Good examples are PEMEX (Mejicano Petróleo Compañiá), which currently is building fifty-two gas pipelines, the Department of Hydraulic Resources (Departamento de Recursos Hidráulicos), which has seventy-three works under construction, and the Federal Electricity Commission (Comisión Federal de Electricidad), which has various Metro lines under construction in Mexico City. None of those I mentioned includes the construction of new roads, the building of new houses, etc. The INAH (Instituto Nacional de Antropología e Historia) currently has 230 investigators in the area of archeology. Only seventy-five of them are degreed, which is a requisite for directing an archeological project; thirty of them are involved in archeological projects.

In addition, during the last ten years the economic crisis has imposed a series of difficulties on rescue archeology projects. Salary costs are so high that, for the moment, archeology that needs to be performed before the construction of dams and gas pipelines has been reduced to surveying the area for the location of sites. Only where it is absolutely necessary is testing being done.

We also are not able to gather tons of material, which would only fill warehouses, since we don't have the personnel to analyze it. As soon as a project is finished, the people involved must go on to another project with equal or more importance.

We have had to learn to be selective both in the study areas and in the analysis. Planning is also difficult because the economic situation does not guarantee jobs. We have had to suspend work for long periods because the companies financing the projects sometimes delay the apportionment of funds for many months, even though agreements have been signed.

Currently, in Mexico, because of the country's great richness and abundance of archeological and historic remains, I don't think we can speak of rescue archeology only in those cases where destruction has occurred due to infrastructure projects. We have more dangerous and permanent enemies, many times unknown and thus incomprehensible. Archeology in Mexico is at a stage where all of it can be considered to come within the concept of rescue.

Let me explain: Economic development, demographic explosion, expanded urbanization, tourism, looters, and other destructive factors continue to destroy our cultural patrimony. Added to this, we have very poor vigilance of our archeological zones. There has been no presidential declaration about the archeological patrimony, which the 1972 law suggested. There have been declarations about historic sites, but without enforcement procedures, the situation continues to deteriorate owing to the lack of legal protection, while the dangers of destruction, invasion, and deterioration grow. Until now, there has been little or no coordination among different federal, state, and local organizations and the INAH. Coordination would allow the groups to plan together the future projects and modifications. The INAH is undergoing internal reorganization in order to redefine its activities in terms of priorities. Besides concurrence with scientific requirements, this reorganization should be oriented toward satisfying relevant sociocultural needs at the national level. This entire redefinition of goals has been outlined in the National Plan for the Conservation of Archaeological and Historical Patrimony (Plan Nacional para la Conservación del Patrimonio Arqueológico e Histórico).

The plan should necessarily be made with the participation of federal, state, and local governments. This would yield a general idea of what monuments exist and how they should be protected. This knowledge would be very useful, particularly for rescue archeology projects and specifically for those projects that must cover large geographical areas where a prior concept of the zones to be worked is needed.

There should be an increase in legal protection after the identification of archeological and historic monuments, sites, or zones, followed by a technical study. All should be required as a basis for legal declaration.

We need to resolve the problem of archeological zones that are not on federal or state land. When the zones are on private or community land, it is possible to protect the known monument but not the surrounding area, which is private land.

We need to create state technical consulting commissions, which would approve projects in accordance with the conservation norms of the INAH. These commissions would be integrated by specific treaties with the Institute, state governments, municipal authorities, and representatives from the Ministry of Ecological and Urban Development (Ministerio de Desarrollo Ecológico y Urbano) and the National Institute of Fine Arts (Instituto Nacional de Bellas Artes).

Restoration and maintenance of these monuments is extremely expensive. It is also expensive to hire personnel to perform the work and to establish a program of priorities.

We need to elaborate a plan of conservation of our cultural patrimony because our people need to have an idea of the importance of protecting and conserving that patrimony. This plan would indicate, clearly and precisely, what our patrimony is, what part of it is protected by law, and how it can be protected by the people themselves. And it should include sanctions designed to inhibit the destruction and looting of sites.

General Discussion

DONALD LATHRAP

I was particularly interested in Bennie Keel's point about the difference in attitude between Latin American and North American archeologists. It is appalling that attitudinal differences exist. Having done considerable work in Latin America as well as in California and Illinois, I guess my attitude is more Latin American, as I survived at the pleasure of the Shipibo Indians when I did my first Latin American fieldwork. But it seems to me, if we're not helping Native Americans to preserve and protect their cultural heritage in North America, it is very hard for me to figure out what we *are* doing. And what I deplore, something I have seen so often among my colleagues in Illinois, is the totally adversary relationship North American archeologists have with Indian groups, a relationship formed before the Indians are even contacted. The scene—and I've just come from a meeting of the Illinois Archeological Survey, a vivid memory—is very much like an old western movie. The Illinois archeologists already have their wagons in a circle and it's shoot before you see the whites of their eyes! I must say that my good colleague, Chuck Barreis, feels exactly the same way about this that I do. If North American archeology is in difficulty, it is because the archeologists have made no previous efforts to contact and interest American Indian groups. These Indian groups have a vast amount to offer to us in our interpretations, and if the situation has become tense, I'd say the fault is totally with the North American archeological community.

BENNIE C. KEEL
I would like to comment in response to Donald Lathrap's observation. I think that if there is one thing the papers presented by the panel clearly indicate it is the failure of archeology and archeologists to communicate with people who are not primarily archeologists. And yet I am amazed, at least in this country, at the tremendous amount of support that we get from the public. I don't know how we're going to improve our image, but it's going to take a lot of change among archeologists in this country for them to finally accept the fact that it is a professional obligation of some priority to communicate with the public. So long, I think, as this profession, at least in this country, considers its highest priority to be carrying out its work, communicating only with land managers or other archeologists, as long as we do that, we're not going to have the real public support we need. We've got to face up to this problem, not only in this country but also throughout the New World. That's the one thing I see that is clearly consistent among all the papers and the different kinds of problems we've been talking about: the problems we have with our individual laws and the ways we go about institutionalizing and structuring how we do our work. It is clearly a problem, a central problem, that we have to face.

MARIO SANOJA
I want to add to what Bennie Keel said; this is a very real problem that archeologists have been unable to respond to. Certainly we have priorities within our society. But I believe there is a larger problem that has to do with archeologists' tendency to ignore everyday reality. The fact is that academic archeology, which is what has been carried out mainly and which has dominated archeological policies and thinking in the New World, tends to deal more with the objects recovered than with man. The conclusions we have arrived at tend to be on a very abstract level, sort of super-structural. We discuss chronology and typology, without considering reality and without using our investigations to address a more urgent problem, the understanding of man himself. I believe that all scientific disciplines have their bodies of theories and methods, but I also believe that archeology in general has always been considered a discipline interested only in what is antique and one having nothing to do with real, everyday problems. Accordingly, the archeologist and his work are divorced from reality. I really believe that

the problem is much more complex than we would like to think, and this is why I say that it is necessary for us to revise the concepts of archeology, its objectives, and its methods so that we can effectively relate archeology to our everyday problems. We should be concerned with much more than the problems that deal strictly with empirical experiences or with solutions to chronological or typological problems.

CARL CHAPMAN

I think you have made a very good point. One of the main problems, as I see it, is that we don't train archeologists to produce the kind of information we're talking about here, the kind of information the public can understand and can actually integrate into their own lives. I'm sure I'm one of those who have been responsible for this because, like those who have taught archeologists in the past and today, I don't think the public's interests are a part of the education of archeologists. Who actually teaches archeologists to write reports that are understandable to the general public? I don't think that is a part of the educational process. That's one of the real problems, as I see it—how we handle the education of archeologists. We teach them how to go about interpreting the things they find, but they're interpreting primarily for their colleagues, not for the general public. I think that unless we change our ways and make the public understand that what archeologists do is important to them, we aren't going to have the public's support.

GEORGE GUMERMAN

I'd like to say that there's also a basic structural problem in U.S. universities connected with this situation, and that is, the prestigious jobs that most young scholars want are tenure-track positions in academic institutions. And by and large, it is the popular, general articles or books that we are encouraging archeologists to write. But because those are precisely the kinds of books promotion and tenure committees look with disfavor on, they do not count in a candidate's favor. This is a major structural problem in U.S. universities.

DONALD LATHRAP

I totally agree with George Gumerman. And I think there's another problem that's become acute. In attempting to be scientific, archeology has become more and more specialized and has tried to develop a theory of its own. It seems to me if the field has any real or broader theory, it would be general anthropological theory. And if the archeologists can't place their findings in an anthropological context, they can't even communicate with the other colleagues they usually share a department with, let alone the general public. So I think there is also the problem, the terrible problem, of tenuring. Tenuring committees do like competitive papers that say nothing. But they can *count*. There is also the fragmentation and specialization that affects academia generally, and perhaps acutely affects anthropology.

CARL CHAPMAN
Another point that was brought out is that laws alone are of no use unless they are enforced. And laws are not enforced unless the people charged with enforcing them actually believe in them and understand what they are about. The passage of laws has been brought up by several members of the panel here today. Passage of some laws has not always been of much use because the laws have not been enforced and many of the people who would normally do the enforcing really don't understand why they should. And so this is another area where we certainly need to work with the people who would normally enforce the laws, to make sure that they understand why the laws were enacted and what the laws were intended to accomplish. I know of many instances in the United States in which, once on the local level, the local sheriff is the one who must enforce the law. Quite often the sheriff doesn't understand the intent of the law and doesn't want to bother with prosecuting someone who's digging out an Indian ruin.

RAYMOND H. THOMPSON
I'm very glad George Gumerman stood up. I'd like to call attention to the fact that we do have some good examples of public interpretation in archeology in this country. In fact, the University of Arizona Press has discovered that it can sell books and make money interpreting archeology to the public. Included in those books is one that George has just written summarizing the works of his very large project on Black Mesa sponsored by the Peabody Coal Company. And I believe that while we can stand here and lament the lack of public interpretation, we ought to be pointing to those instances where it has happened and use them as models for our future activity. And I'd like to congratulate George for assuming that special responsibility even though he does exist in a university where, I think, perhaps they would look for another kind

of publication if he were facing tenure. So we do have some good examples of where we have taken the public into account, and I think that we ought to be focusing on them.

MICHAEL COLLINS

Speaking as an engineer, I'd like to point out a problem. I think what this conference, in part, is all about is the interface between the problems of the engineering and the archeological communities. I think that we do have real difficulty trying to get down to the practical level, which the gentleman was alluding to in his discussion, of trying to sensitize engineers to archeological concerns, to create an awareness in the local engineer, to reach the engineers who are involved in planning activities and make them aware of the problems they need to address in preserving cultural sites. We have to think very seriously about how the archeological community can interface with the engineering community. There are a great many impediments not only in the academic structure, where I'm from, but also in the engineering community at large, problems that hinder the development of good interchange between the scientific and the engineering communities. And I would suggest that one of the things this conference could do is to create some specific contexts, to contact some of the national engineering organizations, particularly the American Society of Civil Engineers or similar organizations, and try to establish some mechanism, some committees, that would look at this problem very seriously and would identify specific ways by which archeological concerns could be brought into the engineering curriculum. I think there is a great deficiency in this area, and it is one we need to look at seriously.

WILLIAM L. FULLEN

I am basically a lay person who touches on the fringe of archeology quite frequently. As a lay person, I believe that to a certain extent the archeologists represent a closed circle. When previously I was president of the Texas Historical Commission I encouraged the staff, which is responsible for archeology in Texas, to teach a course to lay people. And I encouraged academics to get in touch with the local groups they come into contact with in the field. And one of the greatest problems I've had is that while it's easy to identify historic buildings and to interest the public in preserving them, it's very difficult to get the public involved in an archeological site, something that they do not understand.

CARLOS G. ZEA-FLORES
There is something that has not been discussed but that is especially pertinent in Latin America. We have a problem similar to South America's, but much more similar to Mexico's. We have an extensive number of archeological sites in Guatemala and view "rescue" and "salvage" archeology in much the same way as expressed by the representative from Mexico. We have problems regarding priorities of archeological work in various places, problems that become even more difficult when fieldwork is carried out by foreign institutions in our country. There are European and U.S. universities that have worked and continue to work, but on their own terms. They are looking for the sites most important to them and not necessarily most important to Guatemala. About two years ago we had a problem with a university from the United States that was supported by the National Science Foundation. The university wanted to explore a site that did not have a high priority for us. Problems of this kind should be taken into account at this conference, because in any salvage or rescue operation we cannot, in good faith, ignore the priorities of the host country, even if the archeologists have to revise their research priorities.

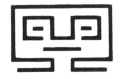

PART II
Rescue Archeology and
Its Interface with Engineering

Robert J. Dacey, Moderator

ROBERT J. DACEY
Our topic this afternoon is engineering's interface with rescue archeology. I'd like to talk about the environment in which that interface and that cooperation has to take place.

In Denver, Colorado, there is an institution called the Thorn Ecological Foundation. Each summer the Foundation runs a seminar on the environmental arts and sciences, inviting people from government at all levels—city, state, and federal—as well as students, private citizens, and contractors. The Foundation brings this group together for seven days. In the morning of each day, each person goes out and looks at a pristine area (i.e., one that has not been disturbed), examines the flora and the fauna, and makes a kind of catalogue of what's there. Participants are given a briefing on the history of the area so that each person can get a feeling for what the prehistoric or historic values of that particular area might be. In the afternoon there is a visit to a similar type of site that has been developed in some way. For condominiums, for solid waste, for ski runs, for logging, for whatever purpose, there's been some development that's taken place. Toward evening the people in the group reassemble, put their notes together, and after dinner sit down to talk about what was seen that day. And they think about how a better interface of all the involved planning disciplines could have improved what actually took place. The amazing thing, after you have gone through that process for seven days, is that every night by midnight you are talking about birth control. And if you think about it, that's where the conversation has to take you. Because when you are talking about providing for the population, whether it's providing homes or jobs or recreation or potable water, you're talking about development. And development, unfortunately or fortunately depending upon how you view the system, always takes place on a crash basis. We don't seem to be able to reach a consensus on what our needs for water will be, for example, in the year 2020 and to begin today to do the deliberate, coordinated, cohesive job of planning needed to meet those requirements. We don't have restrictions on our population, either on its size or on where it can move. So the migration to the sun belt that's taken place in the United States, many planners had not anticipated. Because the movement of our people hasn't been disciplined, it's presenting great problems, and we're coming up with crash solutions to those problems. So as we look to resolving the problems that we face together in planning and in engineering and construction and development, we've got to understand two parameters: first, that the population is unchecked, and second, that the population problems will be handled on a crisis basis when we get to them.

The second dimension to look at is that right now in the United States we're spending twelve cents out of every dollar in the federal budget to service the national debt. Based on current deficit projections, four years from now we'll be spending nineteen cents out of every dollar to service our debt. Now where is the additional seven cents going to come from? Our President, after having been elected, said that he was not going to touch Social Security or cut the defense budget. And if that's the case, then we're going to have to find the extra seven cents someplace else. The President also said that he was not going to raise taxes, so that means you've got to find that seven cents by cutting other areas of the budget.

Today, for all the water resource development in the United States (the area I'm primarily involved in)—including the U.S. Bureau of Reclamation, the U.S. Army Corps of Engineers, the U.S. Soil Conservation Service, and the Tennessee Valley Authority, all of the agencies of the federal government that are involved—we spend less than three-tenths of one cent out of each dollar. I see no reason to think that we won't come up with our portion of the seven cents that's needed to service the national debt. I say that only because I'd like to elaborate on Ray Barnhart's comment made this morning. We have to come up with a mechanism to identify those sites that are really unique and really of value and that should be preserved. And we've got to come up with a prioritization system, because the dollars we would like to have are not going to be available. Resources needed to protect, preserve, and explore every site will not be available. And we, today, collectively, have not come up with a way to prioritize these sites to determine which are the ones we should be applying the scarce resources to. So during our discussions this afternoon, I ask that you put the sites in perspective. While all of us would like to be able to do more, the reality, as I see it, is that we are going to be severely constrained. We'll be handling things on a crash basis—on an undisciplined basis in some respects—and with an austerity of the resources needed to solve all the problems that all of us want to see addressed.

ALBERTO REX GONZALEZ—Panelist
I would like first to comment on what General Robert Dacey just said, because I believe it is very important: the idea of our being able to conduct rescue archeology in South America.

In the first meeting, our first conference in Quito, I spoke with Larry Banks, who attended as a representative of the Corps of Engineers, and we talked about the possibility of army involvement in rescue archeology in South America. I thought it was a wonderful notion, but at that time it was very difficult—especially in my country, which was going through very serious times—to approach the army with our concerns. Argentina was having serious internal problems, a crisis in fact, and it was practically impossible to take up our concerns with the army. But for a year now, Argentina has had a democratic system, and the National Government is going through a complete reorganization of its armed forces. And I believe that now is the right time to approach the army with our archeological concerns. We have a very good example in what has been discussed here, and I believe it is our duty as archeologists to share this awareness we have spoken about. It has to start with us. The army and other branches of the armed forces have been very helpful to us on many occasions by taking aerial photographs, for example, or by assisting in solving logistical problems in some of our archeological projects. But I will acknowledge that frequently our armed forces and our scientists find themselves at odds with one another. Conflicts have their roots in historical factors that do not exist in the United States, where military officials take courses in universities that prepare them for dealing with problems peculiar to rescue archeology. From what I've just heard, it is clear that it is our responsibility as archeologists to take our concerns to the army. Based on my experience during the Quito meeting and during this conference, one of the first actions I will take if I am able to meet with the Ministry of Defense will be to acquaint them with our rescue archeology problems.

Now I want to refer to the problems in Argentina as to rescue archeology in general. When I say Argentina, I also refer to many of the countries of South America. For the First New World Conference on Rescue Archeology held in Quito, I was asked by the organizing committee to summarize the current status of rescue archeology in South America. My main problem was that I was not familiar with the geography of other countries. This meant that I had to study six or seven months and contact my colleagues so that I could get a good idea of what was happening in other parts of South America. The published report includes all the major problems that I could identify. Actually, the problems I discussed are much more complex than my report suggests. Had I gone into detail, the report would have consisted of several volumes for each one of the South American countries where rescue archeology is being done. There are, however, two or three salient points I can make that characterize the problem of summarizing rescue archeology in South America. In the first place, there are great differences among those countries. Even though all the countries are still developing, many have reached fairly high levels of academic sophistication, in archeology, for example. Other countries have not.

There are some countries where there are five, six, or even eight universities that offer archeological courses at the college level. There are many universities in Peru. In Argentina we have a couple; we have reached an enrollment of five hundred students who are taking coursework in anthropology and archeology in the University of Buenos Aires. Yet in other South American countries, especially in Bolivia and Paraguay, there simply does not exist career training in anthropology and, of course, archeology. Therefore, the attitude in these countries toward these disciplines is very different from that in countries where human resources courses are more extensively available and where trained faculty teach and carry out archeological research. The amount of training parallels a country's degree of interest in defending its historic patrimony. Because in the end, the problem of rescue archeology is directly related to the defense of cultural patrimony and the attitude of the national government toward cultural heritage.

There is a great difference between South American countries that have laws, often very precise laws, that defend their patrimony and others that do not have such laws. Accordingly, the problems we are trying to solve in some countries, and the potential for solving these problems, are much different from the problems we have in other countries. For example, in the case of Argentina, the National Government's attitude toward the protection of our patrimony has not included laws specific to rescue archeology, even though we do have explicit laws for protection that have been in effect since the beginning of the century. In fact, in my report to the First New World Conference on Rescue Archeology I noted that, with few exceptions, there are no specific laws relating to rescue archeology in Latin America. In most countries, we have not resolved the problem; we're still creating specific rescue archeology laws that can be designed to complement those that already exist for the protection of the national patrimony. So we find ourselves in a situation that is sometimes very special. We need to create a general law that provides protection for the cultural patrimony, and another that is specific to rescue archeology.

For me, it has been very, very useful and extraordinarily important to participate in drafting new legislation because we began immediately to create a plan whereby we could relate the preservation of our patrimony to the rescue of important prehistoric and historic sites. For example, we have started some programs that are going to transform the lower elevations of the Rio Paraná into a lake sixty kilometers long and sixty kilometers wide. Water impounded behind the dam will inundate a very big area, portions of which contain sites dating from about 12,000 B.P. until the Spanish conquest during the sixteenth century. At the time of the conquest, these areas were inhabited by sedentary peoples, so we can predict that a great number of sites will be found there.

Immediately after the last conference we knew that there were many things we would have to do for the small institutions. The basic task was to create a super organization that would address the problems as a whole. So at the beginning of this year we tried to convince the principal authorities—our Ministry of Culture, in which I had a position—to encourage the provinces that will be affected by the projects in the Paraná to take an active part in a rescue archeology program. What we need to do is to create a national organization that takes into account the different programs that we plan for the future. In the report I have prepared (which I believe is going to be published) I included a very long list of cases in Argentina, starting with the oil fields.

In summary, I want to say that we are trying now to create a national law reflecting the basic elements I have mentioned that are important and concrete. Starting with the case of Paraná, the national meetings could lead to a law for Argentina that provides greater protection for our cultural heritage. The movement has its roots in the First New World Conference on Rescue Archeology held in Quito in 1981.

DARRELL MACH—Panelist
It's an unusual situation for me to be at a conference like this and to be part of the round table in which we are to discuss some of the problems of engineering and archeology and how they fit or don't fit together.

Part of my role as Director of Planning for the Bureau of Reclamation is to accomplish the goals and objectives that we've set as an agency to develop the water resources in the western United States for irrigation and for municipal and industrial purposes. And I think that our agency, as we became aware of and faced up to the issue of preservation and avoidance of damage to archeological sites, had to go back and look at the type of people we had in the organization itself. Being an engineer, I have to say that most of my training has been in the direction of trying to accomplish an objective in the most efficient way possible. Anybody who hires an engineer or asks an engineer to do a job, is expecting the engineer to accomplish the job for the least amount of cost, and in the least amount of time. In our case, all of a sudden, we had a group of people called archeologists who were saying that we needed to take some time to study the area, to look for archeological sites there, and we saw this as a hindrance. We saw the archeologist as someone who wanted simply to pick up objects that were lying around on the ground and put them in a museum. Generally, we saw someone who didn't seem to be very efficient. I think our passive, if not negative, attitude toward archeologists was one of the first things that we as an agency had to overcome. Yet this was our perception of the differences between our disciplines. The disciplines also had different objectives. Again from an engineering standpoint, our objective was to build, to develop, and to do this in an efficient manner. Archeologists' objective was to preserve, to keep something in its original state, so that it could be studied, so that information could be gathered. Early in some of these processes, we literally had confrontations within our own staff, our archeologist actually standing in front of bulldozers with the construction engineer saying, "Get out of the way!" And it took some time for us to learn to cope with these differences in our disciplines and in our training.

Conflicts that developed from these early experiences demanded resolutions. We discovered that if we sat down and discussed our differences and began to look at the situation from the other's perspective, and from the other discipline's perspective, that maybe there were some areas where we could agree and find solutions, and not be in conflict all the time. I think this was probably one of the major breakthroughs we experienced. And I also believe there is a need to develop some archeological information for what is characterized as the general public. Because, in all frankness, we engineers, in many cases, are part of that general public the archeologists have been talking about. We need to be told, to be made to understand in a language we can grasp hold of— we need to understand so that we can sit down and start to talk to each other. As we discovered in our project, once we start to talk, we will begin to see that it isn't necessary to be in conflict, that it isn't necessary for us to be in an adversary position, but rather that we can be mutually beneficial to each other, that we can help each other.

This experience taught me that there are ways that I can accomplish my purpose—develop a project for the least cost, with the greatest benefit that can be put into the project—and yet not destroy things that have significance from a historical perspective. What we have come to realize as an agency, and the point I would like to stress most strongly, is that there needs to be an early dialogue among all of us, not only among those of us who are in development-oriented agencies but also among other people, the general public, that we deal with as well.

I spent some time in planning in the field, part of it as Director of Planning for our Southwest region that covers Texas, Oklahoma, and New Mexico. That is where I received my first exposure to the field of archeology. I found, by going into the field with our archeologists and talking with individual landowners we might be dealing with, that if we explained to these landowners what was happening, what was going on, they soon began to develop an interest in and an appreciation for some of the things we were trying to do. I can recall one man who had been farming a particular field for more than twenty-five years. There were some low mounds in the field that, from his standpoint, were a nuisance because they broke the ground level. He had also noticed that occasionally he would turn up something that was not normal to the area, such as a rock or something like that. When our archeologist went out to that field with him and explained that these mounds had been built by the Indians many years ago and explained the historical significance of those mounds—that they were the clues the archeologists had been looking for—then the problem of getting onto the land, of working with the landowner and trying to do something about the sites, essentially was solved. Within a short time the landowner had developed a great interest in what was going on. We discovered that he had been collecting some of the artifacts that occasionally turned up as he tilled his field, had been putting them away in the barn, and was now willing to let us have them for study. In this way he added some knowledge of the site, and we soon developed a very good dialogue with him. We found this kind of thing happening more and more often as we worked with these people. We found a growing interest in archeology among many of our construction engineers, whose primary purpose was to build a project within a certain period of time and within a certain range of cost, and whose efficiency and productivity were measured on that basis. As they began to read textbooks, to search out books from the library on archeology, and to study the subject on their own, they began to understand what the archeologists were doing and how they as engineers could take part in what was going on.

So I think this is where we need to go: develop a real dialogue between the general public and ourselves and begin to understand each other's purposes and what each of us is trying to accomplish. Having done that, we can work together to meet our mutual goals, not our conflicting goals.

BARRY G. ROUGHT—Panelist
To some, the study of things of the past has always been seen as a window to the future. Others have viewed research concerning the times that were as an interesting pastime for the idle.

Prior to the 1970s, those in management in the United States who viewed archeological and cultural activities as needed and worthy contributions to the water resource program were as voices crying in the wilderness. Then the U.S. Congress clarified the national interest in the country's past through a series of legislative and executive actions directed toward the protection and study of prehistoric and historic cultural resources. Today federal managers in the United States ignore our nation's past at the risk of their personal future. Some U.S. Army Corps of Engineers managers were fortunate enough to have obtained archeologists early in the program, thereby facilitating incorporation of that discipline into the overall agency mission. The U.S. Army Corps of Engineers Southwestern Division was—and still is—one of those organizations staffed with professionals in archeology. This has been the impetus for developing our archeological program.

In the late 1960s the role of the U.S. Army Corps of Engineers in archeological investigation was limited to one of coordinating its construction schedules with the Interagency Archeological Salvage Program of the National Park Service. Some Corps of Engineers districts were more actively involved in coordination than others, but none had any professional staffing or funding authority. It was not until 1970 that professional assistance became available within the Southwestern Division, and that was limited to one individual. The five Corps of Engineers districts in the Southwestern Division began funding archeological reconnaissance projects after 1971. Between 1974 and 1983 the archeological staffing within the Southwestern Division increased to eleven permanent spaces, and the archeological investigations of projects—not of individual sites—now number in the hundreds. The funds spent on archeological contracts alone total approximately ten million dollars. This amount represents eight-tenths of one percent of the approximately $1.1 billion spent on our construction during that period. This figure includes the cost of archeological planning, operations, and maintenance contracts. During this decade we have incorporated the archeological program into the complex planning, construction, and operations of the U.S. Army Corps of Engineers' civil and military work. The Chief of the Planning Division of the Southwestern Division, the element where most of the archeological expertise of the Southwestern Division is located, has become increasingly supportive of archeology. This sensitivity has brought into focus the problems facing the archeologists, as well as those facing the planners, engineers, and constructors who are trying to understand and incorporate archeology into the U.S. Army Corps of Engineers' program.

The institution of the archeological and cultural resources program has required communication between disciplines with apparently opposing philosophies, philosophies concerning the relationship archeology has with the U.S. Army Corps of Engineers' basic water resource development missions of planning, designing, construction, and operation. Justifying the program in order to gain appropriate funding while fulfilling our professional responsibilities has been a distinct challenge. Planning, scientifically investigating, providing good stewardship of our archeological findings during the planning and construction phases, and protecting those remaining cultural resources we are called upon to manage during the operation phase, are the essence of the program in the Southwestern Division.

Managers in the U.S. Army Corps of Engineers are often asked questions about archeology by engineers, planners, and economists as well as by politicians and tax-paying citizens. Why is the Corps of Engineers involved in archeology? Why does the Corps of Engineers need archeologists? Why does it need so many? When has enough archeology been done on any one site or any one project? Is there a justifiable benefit-to-cost ratio for data recovery on sites selected for mitigation? These are tough questions to answer, ones that apply to the rationale for expenditure of public funds on archeology not only for the Corps of Engineers' projects but also for any public works.

The basic question is, how much do the citizens of the United States want to have archeology performed in connection with project development? The public laws of the United States should be a reflection of the sentiment of the public at large. However, most U.S. citizens are likely to be more interested in dramatic findings than in routine archeology. This viewpoint is bolstered by comparing the public reactions to exciting finds with the public interest in ongoing archeological work at many Corps projects. It is obvious that the public is concerned about archeology when its importance is explained. The people deserve to have access to information that explains what is being done in archeology with their tax dollars. In fact, if that access is not provided, one could question if the public's best interest is being served in our cultural resources programs. This information is and should be provided through many media, such as public displays, documentary films, and summaries of publications, written in language that is understandable to the non-archeologically oriented citizen. This support base continues to come from the general public and not necessarily from the professionals. In regard to justification of the Corps of Engineers' involvement in archeology, it should be noted that the Corps' precedents are deeply rooted. During the early history of exploration, the Corps of Engineers set the pace that led to the programs of many of our sister agencies.

The work of the "professional explorers and scientists" discussed by William H. Goetzmann (1966) and referenced by Gordon R. Willey and Jeremy A. Sabloff (1974) as the "birth of the discipline of American Archeology" was performed primarily by Corps of Engineers officers commissioned as topographic engineers in the 1830s and 1840s. The Corps of Engineers' surveys of the 1870s included archeological excavations and mappings in some of the same areas we are concerned with in the twentieth century. Engineer officers at the Corps of Engineers school at West Point, New York, in the early 1800s were trained to be knowledgable about the natural sciences as well as about the principles of engineering. They were fired with a thirst for knowledge and quality. Has such a thirst been quenched? When does such a search end? Surely not yet! When do we know enough about any subject? Knowledge is cumulative and is based on what has been observed and documented either implicitly or explicitly. Who can place restrictions on how much we need to know about our past before we can accurately ordain our future? The rationale for the Corps' involvement in archeology is embodied in the answers to these questions. We must search for answers within the logic of these questions if we wish to maintain a quality historic preservation program.

After that brief philosophical introduction, I shall now comment on specific problem areas that should be of concern to both managers and archeologists.

Perhaps one of the most perplexing problems that face a manager is the question of how much money to allocate to the archeological aspect of an individual project or cultural resources program. This is especially true in the planning stage of a project. Funds provided must be sufficient to avoid inadequate evaluations and to still meet the other needs of the project. Archeologists must understand that archeology is competing with other disciplines for a limited amount of resources in terms of money, people, and time. The manager must know the requirements to properly do the job in the area of prehistoric and historic resources, but to not overdo it.

The manager will ask others for input on other aspects of the project, such as the amount of rainfall expected over a period of time and the rate of runoff into the streams and eventually into the project area; the determination of soil characteristics; the design of outlets, spillways, and the structure itself. These needs and many others compete for those same resources of money, people, and time.

Obviously, the manager would be doing less than an acceptable job if these basic engineering points were not properly considered and the project failed. Would it be equally bad to do these engineering studies and not take into account the history of man that may be lying within the project area? If the manager foregoes some archeological work, the impact will leave a gap in the history of man. This would not necessarily be catastrophic. But if the manager fails to properly analyze the hydrology and hydraulics, or the structural stability of the project, and if the project fails, the result can be catastrophic to the immediate welfare of the people of the area. The manager must weigh these factors when determining the amount of resources to budget for archeology in a given year. The archeologists' knowledge of the data base and their appreciation of the potential value of the archeology of the area are the keys to selecting a proper allocation. If the archeologists can accurately delineate the amount of resources in terms of money, people, and time that it will take to do a good (not just acceptable) job, then the likelihood of obtaining the warranted share of the resources is enhanced.

Routine questions asked of the Southwestern Division staff include the following: Why do we need this information? How long will it take to acquire the archeological data, and what will be done with it? What potential contributions will the information add to the state of knowl- edge? Should all the artifacts be recovered? Why not leave them to be buried even deeper under the soil or under the water? Why spend these resources on archeology? Will archeological work delay the completion of the project? The archeologist must answer these questions during planning, construction operations, and budgeting; he must provide the managers with a convincing rationale that knowledge of the past culture of the area is of value to the future and to the project. Budgeting requirements are then considered with some degree of accuracy and with a determination of schedules—how long it will take to contract, award, and complete the work, and to do the analysis. This information is used in comparing the costs of the archeological/historic program against the costs of the other features of the project before making the final allocation of resources.

Another problem area concerns contract administration. Improper contract administration will more often than not produce a product far different from that expected. This is true even in a project with the noblest of objectives, the best-laid plans, and an excellent contract document.

Contract administration starts from the very moment the manager conceives the project and starts to develop a plan and specifications for the accomplishment of the effort. Preparation of the contract requires knowledge of the amount of fiscal resources that will be available to administer the contract. Administration includes more than the signing of the document and the payment of the contract. It includes the collection of information from the contract, assurance that the terms of the contract are being properly executed during all phases of the contract. It means a qualified person must determine whether the contractor is accomplishing the work in the manner specified. Regular visits to the contractor and the contract site are essential, including visits by a professional archeologist. The obligation here is not only to make sure that the contractor is doing his job but also to guide the contractor in areas of uncertainty and to make modifications, if required, in a manner that will assure timely performance and prompt payments. To assure correct procedures, archeologists should attend a course in administration before they are made responsible for administering a contract. The archeologists, at a minimum, should visit their first contractor with someone who is experienced in the field, to help them through the difficult areas and to teach them how to avoid pitfalls.

Contract administration is very likely the most severe problem area that we have in archeology today. Many contracted projects appear to run over cost without providing the product originally agreed upon. If the contract and its administration are nebulous and loosely accomplished, it is impossible to determine when the instrument has been effectively completed. This area must be given proper attention by the archeologists and the managers.

A third area involves the need for research publication, since a book that is never written will provide little enjoyment to a reader, and a report that is never written will provide little knowledge to the world. The joy of the experimentation and the exhilaration of the exploration are the fun part of a project. It takes an exceptional person to enjoy the analyses and preparation of the report, the scientific verification and documentation for posterity. This may be the separation point between avocational and professional attitudes in archeology.

Visits to museums and to the visitors' centers at government projects, where the findings of archeological and historical interests are displayed, find the people enjoying a knowledge of the past. Documentaries on television and articles in magazines and in newspapers tend to interest the public, letting them share in the excitement of the past. Without this documentation and without this effort, the archeologist cannot build the public base of support that the manager needs to help justify the expenditure of the government's time and money. Findings must be published in a format that enables the world—and not just the archeologists—to know what has gone before.

In addition, preserving the artifacts and documentation of our explorations and investigations is extremely important. A major problem facing the manager is how to pay for curation, and how to have this accomplished in such a way that the best and most important specimens and data are made available for research and for public enjoyment. The critical issue in curation is determining which data and specimens need to be curated. Even relatively unimportant data of today may be important for future research and may warrant reconsideration. Archeologists must make some hard decisions about which materials absolutely require curation. Managers should not decide this issue, but they will if archeologists do not. The universities and associations that are willing to accept the data and materials are becoming so saturated that they will accept material only if compensated. Curation must be considered in the total cost package for the budget outyears. The job must be done properly, and in the most cost effective manner.

Vandalism is a problem at any government facility, and it is a major problem in areas open to the general public. The discipline of economics applies a theory known as "the tragedy of the commons" to this situation. This theory postulates that if a publicly owned resource is made available to all—free, or at a very low cost—then the users will destroy the resource.

This theory seems to apply very well to cultural resources on public land. Today much of the public appears to believe that it is their right to keep or to do what they will with what they find. This is, of course, untrue, and it is our job to communicate this to the public.

Vandalism falls into three categories: casual, premeditated, and destructive. The casual, or unintentional, vandals are those who collect as a personal hobby, with little research, picking up whatever they find. They are apt to stumble onto a site on a weekend outing and enthusiastically gouge and rummage to obtain whatever they can during their short vacation. These vandals can, of course, cause great damage to the resource, and they may illegally appropriate valuable artifacts for their personal satisfaction. The second category is the intentional, premeditated looter. These persons know what will sell or what is needed for their personal collections. They know they are operating illegally and, therefore, must work quickly and secretly. They may know a great deal about archeology but apply none of their knowledge to the sites being plundered. They dig with great efficiency, destroying much. The final category of vandals consists of the true vandals who smash and destroy without apparent logic. The solution to the vandalism problem requires education of the public and strict enforcement of commercially oriented activities. We should also encourage the closer cooperation of the genuinely concerned avocational groups and of the public at large.

Finally, the safety of an archeological project is a constant concern for the manager. The archeologists must practice safety. A manager cannot allow a contract to continue if safety is not a way of life. The Corps of Engineers has a safety manual and a set of safety procedures that are included in the general provisions of any construction or architect-engineer contract. The procedures must be applied and followed on archeology contracts. This means that the field team leader must know the rules and must ensure that the crew is fully schooled in safety rules and procedures. The crew should attend toolbox sessions in which potential problems and questions are discussed. For example, what action should be taken if someone is bitten by a snake or has a stroke, or if there is an accident, a tornado, or a fire? Where is the nearest assistance in terms of police or medical needs? How should sanitation be ensured? When and under what conditions is shoring necessary for trenches or pits?

This system of accountability, regular briefings, and visible, written information is followed by the Corps of Engineers' field crews and construction contractors on all of our work. We will not accept less from the archeology teams.

Some of these remarks have been pointed, but they are intended to demonstrate the deep and continuing interest in archeology of the Corps of Engineers. The Corps of Engineers' early involvement in archeology has been pointed out, and the Corps of Engineers' management concern with budgeting, contract administration, publication, curation, vandalism, and safety has been touched on.

However, the single most important point is that a partnership among the managers, the archeologists, and the engineers is required if a worthwhile, lasting program is to be developed. The Corps of Engineers' motto is *Essayons*, "Let us try." That motto applies to all who work for or with the Corps of Engineers, including the archeologists.

PETER PATTON—Panelist
I would like to talk today very briefly about my role in rescue archeology, which is somewhat different from everyone else's on this panel. As a geologist and geomorphologist, my research interests are primarily in the effects of large, catastrophic floods on river systems. In particular, I am interested in developing long-term hydrological records for river basins that will allow modern catastrophic floods to be seen from a long-term perspective—a very large problem in modern hydrology. As an approach to the problem, I have studied the mechanics of sedimentation along river systems during large flood events, and from this knowledge of sedimentary processes I have identified those areas along the rivers where sediments accumulate during rare great floods. From the preserved stratigraphic record in these areas, it is possible to reconstruct past flood events, a process that has become known as paleohydrology. This assessment of flood potential enables a better risk as-

sessment for floods in a given river basin. What, then, does this have to do with archeology?

I have found that stratified archeological sites adjacent to rivers provide the best data repositories for this approach. One particular archeological site in West Texas illustrates the applicability of archeology to modern geomorphic research. The site is located on the Pecos River at its confluence with the Rio Grande, in the vicinity of Amistad Reservoir. The Pecos River in this area is confined to an erosional river canyon with very few depositional features along the margins of the canyons. The site was excavated by the Texas Archeological Salvage Project in 1965 and 1966 and is called the Arinosa Shelter. With an archeological record that spans essentially the entire Holocene epoch, the Arinosa Shelter provides a continuous record of cultural development in Southwest Texas.

To my eyes, the most significant aspect of Arinosa Shelter is not the evidences of cultural habitation. In my view, the most spectacular features were the nearly pristine, well-preserved sedimentation units that punctuate the shelter. My study of the sedimentology of Arinosa allows the extension of the flood frequency record for the Pecos River over a time span of approximately two thousand years. In addition, analysis of the sedimentary layers enables one to see changes in the frequency of flooding in this locality over that time period, changes that were coincident with climatic changes, which were deduced from other paleoclimatic indicators present in the site. When this information is integrated into the cultural information we have for the Arinosa Shelter, it will allow a better paleoenvironmental reconstruction which, I think, will be helpful to both the archeologists and the geologists. But the beauty of this approach is that the information extracted from the Arinosa Shelter can be isolated from its archeological context and can be used to look at a very practical and pragmatic engineering problem: What is the frequency of large, rare floods in the Pecos River basin?

It is also very appropriate for me to describe Arinosa Shelter at a meeting of rescue archeologists. When Arinosa Shelter was excavated I was eight years old, and the Shelter was inundated long before I could ever visit the site. It was only through the fine, quality fieldwork and reporting of the Texas Archeological Salvage Project (as it was known then) that I was able to analyze the site and extract my information from the data base stored in the Project's warehouse. My specific message is that there is a high-quality data base in the rescue archeology repository that is not being adequately exploited by other disciplines. I can broaden my appeal from this one isolated topic of fluvial geomorphology; there is a range of geological phenomena that occur too frequently to be directly measured, e.g., Quaternary studies focused on hazard mitigation, land stability for nuclear waste disposal, or the periodicity of catastrophic surface processes.

The second part of my message is that geomorphologists can aid archeologists in site prediction. That is, through an understanding of modern surface processes it becomes possible to predict those sites, within relatively large geographic areas, that have the greatest potential for archeological evaluation. If I can go back for a moment to my specific little field of study on rivers, in my current work in New England with a group of archeologists, we're interested in being able to find archaic sites that are separated from the modern plow zone. In New England this is a difficult problem because the rivers have relatively low sediment yields. Sedimentation on the flood plains is relatively slow, and we typically find the entire cultural record in New England mixed within the plow zone.

Nevertheless, one then takes the approach of looking for those areas where sedimentation is most rapid on the flood plains. It is possible to target specific areas, by this I mean on the order of a few hectares, for detailed analysis. Our results have been quite satisfactory in that we have been able to find several archaic sites separated from the plow zone by sediment strata that were laid down during major floods. So we have surfaces that are stable for tens to hundreds of years at a time and then a periodic inundation and deposition by a single geologic event. Again, this approach is not limited to the interplay of fluvial geomorphology and archeology but can be logically extended into other environments. One that leaps into my mind is on the coastal zone. Again, I think this would be an extremely valuable approach. In targeting areas where time and funds are limited, we'd like to get the greatest possible return for the rescue archeology project.

Finally, I'd like to offer what I consider a critique of the status of what might be called geoarcheology. In the academic professions in the United States today both disciplines, geology and archeology, are moving forward rapidly with a new understanding of processes and of the application of new technology. This has meant a new understanding of surface processes and a rapidly revolving theoretical model for landscape development. I am occasionally upset and appalled by the application by some of my colleagues of what I consider to be oversimplistic concepts and models of landform development.

Fortunately geologists and archeologists have a long history of dialogue. And it is of paramount importance for archeology that the archeologist and geologist continue this dialogue so that we can have a wedding of what is best in both disciplines. If this is accomplished, I am confident that the scientific rewards for both communities will be great.

MICHAEL MOSELEY—Panelist

As Lautaro Núñez pointed out, looking at the central Andes, we face a crisis situation in a very arid area along the Pacific Coast where we have been trying to develop some applications of archeology to practical engineering concerns. Rainfall takes place at an elevation of about two thousand meters, and the water cascades down the Pacific watershed. We are trying to develop studies that address irrigation being practiced on the desert coast. The coastal irrigation networks are fed by small rivers; canals contribute to a very productive agricultural system in the context of the world's driest deserts.

We have learned that at one time more than 30 percent more land was under cultivation than today. This was due to two major geological processes. One is the El Nino, which creates heat aberrations coming across the Pacific. Normal conditions then bring rain to the otherwise arid Andean Coast. Because extensive prehistoric canal systems crossed and blocked dry drainages, we are able to get a record of paleo-flooding, evidenced in catchment basins, mud flows, and sequence flooding. By extending the flood record back for about two thousand years, we can come to grips with the fact that the 1982-83 El Nino was really miniscule compared with several events that occurred in the past. Early floods washed out prehistoric canal systems. One section has been repaired, but all subsequent erosion over the last thousand years has not equalled the force of a single event that took place about a thousand years ago. That same event flooded a valley system and scoured out the entire valley floor.

Climatic effects are only one of the impacting forces. The Andes are very active tectonically, with underthrusting going on at a rate of ten centimeters or more each year, such that the mountain range is being pushed up. This has all sorts of consequences for irrigation systems. For example, a major canal system now runs uphill. Where canal systems show fault impacting, we can identify which faults are active; if people are designing canal systems or road systems in the same area, we can provide information on the environmental stress that will affect such engineering works. Tectonics is not simply gaugeable by irrigation works, it is gaugeable by major architectural landforms. We have floors and walls that show accumulative slope change through time.

To understand the varying collapse on a scale of hundreds of kilometers through many of the irrigation systems, we can think of the process simply as opening a fan of agriculture in which the canal system moves water most efficiently to the river on a perpendicular course. As uplift occurs, rivers downcut. The coast uplifts, rivers downcut. So a process of agricultural contraction was taking place over the past 1500 years, as canals were built progressively downslope. Because the agricultural fan contracts through time, leaving less land under cultivation, we can chart the amount of uplift and gauge it against agricultural fans. This allows us both retrodiction and prediction as to what will happen with contemporary large-scale irrigation projects. The closing of agricultural fans in relation to tectonic parameters moves from slow uplift at the top to more rapid uplift at the bottom.

We can also use abandoned agricultural systems to get an idea of engineering, cost, and labor investment. We can see that some attempts at long-term expansion involve great labor and engineering investments with only moderate land gains. Such projects can be difficult to maintain if contemporary engineering is not aware of the statistical periodicity of major floods occurring in the area or of tectonic parameters.

We are trying to apply aspects of archeology, such as pointing out active faults and problems with canal intakes, in order to establish a paleo-flood record. In this way we can mitigate the effects of much of the current reclamation work that is being done in Latin America, and we can do it in a cost-effective manner.

VICTOR A. NUÑEZ—Panelist

I will refer specifically to problems that developing countries face in dealing with rescue archeology. The specific reality of these countries must be taken into account. Otherwise we run the risk of building unworkable theories. The problems differ according to the country. In one extreme, Mexico's situation is not the same as Paraguay's. But there are disturbing elements that are similar in the development of rescue archeology.

One of the fundamental problems concerns not only the planning of projects and how the projects relate to archeology, but also the often dramatic situation of how we as archeologists should relate to the planners and to the existing perspectives in each country. It is dangerous to try to copy models mechanically from more developed countries, models that might involve unrealizable goals. In summary, the concrete reality of each country should be kept in mind when planning how to combat effectively the daily destruction of archeological sites.

To give you an example of the existing situation, in Venezuela, a country of 912,050 square kilometers, we have less than twenty professional archeologists, only five of whom have the doctorate. Let us suppose that we concentrate our efforts on raising the consciousness of planners and government agencies. Then, as an example, suppose it would be legally necessary to perform rescue projects before any construction began. This would be absolutely impossible. To aggravate the situation, a vicious cycle develops because of the lack of human resources. There is no support for the education of archeologists. When archeologists leave the university there is often no employment for them. But at the same time we are unable to plan rescue archeology projects because we lack human resources.

The economic situation of universities and research institutes becomes more acute due to reduced funding that each year affects both types of institutions. But the academic organisms require research results every year. Therefore, the archeologist must content himself with elaborating theoretical projects or with reanalyzing old collections, a series of archeological tasks that may or may not be very important but that are not related to direct work on archeological sites.

There are anthropologists who graduate without ever having seen an archeological excavation. Laboratory practice is also reduced. Today, an underdeveloped mentality would tend to create doctoral-level courses. But this is not the real problem. Rather, we should concentrate on increasing the number of persons involved in rescue archeology projects. Otherwise, in the immediate future, we will not have archeological sites to study.

I believe that there are certain alternatives that can supplant the lack of human and economic resources. I will mention a few of them.

Owing to the number of projects, the few people available, and the scarce economic resources, the archeologist must be like a one-man orchestra. He needs to be a topographer, draftsman, chauffeur, administrator, secretary, and even archeologist. Given this fact, we have to create an interdisciplinary approach designed to utilize the archeologist's work hours more effectively. The incorporation of specialists from other disciplines would permit middle-range projects.

Furthermore, one has to depart from traditional schemes for financing and logistic support in institutes and universities. Funding should be sought from private companies and from nontraditional state-owned companies. Contacts should be established with planners from ministries and municipal councils, in order to raise their level of consciousness.

I share with Rex González the idea that the army could make a very positive contribution. We had such an experience in the rescue archeology project at Corpozulia, which was halted three months ago due to economic problems. Similar experiences occurred at La Guajira and in other regions of the Zulia state in Venezuela. The army helped with men, transportation, and equipment. It donated expertise such as that of topographers. Several areas permitted active participation of the army in this national emergency of the irreversible destruction of archeological sites.

Another possibility that should not be ignored is to explore the extent to which this conference might produce an inter-American organization that would coordinate rescue archeology projects. This organization would serve as an information and action center. It would also be aware of the greater priorities regarding rescue archeology, and it would try to organize inter-American cooperation in order to resolve urgent archeological problems in countries with insufficient economic or human resources.

I have indicated briefly the areas that require action. We should suppress rhetoric and begin concrete action.

LEONARD LARDAVERA—Panelist
I am here in behalf of Clifford R. Miercort, President of the Southwestern Division of North American Coal.

North American Coal Corporation has surface mining properties both in Texas and in North Dakota. These are large-scale mines that supply lignite to electric utilities. We also have several underground mining operations in Ohio and Pennsylvania.

My role as a consulting archeologist with North American primarily involves the development of a comprehensive cultural resource planning process by which cultural resources can be fully addressed prior to their disturbance by mining activities. As others have pointed out, archeology and engineering originally didn't go very well together, and engineers were somewhat hesitant to have an archeologist at a mining site. But we've been able to resolve some of these differences by developing programs to train and orient our engineers, geologists, and heavy equipment operators so that they can recognize cultural resource sites and, we hope, notify the proper authorities prior to any disturbance.

This kind of training involves coordination with the engineers prior to any kind of mining activity; we use the mining company's maps, detailed mine studies, and aerial photographs. We have found that this has been very helpful in locating prehistoric and historic resources prior to mining. We've also been able to appropriate the necessary funds to deal with cultural resources on a year-to-year basis.

By developing predictive models we've been able to determine the amount of funds we'll need to address certain kinds of resources. The training program we're using for engineers and equipment operators is carried out through slide presentations and field tours for the operators and engineers. Through these presentations we've been able to alert our engineers and operators to come forward if they know of prehistoric and historic sites that might be affected by mining. In one East Texas case, some of our equipment operators are native to the area. Since we've started discussing archeological resources with them, many have voluntarily located sites, such as small family cemeteries or Indian camps, on the mining property. The local people have been particularly helpful in the case of cemeteries. There are some heavily wooded areas in East Texas where small family cemeteries or even slave cemeteries are not generally recognizable. But with our operators educated, they've been able to point out these sites well in advance of mining operations.

We've also developed the predictive model that has been extremely helpful in planning research designs and in appropriating funds for other areas within the mine boundary. We are currently mining on a year-to-year basis, so that we can address cultural resources in advance. We have sufficient time to interview local landowners and regional authorities, and to determine the character and location of archeological sites. We believe it especially important that our land agent, who is the first one to go out and negotiate leases, be able to inquire about cultural resources that landowners may know about.

North American Coal hired an archeologist for the same reasons the corporation hired a reclamation specialist, a hydrologist, and other specialists. The corporation realized that it would have to deal with archeology for the life of the mine, and it felt an archeologist on staff would be most suitable. Legally, North American Coal is required to conduct sample surveys prior to any mining activities; the results of the surveys must be presented in North American's permanent application for a particular mine under the Texas Surface Mining and Reclamation Act. The act was passed primarily so that mining companies such as ourselves would have to obey environmental regulations and other legislation. On the federal level, North American Coal is also entering a memorandum of agreement with EPA under the National Environmental Protection Act. Additionally, guidance is being provided by the Texas Historical Commission in Austin.

North American has designed its mining operations so that the protection of cultural resource sites is accorded a high priority. Topsoil, which must be stockpiled and replaced, is generally placed over cultural resource sites whenever possible to preserve them. Fences have also worked out fairly well as protective devices. If we know of a significant site, we take protective measures by fencing it off, thus eliminating the possibility of accidental disturbance by an operator. The fence also deters vandals or recreational diggers from going into that particular site. As mining progresses, we hope we'll be better able to determine the kinds of resources we will need to deal with. The predictive model certainly has been helpful. We hope to be able to develop better ways to address the kinds of prehistoric and historic cultural resources we need to deal with so that archeology won't greatly hinder mining.

GARY L. MELVIN—Panelist

My comments are going to be from the perspective of a large energy developer with two major characteristics. First, our activities are ultimately very land disturbing, and second, those land disturbances are not mobile because they are tied to the location of mineral reserves. Unlike housing developments, highways, and airports, our activities can't be relocated. Fulfilling cultural and historic resource obligations associated with major development probably illustrates better than other environmental concerns the potential for confusion in the complex compliance procedures.

Major rescue archeological programs in the United States have developed not only quickly but also during the period when most environmental control programs were being implemented. The resulting difficulties associated with this rapid growth are not at all unique to cultural resource management programs. However, such programs seem to suffer from a greater number of administrative, logistical, and intellectual problems than do other environmental protection activities. There exist complex administrative problems among the various agencies at the federal, state, and local levels concerned with or responsible for cultural resource management. Over a brief number of years the administrative structure has changed from a near inability to receive guidance regarding compliance issues, methodology, research design, and other subjects pertinent to rescue archeology, to a situation where several agencies claim a substantive role in the implementation of cultural resource compliance activities regarding a specific project. Even more troublesome is the fact that these agencies are usually in substantial disagreement on nearly all the major issues relative to the project. If interagency conflicts are pervasive, it follows that many areas of disagreement exist between individual archeologists.

Decision makers, project sponsors, and the general public who have occasion to read documents prepared by archeologists find that the technical jargon common to such documents rivals that of the medical profession. It is understood that archeologists must produce accurate and comprehensive descriptions of the data recovery programs so as to provide data to their colleagues in the archeological community. However, the community of interested parties consists of more than archeologists. Because management information such as mitigation recommendations and study conclusions is primarily read by laymen, such information must be clearly and concisely written, free from a lot of technical jargon. Final project reports written for general audiences are very difficult to locate, with the exception of a limited number of efforts that produce firsts, or that address very large and very dramatic archeological resources. It also appears that rescue archeology thrusts the cultural resource professionals into the real world, the world of budget and time constraints, and profit and loss statements. Even contract archeological firms are often unable to distinguish a contract from a grant. The viewpoint that the nature of the research dictates the time required for study is also quite prevalent among cultural resource managers. This concept of project timing is not relevant to a rescue archeology project once a decision to develop has been made.

The thrust of my recommendations to rescue archeologists is that the difficulties I've mentioned—and I've just tried to highlight for purposes of brevity here—would be mitigated to some extent if archeologists would (1) unite and take a look at the feasibility of regional research strategies, thus making survey and mitigation procedures and the determination of National Register significance more easily established in the context of what's important in the region where developmental activities are taking place; (2) look forward as well as backward, particularly in time; and (3) develop a consumer-oriented approach to rescue archeology. I believe such a producer-consumer ethic is really an approach to professionalism at all levels. The approach can be applied to any discipline, and it argues for workers to identify not only with the work they do but also with the entity or entities they are producing for. It makes everyone's work an important link in someone else's work and teaches respect for and attachment to the consumer, the ultimate user of the product that's being produced. The approach results in self-generated quality control within the discipline, and in immediate recognition of new or improved products—primarily discoveries, in the case of archeology. The producer-consumer ethic tends to involve the producer in all stages of the consumer's program and vice versa, thus introducing archeology early in the planning process. If overspending occurs in such a scenario, it tends to be for the reasons of necessity and quality.

MICHAEL J. SNARSKIS—Panelist
That there can be successful interaction among planning, engineering, and rescue archeology was demonstrated by the long-range preparation for the Boruca hydroelectric project in southwestern Costa Rica in the late 1970s. Until that time, relations between local archeologists and those in charge of land modification and development were nonexistent or, at best, informal and largely dependent on the subjective interests and personalities of the engineers or contractors concerned with each project.

Boruca was a bittersweet experience that deserves brief recapitulation. When it became known that a large dam project was being planned for the region, Frederick Lang, who at the time was an archeologist affiliated with the National Museum of Costa Rica, made the initial approach and discovered some interest in rescue archeology on the part of the builder.

Shortly thereafter, a North American student, Tony Carmichael, conducted a brief nonstatistical survey of the zone to be flooded. Lang left the National Museum to return to the United States at that time, and it fell to me to write the proposal for archeological salvage. A detailed three-year plan for archeology was laid out, with more schematic projections for up to eight years. The projected archeological salvage was joined by the project planners with a population relocation team composed primarily of social workers and anthropologists. Although the project managers had never formally budgeted archeology into any earlier projects (there being no equivalent to the Environmental Protection Act in Costa Rica), the level of planning for Boruca was impressive. An architect was selected to design a field laboratory for archeology according to our specifications. I was directed to seek out a sixteen-member team of archeologists for field and laboratory positions. As there were not that many trained Costa Rican archeologists available, non–Costa Ricans were recruited. Sufficient vehicles, field and lab equipment were provided for. Through consultation with a former university professor, I designed a stratified random sampling plan for the 390-square-kilometer inundation zone.

Close cooperation was foreseen between the builder's geologist and the archeological team. The same was true for the social workers. After hiring had begun for the archeological salvage, the Boruca hydroelectric project in general, and the projected archeology in particular, were mortally affected by a double whammy. The project failed to attract an expected international loan, and the local currency began a rapid skid to a 500 percent devaluation. Our rosy vision of adequate long-term rescue archeology was dashed, although project managers, much to their credit, did provide lesser funding and logistical assistance for the two U.S. archeologists who had already come to Costa Rica for the project. They carried out an abbreviated, though nonstatistical, survey over the next eighteen months, and many important sites were located.

The Boruca project, although not coming to fruition, stands in stark contrast to the typical and traditional interface of engineering, construction, and archeology in Costa Rica. Although public and private institutions are required by law to notify the National Museum of apparent findings of archeological remains in land-modifying projects, it is almost never done. The Rosen Public Works Institute, the housing institute, and even the light and power people (not to mention private construction firms) routinely bulldoze archeological sites without informing anyone, simply because they don't want their work delayed or the operators don't recognize the sites. In most of these situations, substantial and important rescue archeology could be done if only contact between contractors and archeologists could be made.

Simply knowing when earth-moving work is to be done, assuming that schedules can be slightly adjusted, can result in significant archeological benefits, as was the case with several recent projects in Costa Rica. Some of these projects are described in the published papers of the First New World Conference on Rescue Archeology.

The law dealing with the archeological patrimony of Costa Rica, revised and strengthened in 1981, provides for strict penalties, fines, and incarceration if sites are knowingly destroyed by individuals, companies, or institutions. Nevertheless, destruction—often purposeful—is what happens in more than 95 percent of the cases today (my personal estimate). Ignorance of the law is often professed, and indeed, many local police throughout the country are not aware of the law at all. Companies and institutions typically flaunt their ignorance fairly openly, secure in the knowledge that the law will not be enforced. It is unfortunately true, and can only be concluded from this, that execution, not litigation, is more urgently needed in Costa Rica.

It should be mentioned, however, that during the past two years a series of introductory courses in archeology, instituted by the Ministry of Culture and taught by practicing archeologists, has been offered to police throughout the country. In the San José metropolitan area, there is now a team of two or three policemen assigned only to archeological cases, although the team typically deals with the illegal export of artifacts rather than with site protection.

As head of archeological research at the National Museum for the past nine years, I witnessed many kinds of cooperation (or the lack of it) with land-modifying agencies. The case of Boruca was virtually unique in that archeological salvage was included early in the planning stage.

I do have some suggestions. The creation of a special rescue archeology unit made up of archeologists, police, and laborers is a good idea, because we often find ourselves in positions of law enforcement which can become very delicate and uncomfortable for everyone. But it is an expensive idea with little chance of fruition in Costa Rica's very precarious financial situation. Very few people can be hired for new jobs in Costa Rica today.

As it stands now, increased conscientiousness of archeology among individuals in public agencies is much to be desired. This awareness does seem to be on the rise, because we do project as much as we can. But even if endangered sites are reported, who does the work, and with what money? And there is a negative feedback, of course, when someone goes out of his way to report an endangered site to the museum or another archeologist and then observes that no one does anything about it. There simply are not enough paid archeologists to do the job in Costa Rica—we have around fifteen.

I believe a more practical short-term solution lies with the large, semi-autonomous institutions in Costa Rica, institutions that are part government, part private. These employ hundreds of thousands of people, not one of whom is an archeologist. Two of the major archeological museums in Costa Rica, those of the Central Bank and the Insurance Institute, also do not employ any archeologists. The hiring of young Costa Rican professionals would increase knowledge of the field's importance over the long run. For instance, tourism in Mexico is well developed; Costa Rica can develop in much the same way, but few people seem to realize it.

HARRY HUTCHENS—Panelist

I come to you as part of the neglected public that we were trying to reach this morning, that is, one of those engineers and constructors who have probably destroyed more archeology than realized. The reason is that we most often are involved in the moving around of the earth. So I am here today to try to get educated before it is too late.

Although a great deal of progress has been made in developing a good relationship between archeology and the engineering and construction industry, a great deal remains to be done. The additional progress yet to be achieved is largely dependent on the education of our engineers who carry out the project planning, design, and construction engineering. Clearly the educational process involves considerable time—time to adapt the educational processes to our kind of work and time to reach the practitioners. Nevertheless, I believe we are seeing signs that our evolution is underway and that it will continue.

A parallel exists with regard to archeology. My thinking of it as a parallel may reflect my own ignorance about archeology, but it seems to me that archeology is parallel to the evolving consciousness in the world about the environment—the air, the water, and the living plant and animal species. It hasn't been very long since we were hearing voices of concern regarding the environment that, just a few years ago, were faint cries in the wilderness. Today, in almost every construction project, environmental concerns dominate the early planning process.

There is a very logical correlation between archeology and engineering because the preservation of our cultural heritage and the knowledge derived from its study go hand in hand with the development of facilities to accommodate present and future generations. It is important to remember that much of our current engineering and construction technology is founded on principles that were known and used in ancient times; some of these principles were perhaps even more highly developed than those of today. So it is that planning and engineering firms are performing archeological assessments of designated areas or rights of way for new facilities simultaneously with assessments of other aspects of the environment. However, I think that very few of those assessments are carried out by professional archeologists. Instead, they are generally done by engineers or specialists in the floral or faunal aspects of the environment. And so their assessments are limited as a rule to surface features data gleaned from aerial photogrammetry, which, incidentally, should be enhanced tremendously as we gain greater access to and understanding of the photography that has been done by NASA and the other federal space agencies.

Nevertheless, these assessments constitute a recognition of the importance of archeological data and a good step in the right direction. But we continue to struggle with the fact that, to a large degree, once a project goes into construction, contractors are dependent on good fortune and the keen eye of interested and alert construction personnel and engineers to detect subsurface elements of interest. For example, in a recent year we had two separate and widely diverse incidents recorded in one deep excavation in a limestone substrate for a power plant. We uncovered fossil evidence not too far from here of a reptile—the *acrocanthasaurus*, a three-toed reptile-type of character—that created a great deal of excitement on the site and among the amateurs in that arena. It also provided some samples for state universities and museums.

Another case was the investigation of a right of way for an interstate highway through a swamp in Louisiana. A "beautifully preserved" (and I don't really know what that means) American Indian site was discovered in Saint John the Baptist Parish, buried under a layer of peat. So detecting these things is not the easiest thing in the world for a construction engineer or an equipment operator. Nevertheless, I do believe that if we look at the educational process of the engineering community, both at the practitioners and those who are studying, and attempt to expand their exposure to the issues of archeology, we will over time greatly improve and enhance the opportunities for rescue archeology in the construction industry.

I might add one additional thought in regard to communication with the public. One recent article in *The Texan* magazine of the *Houston Chronicle* was devoted entirely to archeology in Val Verde County in southwestern Texas. It was very interesting because it was written by a layman, for laymen, but it dealt specifically with the archeological efforts there. It was very, very good. I think such communication efforts will be beneficial to the engineering community, to the lay public, and to archeology in the long run.

General Discussion

HENRY CLEERE

I want to pick up a point made by Víctor Núñez, one of the most important points that I've heard today and one that I hope will be considered subsequently, and particularly in the final session when we come to decide upon our resolutions and recommendations.

It was in this very town, and Hester Davis reminded me that it was nine and a half years ago, that I first heard the phrase "cultural resource management" at the meeting of the S.A.A., the annual meeting in Dallas in 1975. This opened up for me a wider horizon. I'd always thought of archeology very much in national terms—I think we all do. But I suddenly became aware that problems in the United States were just the same as problems in Britain, in other parts of Europe, and in other parts of the world that I knew. And I began to look at this problem of what I call comparative cultural resource management—the comparison-contrast between the systems in operation in different countries. A group of us in Europe got together in the late seventies and began to study how we could work more closely together. We worked first on an informal basis, with meetings in Paris in 1981, and identified a number of areas where we could benefit from the experiences of our colleagues in other countries. On matters of standardization, qualifications, training, legislation, and organization, we believed we could all learn from one another. However, just after we met in Paris, I went to Quito, and I saw that there was already such a movement underway, with the establishment of the First New World Conference on Rescue Archeology, precisely for this kind of informal exchange of views. Fired by the spirit of Quito, I went later the same month to the General Assembly of ICOMOS in Rome, and I proposed a resolution to that body. Although ICOMOS's statutes are very broad, the organization has until very recently been the preserve of the architects and architectural historians, who were interested solely in the built heritage, the aboveground heritage. I believed there was a need to persuade the members of ICOMOS that there was another dimension, and somewhat to my astonishment, I proposed a resolution that was received with acclamation in Rome and was forthwith accepted as policy. Since 1981, then, I've been working toward the establishment of an international committee within the framework of ICOMOS in the field of archeology, and I shall be leaving this meeting a little early so that I can be at a meeting of the ICOMOS Executive Committee during which the international committee will be formally established.

So we will have an international committee. But much more important, we are proposing to have regional committees. And this brings me to the point that Víctor Núñez made and a point I know Alberto Rex González feels very strongly about, that is, the opportunity for the exchange of information through an organization that will promote collaboration on a regional basis. What I hope this conference will decide to do at the end of its deliberations is follow the admirable precedents set in Quito in 1981 (and here in Dallas in 1984) and establish an archeological committee for the Americas that can continue on a more formal basis with this kind of interchange of views, this organization of collaboration that we have all recognized as so important. I hope the conference will give me the mandate to go back to ICOMOS in Paris and to say that the Americas are ready to set up their committee, because to do so is immensely important.

THOMAS F. KING

I have a question for Harry Hutchens. I certainly think you make a valid point, that it's a matter of education. Education is the principal fact, the principal matter that we ought to attend to in trying to reach out to the engineering community in order to gain greater credence for rescue archeology. But you also make an excellent point in that this is a long process. Several of the other panel members have made it clear that there is a major crisis among the Latin American countries, even in countries with highly developed and very sophisticated legal structures, like Costa Rica, in which there are, in fact, relatively sophisticated protective statutes but in which archeological sites are not being protected. Sites are being destroyed by engineering works. So my question to you is really a very nuts-and-bolts sort of question. How do we shortcut the educational process, how can we move most quickly to educate the engineering community, at least in those countries where there is a statutory basis for conducting rescue archeology to get it done?

HARRY HUTCHENS

Yours is a very valid query. Because engineers and constructors have a tendency to respond to the control documents on any kind of a project, they will learn as rapidly as they have to. The more leisurely approach is to go through the long-haul educational process. It is difficult, of course, to legislate things of that nature, but certainly the Environmental Protection Act and complementary legislation in the United States have supplied an impetus for that sort of thing. I don't know how rapidly or effectively such things can be achieved, but if lending agencies and project developers—people who finance things—can somehow or other be convinced that that's an important consideration, the engineers will fall in line.

ROBERT J. DACEY

I think an even more basic aspect of the question addresses a problem that's perplexing all of us: the problem of technology transfer. And I don't think there is any shortcut to technology transfer. That's a problem that we're going to have to resolve through education and through better data communication years from now. But in the interim, I think the interdisciplinary approach to the planning problem, as well as the interdisciplinary approach to the problem resolution as you encounter problems during an engineering project, is the only way we've got. I don't think there are any shortcuts in the process. What we're after is a heightened awareness on the part of all of the people involved and, as Harry pointed out, heightened to the point where you've got a dozer operator who now has awareness that he didn't have ten or fifteen years ago, at least in some of the industry here in the United States. It's an extremely difficult question facing, I think, every aspect of our society. If you've read Alvin Toffler's book *Future Shock*, you know we're just part of that microcosm. It's there and it's happening and I don't think there are any shortcuts.

MICHAEL J. SNARSKIS

Our archeological association is about ready to bring out a tourist-oriented, or rather, a public-oriented, short book with beautiful color pictures, on archeology. Amazingly, such a book has been lacking in Costa Rica for many years. Also in Costa Rica, whenever any kind of archeological project is done, we publish a story about it in the local papers—popular accounts of what we think we are learning. In this way we are reaching more and more people. This is especially true for school-age children who tour the museums regularly with their teachers and who are taken to archeological sites near San José where they see real archeology in action, an opportunity very few people have in Costa Rica.

The looting in Costa Rica is absolutely devastating and has been for a hundred years. But I think we are definitely gaining ground there.

Concerning the legal situation in Costa Rica, it is true that the law is not always followed. Let me illustrate a case, a project outside the capital near Guanacaste some 120 miles away, a small cemetery that had been looted. The police stepped in, and we were called out from the museum a couple of years ago and began working. Threats on our lives and property became commonplace. At one point two police guards who had to stay at the site overnight were driven off by more than ten gun-wielding men—extremely unusual for Costa Rica. In such cases one wonders exactly what to do; there is no simple answer. Fortunately, this hasn't recurred in Costa Rica. I can now report that today this same site has finally—over strong protestations by the owner—become public property, and archeological work is about to be started again.

GEORGE A. AARONS

I fully endorse what Henry Cleere said a short while ago. But I would like to point out that there already are regional and subregional organizations that should be part of an ICOMOS committee for the Americas. In other words, I don't think it would make sense at this point to create another new organization when already there is CARIMOS for monuments and sites in the Greater Caribbean, which covers everything from Florida to Brazil. The organization is made up of the National Trusts of the islands and the territories as well as the countries that have an ICOMOS. There is also the Caribbean Conservation Association, which deals with the Caribbean Islands. There is also the Council for Underwater Archeology and so on and so forth. And while I think that it would be a very good idea for us to deliberate what Dr. Cleere mentioned, I think we should take into account the existing organizations, so that we can take advantage of their plans, their proposals, their thoughts, and come up with a really concrete proposal that he can take to the meeting in Paris.

RUTHANN KNUDSON

I am associated with an international engineering firm where we are beginning to talk to each other. I would suggest that the American Society of Civil Engineers has a history committee that so far deals almost exclusively with architecture. I think that if some of us make an attempt to participate in that committee, to make presentations to that committee, as well as to ASCE in this country and probably to other civil engineering organizations, we will have a much more direct and active way of participating in their language and their organizations. We also might find that we have some other kinds of opportunities.

RAYMOND H. THOMPSON
I think that we have had a slightly one-sided discussion this afternoon in the sense that we have emphasized over and over again the need to educate engineers. And I think it's important that someone from the archeological community should call our attention to the fact that we also need to educate the archeologists. If it's going to be important to have engineers learn something about archeology, perhaps we should have the archeologists learn something about engineering. A number of references have been made already to the problems that have emerged in many situations in this country that have stemmed largely from the lack of understanding on the part of archeologists of the problems of engineers, architects, economists, planners, managers, land procurers, etc. And I think that we would be remiss if we were to leave this conference feeling very proud of the fact that we finally have the engineers lined up and that they understand something about archeology, without also addressing some of the concerns that Ray Barnhart from the U.S. Federal Highway Administration mentioned earlier. I am sure I know some of the projects that caused him to have some of the concerns that he expressed to us, because they took place in my own state. I think, however, that many of those concerns stem not from the inadequacies of the law, or from the failure of engineers to understand archeological problems. Those concerns he mentioned to us and those that others have echoed in this meeting have stemmed from the inability and the unwillingness of many members of the archeological community to understand the problems that take place in other segments of our culture. And I would suggest to those of our colleagues in Latin America who are at a different stage of development in the creation of cultural resource management agencies and programs, that they be concerned about this issue *now*, as they begin to train new cadres of specialists. Because unless those new archeologists are as understanding of engineering problems as many engineers are of archeological problems, the archeologists will be experiencing in the Latin American countries the same kind of backlash against archeology that we're beginning to undergo in the United States. Now is the time to get working on that. So I hope that in the rest of our conference we will begin to see some opportunities for members of the archeological community to pluck motes from their own eyes, so to speak, with respect to this issue.

GEORGE GUMERMAN

While I agree wholeheartedly with Raymond Thompson and the engineers and the representatives of the coal companies that I've heard from today that we need to increase this understanding, I am a little concerned about the implementation of mechanisms for *gaining* this understanding. Let me give you an example.

Several years ago, those of us in the Center for Archeological Investigations at Southern Illinois University decided that because we have quite a large coal research center, it might be profitable to bring archeologists together with people in environmental planning and engineering and coal mines, to effect a mutual understanding. We used a mailing list from the coal center at the University and sent out letters to over five hundred coal companies.

What many of you may not realize is that in the United States there are thousands of coal companies, many of which are "mom and pop" operations. We isolated the larger coal companies and asked them if they would be interested in taking part in a one- or two-day conference at SIU, at a cost of approximately $150 to $200, so that we could come to some sort of understanding among ourselves, so that we could understand one another a little better. Our letter simply asked if they would be interested in such a meeting. We got three lukewarm responses. How can we continue to effect this understanding? How do we implement this understanding? That, I think, is the crucial question. We can call for it here, but that alone will not effect that understanding.

SAPOLO ARTUR RAMEA

I'm from Argentina. I want to call to your attention something that often happens at the kinds of meetings you've been talking about, when people from the academic world and some sympathetic engineers get together. We tend to think that the big problem of understanding is an individual problem, that if people have enough time to get to know each other, everybody will be happy. Perhaps we will have another meeting a few years from now, and we hope there will be more engineers and more archeologists taking part and everybody will be much closer together. But I think that if we want to go beyond this kind of wishful thinking to the realities of life, we have to take into account that in the real world things are not decided by individuals alone. Perhaps laws and regulations may not be the solution, but they can help a lot. Putting people into the kind of arena you have mentioned forces discussions of common problems and leads to the problems being addressed, not ignored. Although I am not an archeologist but a social anthropologist, I think it's very important, if we want to go beyond saying, that we incorporate rescue archeology into the engineers' programs, that we get down to the fundamentals of what can help us to realize our objective.

BARRY G. ROUGHT

I'd like to respond to several of the comments we've heard, particularly to the question of enforcement. The best type of enforcement, of course, is the kind you get by voluntary agreement with the law. The law provides the mechanism, but the desire of individuals to meet the requirements of the law is paramount if you really want to have a successful program. So the question becomes, I believe, one of understanding the importance of history and archeology and of ensuring a sense of pride among all the disciplines involved in a public works project. The way that you accomplish this is by *acknowledging* when somebody does it *right*. And yes, we do get some publicity when somebody makes a very extraordinary find in a project. But what about the man from the engineering firm or the one from the construction firm or the bulldozer operator who day by day goes out, watches for these things, and reports them to his supervisor, who tells him he's done a good job? No one ever hears about these people. I think we have a real need to convey to people that there is an intrinsic value, a reward to yourself and your country and your community when you *do* do these things. I think that's where the education needs to occur.

EDUARDO D. BRENES

I have been hearing of problems between the civil engineers and the archeologists; they're very similar to problems we have in Costa Rica between civil engineers and agricultural engineers. It is imperative that these professions work closely together, for example in the case of an irrigation project we are carrying out in Costa Rica. In the areas in which only civil and agricultural engineers work, the engineers have a problem in accepting professionals from other disciplines, such as archeologists, anthropologists, and architects. But in areas where we start working together from the beginning, the pie is being shared by everyone and there's less professional competition.

ROBERT J. DACEY

As Michael Snarskis was saying about the young children, we have to remember that because many of our population won't go to the university, they aren't going to become engineers and they aren't going to become archeologists; we have to sensitize everyone to the problem. When we have young children going to museums and visiting archeological sites as part of their education and development, we can sensitize everyone, and we can sensitize people to the fact that this part of our culture must be saved. So our problem isn't just that archeologists and engineers need to be working together; we collectively have got to find out how we communicate the same level of concern to the rest of society.

DONALD LATHRAP
I think the idea of rewarding exemplary behavior on the part of engineers is a very good one. As the publicity on our proposed dating of Kimbaya Gold spread around the world, we got all kinds of responses: the inevitable *Book of Mormon* from someone living on Wata Wata Road in Auckland, New Zealand, a letter from an expert on coconut agronomy in southern India, and another from an amateur in Sanskrit scripts and their influence on Maya. But the most interesting letter was from the president of the Lucy Boiler Company in Chattanooga, Tennessee, who had been responsible for putting in the boilers on a major hydroelectric plant in the upper Cauca of Colombia about ten years earlier. Because there was insufficient chronological information on the interesting tomb cultures in that area, he and his associate, who was a chemist, took the wood from one of the coffins from a looted tomb—his associate was a very fine chemist—and did the refinement down to the appropriate carbon chemical. They had the results run and counted at Oak Ridge and came up with a date of 500 B.C., more or less. The Colombian archeological establishment got quite hysterical about such a silly early date and just laughed at the engineers. The man was quite gratified that now there was some reason to take his effort, after ten years, seriously. It is also gratifying to know that sometimes engineers are reaching out in ways that the archeological profession does not take full advantage of.

JOSEPHINE FLOOD
In Australia we've developed one or two mechanisms for trying to improve the dialogue between developers and engineers and archeologists, and I want to mention two of them. One is to get the archeologist in at the very beginning of the project, so that in a mining project, for example, during the exploration stage the archeologist works with the developer in planning out the work to try to avoid sites or to mitigate any adverse impact.
   Another thing that's been developed in Australia is a standard con-

tract for archeology. Because all our contract archeologists are members of the same professional association, it's fairly easy to develop an agreement that satisfies everybody. Our standard contract includes clauses that say that the archeologist has to produce a report in what we call "plain English." Although this is for the benefit of the client, the developer, it's also for the benefit of the aboriginal community whose site may be involved. I think it really is helping. The contract tends to be a fairly short document to which the detailed archeological report is attached. Another thing we've managed to do, using the same sort of approach, is to make sure that each report on an archeological project that's done under a contract is deposited in a national archive, the Institute of Aboriginal Studies, so that people have access to these reports.

Perhaps another thing that's relevant is that now archeology is taught in all our universities. We offer at least one course in what we call public archeology, or cultural resource management, which educates the university students—those studying engineering and geology and other things as well as those studying archeology—in the legislation and in all the other facets of cultural resource management.

LARRY D. BANKS
I refer to some of the earlier discussions about the interface between archeologists and the construction industry.

Over the past several months we have sent out hundreds of flyers to people in the construction industry; the only one who has responded is Harry Hutchens of the Brown, Root Construction Company. Mr. Hutchens, we're eager to hear from you as one who represents another aspect of the construction industry. So I have a question: The construction industry holds some sort of regional meetings, doesn't it?

HARRY HUTCHENS
Yes, the Association of General Contractors is one of the organizations that generally meet on a national basis and work through committees, often joint committees, with the engineering community and others.

LARRY D. BANKS
Would it be out of place for me to suggest that perhaps the next time you have one, you invite an archeologist to attend and make a presentation? On the other hand, I think the archeologists ought to invite someone, like Mr. Hutchens, from some other construction industry that's had problems with archeologists to participate in their meetings. I think that until we start interfacing like this, and letting each other see the

other side's point of view, we're going to continue to be two different worlds that come together every five years or so. So I suggest that in some of our archeological conferences we get someone from the construction industry to present programs and that we get someone from archeology to participate in meetings held by the construction people.

HARRY HUTCHENS
I think that's a good idea.

RUTHANN KNUDSON
I think all of us here who are archeologists have different training. I believe I have learned more about being an anthropologist—which is my basic training—in the last three years as I've functioned as a cultural resource manager among a series of subcultures. I think we ought to think a little more anthropologically, frankly, about the power *relationships* of the various interests in this issue and about the *missions* of the various interests, and I would just like to make that suggestion to Larry, to George, and to the archeologists who want to save sites and who want communication with another culture that frankly doesn't have archeology as a primary mission. We must take the initiative. We must ask to be invited to the ASCE meeting to give a presentation and not wait for them to come to us. And I think we must go to the National Coal Association meeting and not ask them to come to ours. Those are some of the basic realities about relationships. A couple of years ago in Australia there was a conference to discuss the development of aboriginal rights and mining, and only one miner showed up. Why? Because aboriginal rights and other anthropological concerns are not their primary mission. Again, I think if we go to ASCE and to other similar organizations we can be more effective in developing some fruitful dialogue.

WILLIAM L. FULLEN
General Dacey, I'd like to relate a little bit of what we've done at the Wallaceville Heritage Park during the last three years. I'm Program Director of the Heritage Park.

Three years ago we entered into an agreement with the Galveston District Corps of Engineers to assist in conducting the Corps' Junior Ranger Program. Our role was to concentrate on the design and development of curriculum instruction for fifth graders in the conservation of cultural resources. Your Federal Ranger, Smokey Cranfill, is an exceptional person in that he is double-degreed (biology and psychology) and produces a very effective program dealing with the conservation of the ecosystem. We worked toward the same goals to match what he'd done in the conservation of cultural resources, and we had two years of successful programs. We held them only in the springtime because we have one Corps ranger at the Wallaceville Lake Project and in the fall he is busy with duck hunters. In the spring he has a little more time to take out classes of twenty to thirty children for outdoor education activities at the Wallaceville Heritage Park. This year we were unable to proceed with our plans because cultural resources were endangered by our activities. Part of the problem is the lack of attention to the Junior Ranger Program that's being developed for the Wallaceville Lake Project. I think that if you look at what's been done and evaluate it, you'll agree that it's one of the most important programs in the Corps of Engineers.

JAMES J. HESTER

I would like to comment on the general topic that concerns the interaction between the engineering community, the construction industry, and archeologists. And I want to relate an experience I had with that type of interaction which did not work very well.

Every year there is a conference of oil shale engineers held at the Colorado School of Mines, and on one occasion we were able to request the director of the conference to schedule a session on archeology and the rescue of sites endangered by oil shale development. Our program consisted of four archeologists giving presentations on their particular concerns in site rescue. The program was a disaster! Several of the audience fell asleep, others left in droves, some fell off their chairs—they could not be *interested* in archeology. Our problem was that we failed to make archeological concerns *relevant* to the engineers. So we have to make it a matter of concern that *they* would interpret as being in their own personal interest. If we can do that, we can communicate.

ROBERT J. DACEY

You've got to be patient with us. There are those who will say the term "dumb engineer" is redundant, but we're trying!

GEORGE A. AARONS

After several hours of listening, I readily think of two aphorisms: "Physician, heal thyself," and "Those who do not know their history are condemned to repeat the mistakes of the past." Today's archeologists—the first archeologists and anthropologists were engineers, geologists, natural scientists, historians—are the children of every single other discipline. I continue to draw from all those disciplines. A few years ago when I was earning my first degree at Cambridge University, three things were impressed upon me as being the essence of archeology-anthropology: "Do not dig unless you research your site"; "Do not dig unless you know how you are going to conserve and preserve what comes out of it"; and "Do not dig unless you're going to publish the results of your work." So I think we have to keep the essentials foremost in mind. Look at how archeology has developed, and do what we need to do. I think it's very simple.

ROBERT J. DACEY

The topic that was assigned to our panel was "Rescue Archeology and its Interface with Engineering." It's obvious that we have not resolved the problem. In fact, we're a long way from resolving the problem. But as long as we can meet and discuss it, I think we are making advances. And I think that's all we collectively and individually can push for.

PART III

The Social and Political Realities of Rescue Archeology

Henry Cleere, Moderator

HENRY CLEERE

Welcome to the session on the social and political realities of rescue archeology. I've been pondering this theme ever since I was asked to be moderator. I suspect I was asked to be moderator because I come from the other side of the Atlantic and therefore can have, first of all, no awareness of the social and political realities of rescue archeology in the Americas. And second, I can have no axe to grind. In other words, I've been put in the hot seat.

It is probably the broadest theme that we shall be considering these three days. It is indeed impossibly broad for us to deal with this morning in the time available. We felt, therefore, that it was necessary to choose from a number of relevant themes and to treat these this morning. Now obviously we have to take general themes because the direct applications are dependent upon the legislative and administrative structures in the different countries of the Americas, which vary considerably. We have chosen six themes. First of all, we want to look at the role of archeology in the establishment of cultural identity. We then want to go on and talk about education—education in its broadest sense, not formal education through schools and universities but education of the public in general. Contact, communication, that's the second theme. Third, we want to have a look at public involvement—how we actually involve the public positively—in rescue archeology, for example by the use of amateurs and avocational archeologists, perhaps, or

67

by the use of local knowledge from people who have lived in the areas, whose families have lived there for many generations. Then we want to switch to the identification of cultural resources. Essentially, we want to touch on the problems associated with the compilation and management of national registers, what we call sites and monuments records in the United Kingdom. Fifth, we want to look at the utilization of cultural resources—of monuments resulting from rescue archeology—in education and in tourism. This is a factor that none of us can overlook nowadays, a factor that can have very dire impacts on the cultural resource generally. One thinks of the Acropolis in Athens, for example, where the marble pavements are being worn away. Or Canterbury Cathedral in my own country, where since the end of the war, the feet of thousands of visitors have worn down the soft limestone floor of the nave by approximately six inches in about thirty years. Finally, we want to give some consideration to the impact of rescue archeology on indigenous groups within the countries of the Americas.

What I have done is assign one of these themes to each of these panel members. But they are not going to speak specifically about the themes. Instead, they're going to give short presentations, something they may have prepared, perhaps stressing the point of the theme that we shall be dealing with. I've asked them to be brief, five to ten minutes, no more. Then we're going to have, I hope, a discussion here amongst the panelists before throwing the discussion open to the floor for just a few questions, then we'll pass on to the next topic.

IRAIDA VARGAS—Panelist
As Alberto Rex González said in his remarks yesterday, the problem of cultural identity is very closely related to rescue archeology. But seldom do those in power, even members of our own profession, consider the rescue of a people's identity to be an important part of rescue archeology. We have heard engineers and archeologists say that we should communicate better with each other and with the general public, to make it clear what archeologists do and what their research means to society. To understand the problem of cultural identity we must consider exactly what archeology is, and to do that we need to use a language that all of us can understand.

We can think of archeology as a historical discipline, closely related to the study of history. And if we were to include archeology as part of history, including it in our primary and secondary schools, in museums, and in other culture centers, I believe there would be no need to go further in keeping the public informed because their own history and prehistory then would be understandable to them. I don't believe we would need to offer special programs just because we are architects, archeologists, or engineers. I don't believe further explanation would be necessary, because if a person has been brought up with a real awareness and appreciation of his own history, he will understand the significance of the archeological objects and what they mean to him and his society. It seems to me that part of the problem is in how rescue archeology is done. There are knowledgable and concerned authorities in positions of power who perceive a lack of understanding among archeologists and therefore consider rescue archeology to be an individual problem for which archeologists are responsible.

This is partly because archeologists use a very difficult language sometimes. And we tend to keep to ourselves and talk with small groups of people. So I believe the problem of identity very closely relates to our concept of what we think of as history. In the second place, the problem of rescue archeology and national identity has to be understood not only by the people who physically carry out the work but also by the people who have the decision-making authority regarding how to incorporate the knowledge of our prehistoric and historic cultural resources so that our national identity will be acknowledged by our people. In the third place, I believe the problem of national identity and rescue archeology cannot be set apart from the professional organization of the people in the field. We have heard that we must take urgent steps to stop the destruction of archeological sites; we should involve students of all ages and the general public, and we should encourage them to participate in this rescue. I also think it is very important that we respond to the public's need to know, as well as make statements that are understandable at a political level, to the people who make decisions. It is very difficult to convince politicians that rescue archeology is a matter that should be considered by their countries. We are fortunate in the case of Mexico, for example, a country that has continually been identified with values that break with what we call traditional values. I believe we must seek ways to join our interests with the political interests of a country. And I believe that the only way we can achieve that is through both formal and informal education.

I believe that the nourishment of a sense of identity in our countries can in large measure be accomplished by creating a network of museums that encourage active participation of the whole population. I don't mean the kinds of institutions many people think of as museums—very big buildings, full of objects. I mean all types of museums: rural museums, farm museums, school museums, big museums, very small museums, museums designed to appeal to the common people, museums that promote the same message of the national identity and the identity of each region of the country.

HENRY CLEERE

Thank you very much for that splendid introduction. I must confess that I was slightly worried at the beginning, when you began to discuss the definition of archeology, because at a gathering of archeologists that is the one topic on which they will never reach agreement. Happily, you carried us into this very, very important area of cultural identity, the role of archeology. Now, may I throw the discussion open to my fellow panelists, first of all, for comments on what we've just heard?

THEODORE STROUP

I totally agree with what was said. But, as a manager who has to enforce cultural resource programs and cultural resource preservation, I would like to ask the following question: looking particularly at the resourcing that has been provided in South and Central America, do we communicate to managers and leaders how we're going to pay the bill in resources of people, pesos, dollars, and other forms of currency in order to offer archeological awareness programs in the schools and small museums as some of you have suggested? I think that's a challenge that we need to address in our resolutions at the end of the conference. Who pays the bill? I have to deal with that question on a daily basis in preserving my own cultural resource staff.

IRAIDA VARGAS

I would like to observe that what we're talking about are the consequences and the facts of life that we have to deal with on a day-to-day basis. I believe that our problems would be considerably relieved if we were to attack the *causes* of the problems. Solutions to the problems will take a long time; you're talking about a quick solution, which is simply not realistic in the Central and South American countries. We must establish effective channels of communication with the public, especially the people who control the money and who pay the bills, if we are ever to develop a national network of museums calculated to reach the different levels of our society. I cannot give you a concrete solution as to how we can approach the people who managed the funds. Obviously, if we had a solution, we wouldn't have the problems that we have in Venezuela.

HAROLD TSO
I'd like to make a couple of comments along this line of educating the public, getting the public involved, presenting a resolution, and trying to resolve the problems created by the ignorance gap. I think that one of the things you have to do as scientists is to make yourselves familiar with the local people. For example, the word *Anasazi* to the Navajo people means "remains of the enemies." Now I don't know what the Navajo say when speaking of the remains of their *own* people. I don't know what that word is. But the word *Anasazi* carries the meaning of enemy remains. So when an archeologist comes to the Navajo reservation and wants to open up the remains of the enemy people, he is probably going to release those enemies upon the Navajo people. The Navajo thought that their enemies were from Washington and from the state government, but now they have a whole lot of other enemies to contend with. So here we have a cultural barrier to deal with. Inherent in the Navajo people's way of life is a reverence for the land and its resources. That reverence is embodied in the deities these people have. This is not limited to Navajo people; it is the same with other people that archeologists, in the course of their work, may visit and work among. The people have a reverence for their nature, for their environment. And that has to be respected. Archeologists must have an appreciation of how the Navajo people feel about their environment so that the people archeologists are working among will provide room to work in, to do the project. Yet probably more important than the land, the connection to the land, is the reverence that these people have for their religion. Here in America we talk about atheists and various other religious groups in a familiar way. Among the Navajo people, there are also various religious groups. Historically, most Navajos belong to the group called the traditionalists—they endorse the beliefs that were in existence before the first blue-eyed Europeans came west in their covered wagons. In addition, there are other religious groups that were probably generated as Indian tribes mixed with one another. The Native American Church, for example, is this type of thing, a kind of migrating theology, just as the Lutheran Church is a migrating theology, having come from Europe to America. And I think that you as archeologists, as scientists, have to recognize that these people have a religion. And you have to respect it. If you are a Baptist or a Methodist you have to remember who you're talking to and address him accordingly.

Let me exemplify what I just said. The connection with the land for the Navajo is personal. It's as personal as that little hole you looked at this morning, just below your abdomen. At the bottom of your abdomen you have a little hole that we call the belly button, or to be nicer about it, the navel. This represents the connection you had with your mother. (I think this is where women have it over men, the power of life over men.) The umbilical cord that connects motherhood and life is embodied in the umbilical cord that Navajo people bury in the land that they wish to come back to. They know they're going to travel, but they come home. Many times, this is a private ceremony; the umbilical cord is buried in a parcel of land, so that the land becomes a very personal part of that person's life. And he comes back to the land again and again.

My wife's grandfather once asked me: "Son, how goes it in the city? How goes it out there where you live with those other people?" And I said, "Well, grandpa, you know that men are on the moon." He said, "Yes, I heard that." I said, "You know, grandpa, that the black men are rioting in Watts." He said, "Yes, I heard that, but you know, son, the black man will never amount to much in America." Now this is a 103-year-old medicine man, who never went to school, never read a newspaper, never saw television. But he said that the black man will never amount to much because he was stolen from his land. The black man left behind his religion; he left behind his ties with his land, so that here in America he is an orphan. And because he is an orphan, he will always be restless. He will always be looking for something. And that is why the black man will never amount to much in America. If he goes home, then maybe he can reestablish the connection he lost when he was stolen from his country.

I think that this connection is very clear; it is something that you archeologists and scientists must understand and appreciate if you are going to do your work with a minimum of interference from the local people. That is my main message to this group. As I said earlier, we Navajos spent at least 120 years of our lives reclaiming the land from the cowboys, the miners, and other interests of society. We have developed a line we call the reservation boundary. Because it has taken us 120 years to reclaim this land, we are not about to open it back up in the name of archeology, or in order to provide the great society of the world with a clearer picture of when man came or how man lived in earlier times. We see the digging of archeological sites as perhaps loosing enemies upon us—enemies that may be spiritual, enemies that may be physical in the form of tourists, enemies called regulation and government, enemies in the name of mineral development who may come when the reservation barriers are relaxed or removed. All this is from my perspective, and I wanted to share it with you.

HENRY CLEERE
Thank you, Mr. Tso, for a most potent and poetic, I must say, evocation of this theme, the relationship between archeology and cultural identity.

IGOR CHMYZ
In one of the rescue projects that I worked on in Brazil, we were thrown out by the Indians who said that we were violating their indigenous lands. Our expulsion was not because of religious motives of the Indians, or because of their roots. Rather, it was because the Indians did not accept the official documents we brought with us, the government papers and permits that authorized the project. That is why we were thrown off their lands.

HENRY CLEERE
It's interesting to me, I must say, coming from the Old World, this sense of cultural identity that is independent of modern national boundaries. The inference I draw from what the panel members have been saying is that we have a need to communicate better with the public. So I'm now going to ask three of my colleagues to give us some short presentations concerning their work and how their work bears upon this problem of communication. And I'll turn first to Bruce Eberle.

BRUCE A. EBERLE—Panelist
I'd like to say a few words from the point of view of someone who works within the federal government in the Federal Highway Administration.

About a decade ago, the Federal Highway Administration looked around for a training course that would sensitize our highway officials and make them knowledgable not only about historic and archeological resources but also about the need to protect these resources. We found that there were no engineering courses treating this subject. We also found that there were no government courses on this subject. Subsequently, both the Advisory Council and the National Park Service made several efforts to fill this gap.

We tried a seminar approach. We brought in a series of experts and set up a course this way. But we found it extremely difficult to manage the flow of information. The experts were not always able to communicate with people who were not already somewhat sensitive or somewhat knowledgable. So we turned around and hired someone who was neither a highway engineer nor a preservationist, but a professional trainer, in fact. Because the trainer didn't know either field, it was essential that he spend some time learning about different disciplines.

We had to train the trainers, and it was an arduous and very expensive task. It also called for continual backup, not only by our organization but also by the Advisory Council, the National Park Service, and state and local officials who were knowledgable about historic preservation. We gave this course a number of times throughout the country, targeted primarily at highway officials. Because of the backup provided by the Advisory Council and the Park Service, we were able to get a real interchange of ideas, and the highway engineers left the course with a fuller appreciation of cultural resources. And those who were actually involved in cultural resource management or preservation left with a clearer understanding, too, of their responsibilities for cultural resources in transportation projects.

I'd like to mention a couple of lessons we learned that might be of use to you. The first is a spin-off of what we talked about this morning and yesterday: You have to target your audience and you have to gain their attention. Frankly, that was a lot easier for us than it would be for many of you from South and Central America. For example, we have legislation that federal agencies must follow. So when we were talking with our own engineers, we explained what a cultural resource was and why it is important. But if they failed to appreciate that importance, we were able to say to them: "Now look, you're still going to have to follow the laws. And you're still going to have to fully consider this resource in your project planning." Now the laws don't say that the cultural resources must be protected, but the laws do say that they must be fully considered. And this is where our engineers were left with a very serious message.

We also found that case studies were very, very helpful. We found in some cases that our highway engineers were becoming very sensitive to historic and prehistoric resources and were modifying their projects to avoid impacts that were sometimes fairly minor. We also found that the preservation people were willing to accept some impact on the resources to avoid serious safety problems with the transportation facility. The case studies encouraged communication and allowed this kind of interchange.

In a less formal—but I think more important—vein, it's very gratifying to see that as our program has developed over the last ten years, there have been more and more efforts by archeologists, historians, and architects to communicate with the general public, as well as with their professional colleagues. They're writing articles that are understandable by the public, and they're being published in places to which the public has access, newspapers and popular magazines, for example. Now this effort should not replace the publication of scientific articles. Site reports, overviews, and surveys are the building blocks of science. And we accept and realize that. But we also believe that there's a responsibility to make the public understand what this is all about so that they are more willing to continue the funding of these efforts. Members of state highway agencies have taken a lead in this area. They've put together brochures, short overviews of what the project is about and what the findings are, in plain, clear language. They've also put together some exhibits, sort of mini-museums, if you will, some of which have traveled around their states. One of these exhibits was placed at a state fair and was viewed by more than fifteen thousand people. That's far in excess of the audience reached by the professional publications. The viewers did not become trained archeologists simply by looking at one of these exhibits, but they did gain a better appreciation of the role archeology has in their lives, making clear to them where their roots are and what's been going on in the area that they call home.

In some cases in which archeological excavation was taking place in the course of highway construction, we invited local groups to tour the excavation, and we even set up some archeological parks to help facilitate this. Frankly, the Federal Highway Administration was at first very reluctant to participate in this kind of endeavor, despite the fact that the President's Advisory Council on Historic Preservation supported it. We thought the tours might siphon off the expertise we needed to get the excavation done, and we didn't want to cause any delays. However, we're pleased to note that the results have been extremely promising and gratifying and that thousands of people have toured the excavations. And while these people have learned a little about archeology in their local areas, and something about their local prehistory, they've also been left with a better feeling toward the local highway authority. They now realize, I think, that the highway officials are not totally insensitive to the cultural environment. We think this is a very positive step. In addition, we're finding that some of our highway archeologists are taking it upon themselves to develop presentations that can be taken around to local high schools and junior high schools, presentations that are designed to explain to young people what their cultural resources are all about and what to do if, for example, the students come across one of these resources—who to contact and how to protect the resources. We're very pleased with these developments, and I hope that the product of our discussions will be a further sharing of experiences.

HENRY CLEERE
On a purely material and mundane level, I think we have an obligation to tell the public what we're doing. Because we are not only disturbing their land but also doing it with their money. We must never overlook the fact that most rescue archeology is done with public money. We are accountable for how that money is spent.

I want to continue with this general theme, moving south of the Rio Grande, much farther south. I'm going to call now on Leopoldo Bartolomé, who will tell us something of the work that he has been doing in Peru. He will be followed by Eduardo Brenes.

LEOPOLDO JOSE BARTOLOME—Panelist
I believe Bruce Eberle's comment is very important. He stated that a common ground for discussion is found in the existence of legislation that requires administrators and engineers to consider rescue archeology even if they don't view it favorably or see it as legitimate. This creates a very different attitude than if someone has to be convinced that something is important.

I am thinking of a problem that concerns rescue archeology but that is also part of a broader perspective that may not be directly related to the primary goal of a particular project. For example, hydroelectric dams have two basic peculiarities: they are works on a large scale, and they have a definite deadline for completion. Investments in these projects are enormous. Ad hoc organizations are developed for their completion. This creates what we might think of as the "project ideology," which has a special time sense, since these projects do not last forever. Also, these projects, be they national or binational, are based on a power structure and a decision-making process that is oriented toward the global ideology of the project, rather than toward the individual wishes of the executives or decision makers.

I think that a social scientist or an archeologist or any specialist who isn't linked to the central theme of a project knows that what he has to say is something that he has to take part in to make it viable. He must accept the fact that his involvement is not the kind of thing he does in academia and that what he must do may not necessarily enhance his academic image. In addition, he will not usually have as much time to complete his part of the project as he is accustomed to having in the university.

A large project can easily cost several million dollars. But when we take into account the ecological and social costs, rescue archeology costs are not significant. Nor do they appear significant when we consider cuts made because the project lacks "legitimacy" from the point of view of the "ideology" of the project. I say "ideology" because it's not a matter of simply convincing the project manager or the chief engineer; there may be many others who must be individually convinced that rescue archeology is needed. Clearly, the decision-making process is not limited to two or three people. But even if a strong argument is made, ultimately what is important is the project's "ideology" as such. In the light of more pressing concerns, rescue archeology is not seen as being very important, at least not as important as the ecological, economic, or social aspects. Failure to take these project impacts into proper account could lead to serious political ramifications. People might get upset about it and could cause problems. Costs can also become a major factor when a project is delayed by a strike or when the affected population starts a disruptive protest. Our goal, as I see it, is to promote the legitimacy of our objectives in large projects, even if those objectives do not appear to be central.

An enterprise of this nature, such as a dam and reservoir project, is not just a technical work. When we remodel a home and we decide whether or not we are going to build a wall, we have a technical or esthetic problem, depending on how we see it. If we build a wall that crosses the street, we create a social phenomenon that exceeds the technical. What happens, then, is that we must modify our plan and spend more money.

The solution, I think, is not really a matter of funds or lack of funds. In terms of cost, rescue archeology is not a significant item in very large projects. But the pressure of many years has made it necessary to take ecological costs into account. In other words, in making a feasibility study of a project, we can establish some parameters for ecological costs. Ecological costs have a reality from the broad point of view. Although large amounts of money must be invested, no investor can own the entire project. We will not realize great or immediate benefits from taking into account the ecological costs, the social impacts, or the preservation of our cultural heritage through rescue archeology. Investments of monies for these purposes do not appear as profitable in the overall accountability of the project as investments for other purposes, especially if we do not take the whole nation into account, using it as a frame of reference for our accounting.

So we must create a national conscience—an awareness of the benefits of preserving our cultural heritage, an awareness that rescue archeology must be considered as part of the overall planning for public works projects. A broad national consciousness would lead to protective legislation and performance standards that would enhance the legitimacy of rescue archeology and historic preservation, which is essential to communication with the various specialties or professions involved in these activities.

But I believe it is very important to discuss these concerns from our point of view. If rescue archeology is important, so too are social concerns. It is just as important to protect the environment. These components must be seen as part of a system but not as something we must defend in academic terms. And when we find deficiencies in a project plan we must propose feasible solutions. We cannot propose solutions that call for changing the entire society.

EDUARDO D. BRENES—Panelist

What I have to say is related to Leopoldo Bartolomé's earlier remarks because we work in similar fields. My experience with rescue archeology in Costa Rica has been fairly recent. It involved construction of a hydroelectric project that was planned to commence after 1983 but that was delayed due to an economic crisis in my country. Under an agreement worked out between the National Museum of Costa Rica and the Costa Rican Institute of Electricity, a rescue archeology program was developed for the two-hundred-square-kilometer project area, an area that has long been densely populated. The agreement provided for two and a half million dollars to be spent over a minimum of three years or a maximum of eight years. At the moment, I cannot say if that much money is enough or if it is completely unrealistic. But the agreement represents a laudable effort that could be duplicated in other countries where a public civil works agency, particularly one responsible for hydroelectric projects, enters into a contract with a museum or an institution of higher learning to conduct rescue archeology in the area affected. In this case, public funds were made available to cover all aspects of the archeological work.

I will not give you all the details of the agreement, but I would like to emphasize several points. I fully agree with Leopoldo that, like ecological studies and the consideration of the social effects of large public works projects, rescue archeology should be an integral part of the planning for such projects. Obviously, there must be adequate financing. There is also a problem in that the scheduling of a civil works project does not take rescue archeology into account.

A large public works project in Costa Rica, as well as in other Latin American countries, is generally financed by one or more international lenders such as the Inter-American Development Bank, the World Bank, or the U.S. Agency for International Development. But these institutions have their own ways of doing things, including the ways in which they carry out their feasibility studies. We receive the money only after it has become quite clear that the project is feasible. Prior to that, we don't receive any type of investment. Here is where there is a great difference between the objectives of engineering and those of archeology. Obviously, rescue archeology should be completed well before project construction begins, but if there's no money to work with, there's no way that the archeology can be done.

In the agreement between the Institute of Electricity and the Museum of Costa Rica, we tried to arrange for time to carry out the rescue archeology before the beginning of construction. I recall that one of the great concerns of the project administrators was that archeology not delay project construction. From their point of view, that was reasonable. When the agreement was signed two or three years prior to scheduled construction, we supposedly were given a reasonable period of time to carry out our rescue archeology program. We hope the time allotted will be enough. Yesterday one of the speakers said that in his country the police and the people in general had a broad knowledge of what rescue archeology was all about. I am glad for him and his country; in Costa Rica that is not the case. Nor is it the case with other disciplines. In general, the contributions of rescue archeology to the reconstruction of the culture in an area are seldom appreciated. Clearly, it is important that the population that lives close to the place where the rescue archeology is being carried out knows what is being done and what the work means to them.

In the area where this hydroelectric project is to be built, something terrible is going on. The rural population lives off *hauquerismo* more than their agricultural work. It is really quite simple. When crops fail, the farmers devote their time to looking for archeological items. Artifact sales yield more money than does agricultural work. A major problem is how to deal with *hauquerismo* when it provides a regular income for a farmer's family.

To conclude, I would like to say that one of the most important things we need to consider is the adoption of a common language by which we communicate with those who carry out projects and those who practice rescue archeology. But we must also understand that most public works projects are financed by foreign institutions and have a very short construction schedule.

HENRY CLEERE
I don't believe one can prepare any kind of strategy for rescue archeology, for communication with the public or whatever, until one knows something about cultural resources in one's own country. In Europe today there is a great deal of emphasis being put on the compilation of national registers or, as I said earlier, on what we call sites and monuments records in England. Now obviously, in an itty-bitty country like England, which would fit into the average-sized county in Texas and disappear entirely in Brazil, this is slightly easier. Though I do think we probably have a bit more archeology in depth. Nevertheless, I think national registers are very fundamental to any consideration of rescue archeology or of archeology in general. So I'm going to ask Hugo Ludeña to start us off now and give us some idea of the developments in the compilation of a national register in Peru.

HUGO LUDEÑA—Panelist
So far, the conference has addressed the rescue of monuments and immovable goods in prehistoric and historic sites of interest that are in danger. Not much has been said regarding rescue and recovery of prehistoric and historic objects that are movable.

When I attended the Quito conference in 1981, I was very concerned because the year marked a decade when many historic and prehistoric objects had left the country illegally. Peru's loss of these cultural resources was irreversible. The loss was not only of objects but also of resources important to the cultural identity of the Peruvian people.

Following the Quito conference there were several important repercussions. In September 1981, Peru signed a treaty with the United States for the recovery of our cultural patrimony. Later, Peru was able to recover an important collection that had left the country illegally bound for the United States. In his keynote address, Galo Plaza mentioned how Ecuador had been able to recover a very important collection of archeological specimens that had been illegally shipped to Italy. Recently, I understand, Guatemala has signed a treaty with the United States, which is very similar to the one signed with Peru and Mexico, for the recovery of stolen objects that are part of the country's cultural patrimony.

In this respect there has been an important and positive reaction to the First New World Conference on Rescue Archeology. Perhaps the most important news for our countries that are often looted is that the United States has ratified the UNESCO treaty that prohibits the import and export of stolen prehistoric and historic cultural resources.

These are practical and effective steps, which inspire us to think that meetings such as this one are beneficial and can produce quick results. But one of the fundamental problems of rescue archeology is the lack of registries or inventories. It is difficult for countries to recover their cultural resources if the pieces have not been inventoried, photographed, and described.

We have recently developed some important agreements with institutions, such as the Institute of Art Research in New York, to register the collections of the Church in Cuzco in order to have precise identifications of objects from the colonial period. But the problem still exists for other resources because of the lack of registries in some museums. In summary, there is a serious problem regarding the registry of movable pieces, and it should be resolved quickly.

I also want to refer to the necessity for registering the prehistoric and historic monuments in each country. I had thought this was an ancient and permanent activity, as national laws would indicate. For example, Peruvian Law 6634, enacted in 1929, indicated that an archeological map would be made for the entire country. Later laws also provided for a national map and for a budget to support its preparation. But to our surprise, these registries were only partially done during the 1960s and 1970s and are of monuments that exist in a valley, in a province, or in a state. This is clearly a contradiction if important and unimportant sites have not been registered; so how are we supposed to provide special treatment to monuments that are considered unique?

Peru is a party to the World Heritage Convention. I believe many countries are adhering to this Convention, in which the most important monuments of the world are being indexed. Sites include unique monuments and monuments that merit being on the World Heritage List and receiving special treatment. It is true that the necessity to protect and better manage sites such as Machu Picchu and Cuzco has led Peru to include both of them on the World Heritage List.

But there are hundreds or thousands of sites that still are unknown and not registered. A plan for registering both mobile and immobile resources of our national patrimony has always met with economic problems. Yet UNESCO conventions like the World Heritage Convention and the convention of 1970 insist on the necessity of registering the monuments. Presentations at the Quito conference on rescue archeology underscored the necessity of registry.

Because of this, in Peru today we are working toward promulgating a new law that will update the old laws for the protection and conservation of the nation's cultural patrimony. But I can say that there are problems with introducing articles that make registry mandatory so as to comply with these conventions and develop the points established in the old laws. It is evident that possible resistance from the general public and the legislators is due to the fact that mandatory registry by law would mean economically implementing this activity. Moreover, it would mean that the public at large and public and private institutions would have to submit to the law and would have to respect and conserve these sites and carry out the work that each case would require.

I would say that this lack of registry presents a good opportunity for collaboration with countries that have already developed a national registry of historic and prehistoric sites. At present we are working hard to carry forward the registry, the inventory of monuments, and the publication of the results.

In 1983, a first volume was published of the sites located in northern Peru. This year, a second volume is in preparation for the coastal region, and we are counting on a budget for the publication of the registry in 1985 for the southern region. But we have one concern: Are we trying to discover or invent a system of registry, when there are already established, known, and developed systems?

We are acquainted, for example, with the National Register of Historic Places in the United States. That program has reached a high level of sophistication, with a refined process of selection. But, we have not seen any significant efforts to exchange information, nor have we seen any scientific or technical collaboration regarding this activity. I leave a point for discussion: In the future, all the Latin American countries have, in my opinion, the task of registry, because we cannot protect or defend sites when we don't know their characteristics or importance.

HENRY CLEERE
We're talking about two types of registers. First, the register of what in England we call portable antiquities, and second, the sites and monuments registers. The first group is very important for many reasons. This type of register was, of course, a subject that recurred in every session in Quito because at that time the U.S. government had not ratified the UNESCO convention. Congratulations from my country, which hasn't yet ratified it, to the United States for having done so.

I would like now to concentrate our discussion on the second aspect of the register, the inventory of sites and monuments. I took very much to heart the point that was made about the necessity to create a system afresh when others are already in existence. In Europe, or indeed in my own country, there is a distressing tendency on the part of those responsible for the compilation of inventories to reinvent the wheel. The compilers always believe they must have their own unique system, which is not only a waste of time but also counterproductive because archeology, in academic terms, really does not respect, or should not respect, national boundaries. And if one is doing research, one wants to know about a certain type of monument spread over a continent or a part of a continent, so that one can interrogate these inventories to find out what is in them. Now what is the use of such sites and monuments records? First of all, there is the obvious use for planning. We in Britain now have compiled for most of England what are called constraint maps, which identify all the archeological monuments and sites, as well as areas of archeological sensitivity, so that when there is any planning decision to be made—a new highway, a new housing development, a new industrial development—it is possible for the planning authority to consult this map and say, "Don't put it there, or try not to put it there, or if you do put it there you will have to pay a lot of money for archeological excavations because there is something of archeological importance there." So that is one value, I think, of an inventory of this kind. And there are other values.

BETTY J. MEGGERS
One of the problems this brings out is that Latin America is not a uniform entity or area. In the Andean area, particularly Peru and possibly Bolivia, and in Mesoamerica, we have monuments of the kind we are describing, monuments that can be identified as important. But when you go to the lowlands, to Brazil, to Venezuela, to lowland Argentina, and to many other areas, there are no such sites. So what are we to put on an inventory? There are simply scatters of pottery on the ground; there are no structures. There are a few exceptions. For example, areas with very remarkable rock art could serve as monuments and deserve to be protected. There are impressive shell middens on the south coast of Brazil, for example, but aside from that, we don't have the kinds of things that one usually thinks of as being put on a historical register. What we need are general surveys simply to locate sites, to get information from them. Whether any of the sites really need to be preserved is a question I think we will have to consider. Inventorying sites in the lowlands causes a very different kind of problem from working in the Andean area. In some cases in the lowlands, there aren't even portable objects that are

of sufficient significance to make an inventory. So these two different areas are really quite different in the problems they raise and the kinds of approaches we need to use to deal with them.

One of the handicaps in Brazil is that the country has had a mechanism in the federal government for fifty years for recording significant monuments; however, the monuments recorded have been exclusively historic Colonial buildings because no archeological sites were deemed sufficiently impressive to be considered. And, when listings were made, a site was simply indicated here or there, with no additional information given. So while an emphasis has been put on registers, no information dealing with archeology has been included, which I think not only wasted money but also may have placed archeological sites in jeopardy.

IRAIDA VARGAS
With regard to the problem of a register of monuments and portable property, I would like to mention again the concept of what constitutes a nation's cultural heritage.

Venezuela is perhaps the only country that has not signed the UNESCO agreement. Its failure to sign is related to what the government and the public in general consider to be the cultural heritage of Venezuela. Most Venezuelans believe that culture refers only to the fine arts. They do not really appreciate the culture of the indigenous people. Instead, they believe that the only part of the nation's cultural heritage worth preserving is that which began when the Europeans arrived on our continent. Therefore, it is no coincidence that Venezuela is the only country in South America that does not have a register of archeological material—a country in which archeological sites are very dispersed and that does not have much material that can be considered impressive. I repeat what I said earlier: these sites and materials must be considered part of our cultural heritage.

In some ways we're speaking two different languages. Here in North America, no one has to explain what it means to be North American. Even in Latin America there are differences. No one has to tell a Peruvian what it means to be Peruvian. Or no one has to tell a Mexican what being Mexican is. But Venezuela has been brainwashed. Many Venezuelans insist that being from Venezuela identifies them with a national culture that is limited to the fine arts, to dances and paintings, so that all the cultural aspects of the nation are seen in a very deceptive way.

So how can we deal with the problem of a national register for archeological sites, when it is something that is interesting only to archeologists? The authorities do not care about archeological sites but prefer to leave the sites in the hands of specialists who do. So I believe that in the development of a national register, the problem of rescue archeology must be focused in a very different manner, at least in the case of Venezuela. In this way, we are in the same situation as the Caribbeans. It is an ideological problem. It must be focused on reality. It is not a problem of money. We all know that Venezuela is a very rich country. We have many resources, not only for archeological research, not only for rescue archeology projects; however, there continues to exist a distorted version of what constitutes our cultural heritage, and it is reflected in what the government is willing to teach in our schools and museums so that our people really understand what it means to be Venezuelan. We must incorporate the results of our archeological research into the knowledge of the country by including the research in the teaching of history, and we must convince our government that a register of archeological sites is necessary. Again I repeat, it is not a coincidence that Venezuela is the only nation that has not subscribed to the UNESCO Convention.

HENRY CLEERE

This problem of the definition of the cultural heritage is, of course, not unique to Latin America. Perhaps as a representative of an ex-colonial power I could tell the story of India. Great Britain left India with halos; it was the only country we did leave. Nevertheless, after independence, the archeological survey of India, one of the earliest and finest bodies of its kind in the world, totally neglected a heritage of about two hundred years of the British raj. And it has been only in the last two to three years, some thirty-five years after India's independence, that the country has realized that it needs to inventory and to conserve the buildings built by the British in India, which are very fine buildings and which India now acknowledges to be a part of its history. India had the British there for two hundred years. And we did leave our mark. And these buildings are magnificent: the Writer's Building in Calcutta, the many dark bungalows that were built, the clubs, the residences. India is beginning to inventory them—a bit belatedly, because the climate of India is not very kind to buildings of this kind—and is beginning to conserve them.

IGOR CHMYZ

Regarding the registry of archeological remains, since 1937 in Brazil we have had a National Historic and Artistic patrimony, which is in charge of the registry and protection of all cultural, historic, archeological, and artistic resources. However, we make a distinction between a registry and what we call a *tombamento*.

The word *tombamento* is used in Brazil to indicate an archeological site that can never be developed. For that reason, archeological sites in Brazil, after having been registered, are not yet *tombados*. If they were, the sites could not be excavated by archeologists. Often, sites become *tombados* after partial excavation, at which time a small part of the site is preserved for posterity.

HENRY CLEERE
I'm going to ask George Hasseman to talk now about his experiences in Honduras. I've asked him to look in particular at the impact and role of tourism in relation to rescue archeology, and at cultural resource management in general.

GEORGE HASSEMAN—Panelist
Rather than follow Henry Cleere's very precise instructions that we speak generally, I want to speak specifically about the situation in Honduras.

My employer, the Honduran Institute of Anthropology and History, is a semi-autonomous dependency of the Ministry of Culture and Tourism. This structure would appear to be ideal for generating a mutually beneficial relationship between the goals of investigators of the Institute and those of the promoters of tourism at the ministry level. For the past few years we at the Institute have promoted the practical necessity, as well as the professional obligation, of educating the Honduran public, of stimulating cultural consciousness at all levels of society, in order to gain these mutual benefits. Or, in other words, we have promoted a reciprocal exchange between the public and the investigators. This exchange would mean providing the public with a legitimate base for developing an awareness of cultural heritage as a result of our investigations. In turn, we would expect the public to respond with a sensitivity toward our efforts to protect or salvage the cultural patrimony. If anybody has any doubts, the word *sensitivity* here means money.

As a means of education, we are beginning to consider the potential of domestic tourism, even though tourism officials are primarily interested in generating revenues from international tourists. Yet officials in the Ministry are now expressing an interest in the value and necessity of involving the entire population in the development of the tourism product. One step toward this end has been the creation of museums dedicated *expressly* to the education and stimulation of children; the emphasis is on children. One of the realities we face in Honduras is that we cannot afford to direct our efforts at all age and interest groups and still do a worthy job. We prefer to concentrate on the children, and in all probability the general public will gain as much from the exhibits as will the youngsters. What we are decidedly avoiding is the creation of museum exhibits for archeologists. These museums—one is now in the remodeling stage—include hands-on exhibits, slide lectures for school groups by appointment, demonstrations of primitive technology, and reconstruction of full-size prehistoric dwellings on the museum grounds. Of course, these ideas are nothing new, but in Honduras they are revolutionary.

We also want to promote through the Ministry the development of small villages representing different time periods of Honduran cultural history. We would like to relocate and preserve examples of primitive industry such as pottery, sugar and lime manufacture, etc., which still exist scattered throughout the countryside but ordinarily far from the main tourist line. These exhibits—the villages and the industries—would be located near proven centers of international tourism, such as the Mayan ruins at Copán and the Bay Islands of the Caribbean. This strategy would provide even greater tourist appeal for the international sector as well. We also hope to establish craft guilds and industries, again at these same tourist centers, that would develop indigenous motifs on quality products, but not necessarily through the application of indigenous technology. This is an approach that has been used very successfully in Jamaica. I think this may also be an effective means for involving the economic capacity of a frequently overlooked labor force in Latin America, the peasant woman.

Now as I've mentioned, these ideas are certainly not new, but they involve the development of tourist-oriented programs derived from the results of several groups: professional investigators at the Institute, historians, ethnographers, folklorists, and archeologists. This process of education is a long-term solution to the problem of protecting and salvaging cultural patrimony.

I want now to depart from the topic of tourism and offer an alternative, short-term solution to the immediate problems of rescue archeology. We face a number of social, political, and economic realities in Honduras. I'm sure we're among distinguished company throughout the rest of Latin America. These are realities that make rescue archeology on a reasonable scale practically impossible to contemplate if we must depend upon our own resources and upon the traditional attitude of our own government. We are plagued with all the usual problems: looting, urban expansion, public works projects, agrarian reform, lack of interinstitutional cooperation, which is very important, lack of personnel, and of course, lack of funding. But more generally, Honduras is simply a very poor country which cannot be expected to consider rescue archeology a priority matter. Therefore, to solve our immediate problems we must rely upon that alternative. Because my model for this alternative is the World Bank—I'm grateful to see that we have a representative of the World Bank here.

In the 1970s the Honduran government negotiated a loan of $650,000,000 for the construction of a hydroelectric facility in the central highlands. The World Bank, one of the principal funding institutions, established as a condition to the loan that the National Electric Company, through the proper competent agencies, complete a series of environmental programs. As a result, the Institute was awarded $326,000 for archeological salvage in the El Cajon Reservoir. Now $326,000 is one-twentieth of one percent of the original projected cost of the project. But it was the first salvage project in Honduras *ever* financed by anybody other than the very, very poorly funded Institute of Anthropology and History. Now, if the World Bank can take this initiative, so can the Banco de Americanos de Investigaciónes Económicas and the Inter-American Development Bank, to name just two funding institutions that are active in the area. I also think we should expect this same degree of responsible initiative from intervening governments. U.S. AID is channeling an enormous amount of money into Honduras for economic development, and none of it will go toward the preservation of cultural patrimony, even though the economic programs potentially endanger this cultural patrimony. To mention another outstanding oversight, the U.S. Army has been constructing military installations in Honduras for the past two years. Contrary to the laws of both the United States and the Republic of Honduras, no rescue archeology efforts have even been discussed between the competent authorities.

I would recommend, therefore, that intervening institutions or agencies, such as those I've mentioned, be encouraged to develop policies that *oblige* them to establish direct contact with the national institutions responsible for the defense, protection, and salvage of cultural patrimony. Their policies should require intervening institutions to respect the laws of the host country while at the same time assisting these host countries in the fulfillment of their own obligations within the context of their whole society and environment.

THEODORE STROUP—Panelist
The Corps of Engineers is not in the tourism business, but in Texas, for example, at twenty-two reservoirs that we have built and are now operating, we entertain about fifty-seven million visitors a year. The number grows each year to be bigger and bigger. But we have created a visitor center at each reservoir that is open to the public. And we provide an educational message there on the archeology and the historic preservation background of the area we have inundated and built over. We have a continuing reclamation process to identify sites and catalogue specimens. We have printed brochures, and we offer interpretive presentations during the peak summer months that deal with the whole panorama of the past. We do participate in that area. And it's very effective.

GEORGE A. AARONS—Panelist
Tourism started in Jamaica about fifty years ago with Americans and Canadians arriving on boats to pick up bananas. At first the Jamaicans made a great effort to give the foreigners what they wanted. But about fifteen years ago, we started to rethink this very carefully because tourism in Jamaica and the Caribbean within the last ten to fifteen years has been going through a very serious recession. We finally came to realize that what fascinated people about Jamaica was Jamaica: the country, the beaches, the history, and so on. So we began to make a conscious effort to project what was truly Jamaican. We began to replace museum exhibits that were of great interest to Jamaicans, and like Honduras, we focused on the children because, after all, they are the future.

In this we have been very successful. Yet, although the number of visitors in the last two years has doubled, like many other countries represented here, we are experiencing a very serious economic crisis. But the government and the people of Jamaica realize that a lot of money needs to be spent on the preservation of all aspects of our movable and immovable cultural property. Obviously, only a small percentage of this money can come from government coffers. So for the last five years we have been planning a major program in cultural tourism focused on three major sites: Port Royal, New Seville—the oldest Spanish city in the New World—and Spanish Town, Santiago de la Vega, the second Spanish capital.

I am privileged to have been one of the members of the planning group for this program. In fact, I wrote the basic document for Port Royal. So in this case, the archeologist did the planning, and the planners corrected the mistakes. Part of the program will be the sale of arts and crafts. We will be reproducing arts and crafts from all periods of our prehistory and history. From cultural tourism we hope to generate sufficient funding to embark on major preservation programs on the rest of the island, on sites other than Seville, Port Royal, and Spanish Town. We have submitted proposals to the Inter-American Development Bank and the Caribbean Development Bank. I think you will be pleased to know that our proposals are receiving very serious consideration.

HENRY CLEERE
I think it interesting that no matter where we start these discussions, we end up with cultural identity and with children's education.

HAROLD TSO—Panelist
I might say that throughout recorded history archeologists have had the floor more often than the so-called indigenous groups. With respect to recorded history, certainly, there are many things to preserve.

I feel somewhat like the crocodile at this conference because those of you who study reptiles tell us that the crocodile is a living fossil, a survivor from a previous age. I can relate to that notion, because I think that the cultures you're studying have either survived from another era or have died, leaving their remains behind for you to exploit or to use for enlightening the peoples of the world. I think that Indians, as "living fossils" of an earlier time, have a different perspective. I'm glad that we have a government that allows us to give voice to our expressions. Sometimes our voices have resulted in legislation that has helped to preserve Indian rights and Indian sovereignty. I call to mind the Indian Religious Freedom Act and the Archeological Resources Protection Act. These acts include measures to preserve American Indian resources. And I'm glad for that.

I want to leave with you something I mentioned earlier, the idea that there is a sense of religiosity among the native people. There is a closeness that the native peoples feel for their lands. What I didn't tell you was that this closeness governs decisions by the native peoples, decisions such as whether or not to disturb something they feel very close to. Native religions are so strong that the decisions made are almost always to leave things alone.

In recent years we've approved something like one hundred thousand acres of tribal lands for coal leases. We have four coal mines active right now. Coal mining on our land, Black Mesa, has resulted in a book by one of your colleagues and has resulted in sudden fame and notoriety for other members of your profession. In Navajo history, Black Mesa was a place where Navajo medicine men had their retreats and where they collected herbs and medicines for their medicine bags.

We are also concerned for the ancient ones, as we call those who have passed on, those who will never be put to rest. We are concerned for individual graves as well as for cemeteries where there are many, many remains.

I talked to a lady yesterday in the bookstore. And I said: "Why don't you get the author to sign this book? He's here in attendance." And she said, "Oh no, I don't feel that that is right." Then I told her, "Well, he already has sold his soul, he has put his words down in black and white, so why should signing his name be any more of a sale?" But nevertheless, there's a sense of propriety. In terms of archeology and cultural resources, the same feeling carries through. Please don't take our culture and record it. We don't want the rest of the world to know about us. We prefer to be our own selves. We prefer to be our own people. We prefer to set our own course. We do not want it dictated to us. If we open up the lands for coal resources to extract the coal, extract the uranium, extract the oil and gas, extract the timber, convert grazing lands into farming lands, we have to open up something that we have put aside—loved ones, the ancient ones. We're essentially doing surgery on ourselves. We're opening ourselves up to people who say they want to know more about us. What if we don't want you to know more about us? That's the feeling of my people, the people I represent. You have done well in telling our story, but I think that in telling the story you have exposed us unnecessarily for your own reasons. One of our problems, and one of the problems of other native peoples, is that we have created reputations for some or all of you; we have allowed you to collect information and to exploit us for the benefit of yourselves, your institutions, or your governments. I think that's your personal problem, but we see it as an assault on our personality. Because you use us to further yourselves, we are resistant. You or your colleagues come to us wanting to know more about us in the name of your science. But we prefer not to be exposed. We're a private people. I wish that we could go back to the time in American history when we were truly private. We can get along well as people, but we ask that you respect our culture, respect our desire to be ourselves, our desire to hide ourselves from everybody else.

There are places on Navajo lands that we consider sacred, places we want to remain unlisted because the great American desire for knowledge causes people to come and destroy those places. There are places that have to be disturbed because we agreed to the exploitation of coal and minerals. But we ask that you stay inside the area you're authorized to work in when studying our culture. In conjunction with our cultural resources program, we have been able to enact tribal legislation that details how to behave while you're digging up our turf. We have a museum, not a very big one, but one of these days we'll have a big museum for you.

HENRY CLEERE
Thank you, Harold. I've never had the privilege of meeting a living fossil, and I had no idea one could be so eloquent.

I'm going to ask Josephine Flood if she would like to say just a few words about the way archeologists are dealing with this situation in Australia.

JOSEPHINE FLOOD—Panelist
Yes, I would be delighted to, because I share the feeling that our Navajo representative has expressed. So on behalf of Australia's indigenous people, I have to say that I've been a bit shocked, frankly, by some of the things I've heard here. I think we're way ahead in certain respects. The word *primitive* has been used here, and everybody seemed to listen and accept it as a normal term. But *primitive* is a dirty word in Australia. We don't call indigenous people primitive or savage because the use of those terms can leave the impression that we believe we are the civilized ones and that indigenous people are not civilized. In fact, I've been asked on occasion during public lectures why the aborigines haven't become civilized.

On the question of sites, our aborigines also don't want human remains on display anywhere, and they want the opportunity to rebury any human remains that are uncovered in the course of excavation. That is one of the matters being disputed at the moment. The reason is that although reinterment is acceptable in most circumstances, when you have to deal with human remains of great scientific importance, you've got a problem: the scientists want to preserve them for study purposes, and the aborigines want them reburied according to traditional rites.

Another problem we have is that in Australia aboriginal people don't like the concept of museums. It is a totally foreign concept to them. They don't want their culture on display for the tourists. And the way we're getting around the problem now is by the very strong participation of and consultation with aboriginal people. We have them employed by our state sites agencies, and they are fully consulted about what sites, if any, are open to the public. In fact, one or two sites that used to be open to the public now are being closed in accordance with aboriginal wishes.

There's just one other point that I'd like to make: we shouldn't presume that we know what aboriginal people want. We do have to ask them. We've just had a situation with a dam in western Australia in which the archeologists and the museum authority thought the right thing to do was to remove some petroglyphs from under the waters of a lake, lifting them out by crane and preserving them in an open-air museum. Somebody finally got around to asking the aborigines what they wanted, and discovered that the aborigines were most upset by the idea of moving the sites. Because it wasn't just the petroglyphs that were important to them, but the rock and its connection with the earth. They said they wanted their petroglyphs to be underwater because the petroglyphs would be happier there. The petroglyphs would be cool and people wouldn't be staring at them. So I think we have to try to become more sensitive to the wishes of the people whose remains and culture we're studying.

HENRY CLEERE
I want now to move to Igor Chmyz to hear from him about the work and the problems in Brazil.

IGOR CHMYZ—Panelist
In Brazil we have a law that has brought some discipline to archeological work. It has made possible the inventory of archeological sites and the excavation of the most important ones. In the beginning, the few projects undertaken were supervised by governmental agencies. It has only been since 1975 that projects have been financed by the private sector, and most of them have been connected with hydroelectric plants. Problems in conducting archeology arise because the developers are not eager to finance such work. We were most successful with the archeological project at Caracol, when an international agency provided the necessary funds to carry out the project.

On other occasions we have not been so fortunate. We have been unable to obtain supplies and equipment, and we have been unable to pay archeologists and other specialists, even on a part-time basis. A few college professors were the only ones who could work on one project. But the results were satisfactory, and reports were published. Some problems did arise during this project that were very difficult to solve, for example the displacement of the inhabitants who were affected by the formation of lakes. Having to deal with these people made the project more difficult. Another serious problem was the widespread belief that there was buried treasure near the archeological material, which made it more difficult to develop good, and very necessary, public relations. Part of the problem was that Indian groups who lived in these areas were dispossessed and removed to areas far away from their cemeteries and sacred places. In general, we are facing many difficulties with rescue archeology in Brazil.

HENRY CLEERE
We've heard about cultural identity, we've heard about education, but behind everything we've talked about this morning has been this terrible problem of money. Jim Lee can probably tell us something about money, coming as he does from the World Bank.

JAMES A. LEE—Panelist
Although it is the largest, the World Bank is just one of a number of multilateral and bilateral economic development assistance institutions whose policies and practices are increasingly reflecting a concern for the environmental, the health, and the human ecological aspects of their development work. Since 1970, when the World Bank initiated its environmental work, the institution has included archeological sites under a broad definition that has been accorded the environment. The World Bank has recognized and continues to recognize that archeological sites, including the artifacts and other material they contain, are vanishing resources. And an effort should be made to protect, preserve, rescue, or otherwise appropriately manage them. In addressing the archeological concerns within the context of economic development work, two principles are seen as being important.

First, each archeological site has its own intrinsic value in the overall scientific study of the development of civilization. Sites with few material remains can be just as valuable or more valuable, from a scientific point of view, than sites that exhibit a very rich artifact inventory. And because such sites are harder to detect, they are often overlooked or accorded scant attention. Because they are easily overlooked, and their importance little understood or appreciated by decision makers, these sites constitute special concern to the Bank. Second, the destruction of a site is an irreversible action. And all sites are unique. Once destroyed, they cannot be replaced. Their value and the information they contain are lost forever. Hence, the Bank is guided by these two considerations and seeks to accommodate provisions for archeological sites within its projects and its technical assistance activities.

The Bank has noted what all of you have said, and it knows only too well that most nations do not have well-defined policies for dealing with the archeological aspect of their cultural heritage. Most nations, however, do have laws or regulations. But the problem in many of our developing countries is that these laws or decrees are all-encompassing, general prohibitions and often lack the provisions for enforcement. We've heard this from many of you here at the conference. Experience reveals that most of the Bank's member developing countries and their borrowing entities do not have well-defined policies, procedures, institutions, technical personnel, or most important, funds for dealing with the needs to preserve their archeological heritage threatened by development. It is for these reasons that the Bank endeavors to play a surrogate role, including providing funds within the context of the loan, to carry out the archeological work.

Now what typically happens when an archeological site is involved in the preparation and appraisal of a project proposed for Bank financing? The government may wish to follow something similar to a preservationist's course, i.e., to redesign, to relocate, to defer, or even to delete a development project because it will irrevocably degrade or destroy the site. However, a more typical scenario is one in which the implementation of a project goes ahead, and a rescue operation is mounted to recover as much scientific information as possible before or during project implementation. So the Bank, in providing for this kind of operation, seeks to have the work go forward in a sequential fashion, as follows: a regional recognizance-type survey including the mapping and sampling of all sites; an evaluation of sites in or near the project zone of influence to determine their importance and potential for preservation; the determination of the impact of the proposed development project on the sites; the excavation and retrieval of information, data, and materials from the sites likely to be negligibly affected; the preservation and subsequent study of the evidence that has been gathered by competent authorities—and here I'm referring to a national museum or the ministry of antiquities or whatever; and last, the provision for the appropriate incorporation and/or utilization of the site within the framework of the project itself.

So let me briefly summarize what the Bank desires as regards financing proposals for archeological sites that are encountered in development projects. An archeological survey should be a routine element in any project consideration where the presence, construction, and/or operation of the project could adversely impact the site. All such surveys should be directed by professionally trained archeologists. And should a government not have such a capacity, the Bank can assist in providing the appropriate assistance. If a site or sites found through a survey are judged to merit salvaging and rescue, the necessary time, expertise, and financing should be made available within the framework and terms of the loan. Not to be ruled out is a consideration of how or if the site or sites can appropriately be made a part of the project, that is, how the site can be included in ways that will not demean its significance or diminish its value.

We are currently in the process of drafting more detailed guidelines, based upon our own experience and upon the recommendations of those who are knowledgable in a practical sense, as to what realistically can and should be done to responsibly address this dimension of economic development. And I would like to think that more of the development finance institutions in both the public and the *private* sectors—let me stress the *private* sectors—would begin to make provisions for rescue archeology a normal part of their practice. We in the Bank have attempted to show some leadership in this regard over the past decade. We have attracted some favorable attention, but I had hoped for a much greater spinoff.

HENRY CLEERE
Thank you, Jim, for that very succinct and lucid exposition of the Bank's policy. If I may, I'd like to bring us back from the harsh realities of finance to the subjects that we were discussing earlier. Mario Sanoja will give us his views on the matter of cultural identity.

MARIO SANOJA
I have been listening with great interest to the members of the panel as well as to the audience, and I have been thinking about the topics that have been presented. I have reached a conclusion that I think we have all reached: the problem of rescue archeology must be a fundamental aspect of global policy, including various strategies at different levels in order to achieve various objectives. In view of what we have seen and heard, it is evident that rescue archeology cannot be thought of as alien to the ideological problems of each country or to the historical problems of each country. In every nation, the concepts, objectives, and practices of rescue archeology should have very specific characteristics. In my view, an important and fundamental aspect—one that I spoke of during the Quito conference—concerns the matter of rescue archeology and national identity. I say this because archeology is clearly within the historical process; it involves cultural identity and has both archeological and ethnographic elements. I recall the words of my colleague

representing the Navajo tribe. In the archeological as well as the indigenous sense, the Navajo have grounds for the formation of a national identity of a country. For instance, Harold Tso spoke of himself as sort of a living fossil. I don't think he is a living fossil; he does, in fact, represent one cultural identity that is viable in the present day. It is not because he is a native American Indian that he is concerned with the past ways of his people. It is because he is indigenous to North America; he and the Navajo tribe have a very pertinent place in the cultural identity process. Archeologists contribute something fundamental to a people's cultural identity by explaining the historical basis of the culture of that country.

The indigenous people themselves constitute a very concrete and objective testimony of their way of life and their way of being, one that characterizes an important part of the national being of the country. Mr. Tso's words bring to mind what I have always asked my students: What would have happened if the indigenous people had not existed? In our particular case, if the natives had not existed, a large amount of the cultural makeup of our society would not exist either, because we would not have had their influence on dwellings, food, music, agricultural practices, plants—on any number of things. We simply would have become a different society. What is indigenous is not a fossil but is something that lives, something that is very real in our lives. Unfortunately, in North America because of the violent relationship that once existed between the Native Indian and the Anglo-American cultures, important elements of native culture were exterminated.

In the case of Latin America, contact with Europeans was expressed fundamentally through a process of gradual annealment in which the natives, as well as the Spaniards and the Afro-Americans, contributed to form the national culture of the various countries. Now it is time that the facts of their very considerable contributions be shared with the people. That is why I say that one of our first strategies is to conduct rescue archeology in such a way that the identity of the people is reflected in state policy, and their history and prehistory, as well as the manner of discovery, are shared with the public, not in an isolated way but through mechanisms that are generally used to educate people. I am not suggesting something casual; there should be clear strategies. I'm working now on a UNESCO program to see how we can incorporate into the educational system of my country, and that of other Latin American countries, the concepts of what cultural heritage is and how national identity can be considered in the formulation of these policies. Once people are made aware of these things—especially the young people—those who belong to other generations or those already immersed in other things can be regained for this type of thinking. In the way that Iraida Vargas expressed, if the rescue of the national identity is legitimized, the specific practices of rescue archeology will also be legitimized. Ethnic values and customs and the development of urban life would be used progressively in this educational strategy. It would be a way of enhancing the people's knowledge of their history and of broadening their perception of their own being and of what it means to be nationals. It is also very important that the notion of cultural identity be understood as a diachronic or historical process, one in which identities are not stable, but changeable; our cultural identity in the twentieth century is not the same as it was in the nineteenth or eighteenth or seventeenth centuries because with time identities become richer. It is important that people understand that this enrichment is the sum total of the achievements of society, not only of the contemporary society but also of the previous societies. And in the measure that we make this clear and make this specific strategy effective—to rescue the endangered cultural values that are the national heritage in our Latin American countries—we can resolve the problems of financing for the various rescue programs. I believe this is a very important element since the problem is not that there is money or that money is or is not accessible. It is not accessible because those who control the money are not willing to give it for something that they don't feel is important, as my colleague from Argentina was saying. Within the functioning of the modern economies of these countries, rescue archeology is marginal. Such things don't have a specific weight unless the public, as happens frequently, makes an issue or a scandal.

I would like to close by insisting, as I have before, that we agree on the necessity for increasing educational opportunities and for recognizing the cultural values of the people. In a private conversation I had with Henry Cleere and with other members of the round table, and also with Iraida Vargas a short while ago, I said that one does not have to ask a North American why he is an American. You don't have to ask an Englishman why he is English. This identity is given to him by his education. I have lived in the United States, and I have seen closeup how the educational process functions. And I may be mistaken, but I believe that one of the objectives of primary education, among other things, is to give the child a clear idea and notion of national values.

It is for this reason that, although the United States is a melting pot of various nationalities, those who arrive, whether Polish or Chinese or Mexican or German or what have you, can continue to live within the cultural standards of their microidentity. But at the same time, this microidentity is subordinated to a series of national values that are the roots of being North American. That is why when an engineer, or a planner, or an economist is presented with the problem of having to finance, for instance, a rescue archeology program, you don't have to explain that it is important for the nation's cultural heritage, because he already knows it is. The problem is one of managing the resources so that rescue archeology can be done on a larger or smaller scale. For this reason, in the United States there is a body of legislation adequate to protect historic sites and values. There are museums and other institutions where it is a normal, professional practice. It is not thought of as a product of the concept of national identity or the concept of cultural identity of the country. This leads us to believe that evidently the problem is not a technical one, but that a state should conceive it as a global policy in which all these strategies have their place, their importance, and their objective. For this reason, I want to say in closing that if we are to have another worthwhile conference, this matter should be considered basic, since we are in agreement on what rescue archeology means. The next conference should address itself to the design of concrete policies that will be used for rescue archeology in its broadest sense.

HENRY CLEERE
Thank you, Mario. One of the nightmares of a moderator is having to sum up at the end. Mario has just done it for me. Not only that, he must be psychic because what I was going to say was that the next conference should be devoted precisely to this theme.

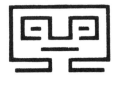

PART IV

Rescue Archeology as a Dimension of Development Financing

Raymond H. Thompson, Moderator

RAYMOND H. THOMPSON

The session on the social and political realities of rescue archeology turned out to cover a little bit of everything. The organizers of this conference tried very carefully to get us to focus on the relationship between the different professional groups in one session and on funding in another, but they were only partially successful, because one of the things the previous session did for us was demonstrate the interrelatedness of all these facets of rescue archeology. In fact, we are now going to find that instead of just talking about funding, about the financing of cultural resource management activities, we are indeed going to focus on a number of different aspects of rescue archeology.

We're going to start our session with a very interesting contemporary example of rescue archeology. Our Quito conference focused much attention on the problems of the looting of the national patrimony of many nations in the world. We have only peripherally addressed that problem so far in this conference. And I'm very pleased that we have with us today Miguel Orrego, an archeologist from Guatemala, who's going to tell us about a kind of rescue archeology that is a little bit different from what we have been dealing with.

MIGUEL ORREGO—Panelist

It is a pleasure to be with you and to represent my country. During these days we have heard much talk on what archeological rescue is. I believe that Latin America in its entirety has the same problems, some countries to a greater degree than others, but they are the same problems. Specifically, Guatemala has problems similar to those of Mexico, with whom we share the same culture. In this case, I want to discuss a type of rescue archeology that has been carried out in Guatemala since the 1960s. We have found some solutions—some that are quite practical, others that are very difficult to implement because of the economic problems they present. We have divided rescue archeology work into three very important parts: The first is the rescue of sculptured monuments called *stelae* and of other things made of stone. The second part of rescue archeology in Guatemala deals directly with illegal diggings carried out by what we in Guatemala call *huaqueros*. The third type of work is archeological claims, that is, the claiming of all cultural, historic artifacts that have left the country illegally.

Now I am going to discuss the various phases of the rescue of archeological monuments. Around the middle of the 1960s and the beginning of the 1970s, most of the archeological sites of the northern part of Guatemala were looted and savagely vandalized without any concern whatever for the importance of the monuments. As a result, rich works of classical Maya architecture and art were reduced to rubble, and today others are incomplete and can be found in foreign museums and private collections. One piece, which was completely fragmented, came from an archeological site called Macha Quillan. The piece was cut into very small pieces to facilitate its transportation out of the country. In this case, it was confiscated by customs officials at the frontier of Guatemala and Belize. It was being shipped to the United States in a box that was marked as containing machinery. This was a rather ridiculous case. Unfortunately, fragmentation also destroys many tracings and details to the extent that these pieces can never be fully restored.

In many cases, when the looters did not have axes and other tools, they burned the stelae in order to break off and carry away only the sculpted parts. This is even worse than breaking with an ax because when limestone is burned it becomes lime and in the process the monument is completely destroyed. In many cases we have lost almost everything. And because no photographic record has been made of many sites, we have no provenience data. Without any clear evidence, these monuments lose their place of origin.

The Guatemalan Institute of Anthropology and History is well aware that El Petén is a dense jungle of more than fifty thousand kilometers that we cannot control. It is very easy to sneak stolen pieces across the uncontrolled frontier between Guatemala and Mexico or Belize. Well, the Institute came up with a plan we called "operation rescue." Its purpose was to try to recover all the monuments that had not been exported and to transfer them to the National Museum of Archeology of Guatemala for display and storage. This was an immediate solution to our problems. Plans were drawn of the exact locations of the monuments, with the hope that some day the monuments could be returned to their original sites. The Institute's rescue operation had a very strong impact on the clandestine organizations involved in the illegal traffic, and by the middle of the 1970s their activities had come to a halt. Now, however, a new wave of depredations has occurred, most frequently in the form of excavations that focus on the most important structures at each of the sites with the purpose of sacking the offerings left in the tombs. We believe that many of the depredations relate to archeological projects that were carried out in Guatemala several years ago. Many of the workers at these projects, because of their years of archeological fieldwork, became quite expert in locating tombs and in the basic techniques of archeology. A very serious problem can develop when a project ends and the laborers are suddenly laid off. Because the workers are left without work, they simply go into the archeology business on their own.

Around 1976 Tikal National Park, one of the most important archeological sites in Central America, also suffered from this wave of archeological looting. We initiated an emergency "operation rescue" in the park under my direction. In one of the sites, Tien Tikal, we had excellent results. A great deal of digging had taken place, but we could see that it had been done by looters whose objectives had not been totally achieved. In this case we decided to continue the excavations, and to date it has been one of the most successful operations in Guatemala.

We have another kind of problem with looting by excavation, as evidenced by a structure at a site called Naranjo. Typically, the looters' excavations will go completely through a structure. In some cases, when the looters have a little experience and they can't find something on their first attempt, they will dig a series of internal tunnels, which can undermine structures and leave holes. This is a serious problem because, in addition to losing valuable archeological data and artifacts, we must move quickly to backfill the excavations in order to prevent a collapse and a loss of the structure itself.

In Guatemala, when we execute "operation rescue" we also endanger our own lives because the looters usually are well armed and willing to defend any of their operations that we might interrupt. So we are forced to have the police and the military authorities accompany us, as well as civil authorities. In one case, we uncovered a tomb that was almost found by looters. The tomb gave us quite a bit of information on prehistoric trade between Guatemala and the valley of Mexico.

Early in 1984 we learned that a very important site in El Petén was being looted. The University of Texas at San Antonio offered to carry out an emergency rescue operation. The project was directed by Richard Adams. The site is made up of about 350 structures, of which half have been extensively looted. El Petén is part of a great Mayan culture, and most of the sites include large architectural features. One of the principal temples has been totally looted. There are tunnels that go from one side to the other, and inside are some fabulous tombs, dating around 426 A.D. and containing murals or paintings. Dr. Adams's expedition found an intact tomb that contained a wealth of data, most notably some human remains bound with aromatic leaves that were held onto the body by a piece of cloth, possibly following the style of a mummy. This is the first time that we have found such data in this area. The organic materials are now being analyzed. One of the pieces found in the tomb is considered unique in America because of the way the top is opened. I remember when we found it, we tried to open the piece thinking that it was a pressure closure. Fortunately we didn't continue to try because we probably would have destroyed it. There are some incisions on the sides in the form of an el that form a half-turn, thus the piece is hermetically sealed. It is the only piece of this type ever reported from Mesoamerica.

There are many things that the tombs have revealed. For example, we have found many styles of an ethnographic type that have helped us to identify several pieces that are being shown in the United States, particularly some pieces in an art gallery in New York. Our good relationship with the United States has helped us to recover many objects taken from Guatemala; we are trying now to rescue the upper part of stela number eleven from Los Pinos.

Finally, I want to recognize my Guatemalan colleague Carlos Lucea, who is present here and who supervises the government official responsible for claiming all those pieces that we know came from Guatemala.

RAYMOND A. THOMPSON
Thank you for describing a form of rescue archeology that I'm sure we all regret but that nevertheless is a part of what we must consider as rescue archeology. We are now going to hear from Victor Smirnoff, who

is a professional architect involved in historic preservation in his home country of Peru.

VICTOR SMIRNOFF—Panelist

First I would like to say that I am not an archeologist. But I am very grateful for having been invited to this meeting to participate and to share your concerns. I am certain that this experience will enrich my professional career.

Several of you have discussed the meaning of rescue archeology, noting that a civilization that does not study its roots is an orphan. The more solid a nation's understanding of its past, the better will be its future. In my professional practice I have participated in projects in which I have encountered archeological problems. Now there is an attitude among professional architects; they feel that they must take part in the physical developments that, ultimately, reflect the cultural evolution of the country, of the civilization. Urban development is the testimony that our civilization leaves for the future, in much the same way that we have inherited the physical testimony of past civilizations.

That is why the understanding of prehistoric and historic cultures is important and why we architects must be aware of how civilizations developed. But I have proven that just being aware is not enough. The fact that I was invited to come here and to participate is really not enough to give me what I need to know about archeology and what it means to a nation of people.

I would like to tell you of a case in which I was visiting an area where a physical development was going to take place. I had been invited by a government official who had the power to make decisions. While looking over the area that would be affected, I noted some archeological remains. But the politician decided—despite the fact that the site might yield valuable information and that archeological work should be done before we created a new civilization—to begin construction immediately.

Let's not say that this case represents a lack of sensitivity or appreciation of culture on the part of the government official who was making the decision. It is true that he had to think, had to choose between our cultural heritage and politics. But at that point, politics was more important to him. What I am trying to say is that if we make archeology our first priority, given the fact that we are gathered here among archeologists, the architect is very close to his interests. He is the creative part of the development. The engineer is the executive. The politician is on the other end. The architect understands the archeologist. But even though the architect is a bit farther from the engineer, it's not that the architect doesn't understand him, it's just that he's a bit farther away. The point I want to make is that on the one end we have the archeologist, who enjoys analyzing past cultures, and on the other we have the practical, pragmatic executive, who is interested in the here and now and who often must take actions that have a negative—and permanent—effect on archeology.

Your activities, like those of other professionals, usually argue for deviations from the norm. The professional enjoys the results of his work. But that's not enough. It's not enough that he gets satisfaction from his work. He should concentrate more attention on educating decision makers in the government, persuading them to his point of view, showing them that his work is worthy of consideration and support. If we insist on being nothing but intellectuals, we make no progress, but if our activities are shared with society, we will progress. We should always keep in mind that the politicians condition their actions according to the reactions of their constituencies; they are in their positions *because* the people have put them there. So they attend to the people's needs before they attend to those of the intellectuals, regardless of how important we think our concerns are. So we need to make our concerns known as fast as possible to the people we are serving. We need their backing.

It is also very important to consider the costs of archeological work in the development of a community. We know that such costs can very easily be taken out of the budget. Unfortunately, we cannot quantify the benefits of archeology to the public. For example, we say that tourism is one of the benefits, that archeology would be an economic development that would encourage tourism. But we cannot really compare such benefits with the costs of the projects. Most recent civilizations look to previous civilizations as the roots of their modern cultures because they believe they are good foundations to build on. If they were not, there would be no reason to study them. I don't believe that archeology should be motivated only by curiosity.

We can agree that a brilliant past is a good foundation on which to build a good future. Yet in my own country, for example, despite the spectacular evidences of its brilliant past, the consideration of cultural matters is last on the list when economic developments are being planned. What I mean to say is that poverty is one of the biggest threats to conserving our cultural patrimony. We have heard an example of the present civilization selling its past, from which it gets more money than from selling its crops. So some countries have a very developed culture but do not have the capacity to discover and preserve vestiges of their past civilizations, vestiges that consequently are doomed to disappear. People in these countries talk about looting. They talk about how their cultural heritage is disappearing. But they must recognize that someone who is hungry thinks only about a way to get food, and if he has to sell his past to survive, he will. This is a serious problem. This is a reality.

So, while we need a budget to cover the costs of protecting our cultural heritage, in reality we simply do not have the resources. The challenge, therefore, becomes an international one. We need an international understanding concerning the imbalance in the richness of cultural heritage among the nations of the world. I would like to conclude with the suggestion that we promote the establishment of an international fund to be used in cases in which a nation cannot afford to protect but cannot afford to lose important evidences of its cultural heritage.

RAYMOND H. THOMPSON
Thank you, Mr. Smirnoff. We are now going to hear from Betty Meggers, who will discuss for us some alternative justifications for the role of the archeologist in certain kinds of projects in Latin America.

BETTY J. MEGGERS—Panelist
We've been hearing a great deal during the conference about justifying archeology in terms of its tourist value, about the need for educating young people, and so forth. Another aspect we all know about but perhaps are not thinking of as relevant in this context has been brought to my attention in two instances in Latin America. In both cases, the archeologists did not go to the planners, the developers, or the universities to sell themselves; instead, other people saw something in archeology that the archeologists hadn't thought about. Specifically, these people realized that with our modern techniques we can do a great deal to reconstruct what happened in the past; we can shed light on possible problems that may not be evident in the short term but that, in the long term, need to be taken into account in various kinds of development projects. Michael Moseley mentioned some findings about tectonic uplift and climatic change on the coast of Peru that are critical for long-term success of agricultural expansion in that area.

I'd like to give you the two examples that have come to my attention. One involves the Universidad de Tarpica, in Arica, North Chile. The rector of the university is not an archeologist, but he's a very well-educated man. He had been looking at the very arid north coast of Chile and at the problems the country was having in trying to increase its productivity for the benefit of the modern nation. It occurred to him that if we knew more about the pre-Columbian use of this land and about how people in earlier centuries, with different patterns, established themselves (apparently quite successfully), we might be able to adopt some of those methods or improve upon them or take off from them. As a consequence, he has decided that archeology is one of the priority disciplines at the university, and he is supporting archeologists in a research capacity. Although archeology is not yet taught, the university is planning to start doing so. Now here is a person who is looking at archeology as something that has a potential for practical utility and who is willing to gamble by putting some money into archeology. As you probably know, this is a part of Chile in which preservation is fabulous. Archeological research can provide a great deal of information to us not only for our own research interests but also for these practical purposes.

Another interesting example is in the southwestern Amazon River area in Brazil. The Smithsonian Institution and the National Research Council of Brazil have been conducting archeological surveys in the Amazon area for several years. They planned simply to develop a basic time-space framework from which to start finding out what went on in the area and how this related to the various problems of New World cultural development. The archeologist who was working on the Guaporé—the boundary between Brazil and Bolivia—encountered, much to his surprise, an area with immense shell middens made from freshwater mollusks. When he mentioned his discovery to the Ministry of Culture Department in Pôrto Velho, capital of Rondônia, they said: "Hey, wait a minute. There's something interesting here." In Brazil they had been doing a lot of mapping of soils and vegetation and other things with radar photography, and they had found that this region was deficient in calcium. They now concluded that if there were enough mollusks to afford a subsistence base for pre-Columbian populations, these mollusks had to be getting calcium from somewhere to make shells. They decided they had better look into this phenomenon, that maybe the information they had about the potentiality of the area was not accurate. So they decided it would be a good thing to have an archeologist on the staff of the Ministry of Education, Culture and Tourism in the state of Rondônia to give them some feedback of this kind.

These are two examples in which archeology was observed by total outsiders as having something to offer to the planners and to the people who are investing the money.

RAYMOND H. THOMPSON
We now turn to Esther Kirkland from Panama who will share with us some observations concerning rescue archeology in her country.

ESTHER KIRKLAND—Panelist
Thanks to your invitation, I have the opportunity to represent my country at this conference. Panama is one of those countries that unite the Americas. We are a melting pot of Indians, Asiatics, Spaniards, and Blacks. Our constitution establishes that there is no distinction among the races. And this is carried out in practice. The majority of our Indians are separated into reservations that permit them to develop individually even though they are integrated into the rest of the country through educational programs and roads. Both Blacks and the mixed races participate in the government and in the making of decisions that benefit the population of Panama.

Since we are a bridge for the world, we live in harmony with our brothers of the Americas. But even though we are part of the family, we have lost our cultural identity. We are not like, nor are our Indians like, the first Panamanian natives. We are not like the Spanish who lived in Panama for more than four centuries, nor are we like the Colombian Indians. Until the past decade we have had the presence of the United States in our country because of the California Gold Rush and because of the construction and operation of the Panama Canal. As Mario Sanoja said earlier, we are the sum of all these cultures, and we are proud of it. But in recent years Panama has been looking for its roots. We're a young nation that is still developing.

We have two hydroelectric plants, one in the North and one near our border with Costa Rica. We have the Inter-American highway, which will unite the Americas. Construction of the road through Darién to Colombia was halted a couple of years ago, but we are negotiating an arrangement to protect our investments until the highway is finished. The United States provided two-thirds of the funds for this project and Panama one-third. We built an oil transmission line in 1983, and we are taking into consideration its environmental impact.

But we have not always taken care to protect prehistoric and historic sites. We have opened communications with the ministry that undertakes large construction projects and have pointed out the danger of further losses of the nation's resources. We do not have university programs to train students in archeology. Our very few archeologists usually do not address rescue archeology in their studies. But we do have a law for the protection of monuments, which I would call adequate.

One year before Reina Torres died, the organization she directed was given custody of all prehistoric and historic sites. Unfortunately, no funds were made available to the organization, and consequently, the archeological park El Caño has deteriorated and important architectural sites are suffering from neglect.

In our country, as in others, there is a problem with education that promises long-range results. Ideally, in large land-modifying projects, funding should be included to cover the costs of archeological investigations. Although this would not solve our problem, it would give the country the cultural benefit of archeological explorations that without such financial assistance would have been impossible. An adequately funded rescue archeology program would expand the horizons of local archeologists who could survive economically while practicing their specialty. It would permit them to relate to their colleagues and to cultural preservation organizations.

One of my assignments has been to coordinate restoration work in the historic center of the City of Panama: eighteenth-century monuments, convents, public squares, and a military fortress, directed by the Panamanian Institute of Tourism and the Inter-American Development Bank. The archeologists delayed construction work in the project for more than eight months in order to complete excavation inside the Santa Domingo Convent.

We have a long way to go in Panama. And although we have lost some archeological evidence, it's not too late to promote rescue archeology and related multidisciplinary activity that, supported by this meeting, would also be multinational.

When I return to Panama I will be meeting with our archeologist. We will open communications with the engineers and architects who work for the Ministry of Public Works at a national level. I appreciate your invitation to participate in this conference. You can be sure you have a friend in Panama for any exchange of expertise we might plan for in the future.

RAYMOND H. THOMPSON
By now it should be quite clear that the bottom line on all of these projects is money. I believe, however, that we have not fully recognized that money is a *political* matter. We've talked a good deal about the role of

public education in providing the base for archeological appreciation, but we have seldom focused on the need for political action in generating the necessary money.

I've been very interested to see and hear the members of the Corps of Engineers speak at these meetings. The first time I heard one of these distinguished gentlemen speak on the subject of archeology was at a congressional hearing about twelve years ago. At that hearing, when the chairman of the committee asked the general who represented the Corps of Engineers why they were not carrying out adequate archeological and preservational work, the general responded in what I believe was a most appropriate way. He said: "Congressman, you have appropriated money to the National Park Service to pay for archeological work. You have not given money to the Corps of Engineers."

Now, we saw two of our colleagues recognized this afternoon because ultimately, through their efforts and efforts of others, Congress did pass legislation that authorized the Corps of Engineers and other organizations to spend the money appropriated to their agencies for archeological purposes. This is *political* action. And that's ultimately where all of the money comes from. And we notice the very good comments that have come from our colleagues in the Corps of Engineers during these meetings—once that political decision has been made, the Corps is indeed very capable of carrying out sound archeological work. In fact, as we were reminded this morning, the Corps has even come to describe itself as a conservation and preservation agency that also does construction. So I believe that it is very appropriate for us to consider not only the concept of where the money comes from, but also the fact that the money comes through political action of one kind or another.

To start off our discussion this afternoon we have Jerry Rogers, who is Associate Director of the National Park Service for Cultural Resources. He is also the Keeper of the National Register of Historic Places of the United States. He is a historian by trade, and he is often referred to as a bureaucrat because of his elevated position in the U.S. government. I would, however, like to have us consider him as a leader in the kind of political action that is necessary to produce the funding that is needed for our archeological projects. Jerry, will you share with us your leadership experience in generating funds for archeology?

JERRY L. ROGERS—Panelist
I don't mind being referred to as a bureaucrat. I consider it an honor

to work in bureaucracies on behalf of the things about which I care very deeply, such as the archeological, historic, and architectural treasures of the United States and of the world.

Before getting into funding—because, as a matter of fact, I think funding is one of those subjects on which I may be least expert—I would like to express my envy of the people who have been discussing planning issues, the subjects about which I truly care the most. I wish I had been able to participate to a greater degree in those discussions.

I want to suggest that you go back and read the record of the 1981 New World Conference. Many of the questions that are being asked in *this* conference were answered in *that* conference. So it wouldn't surprise me if some of the questions we have been discussing here could be resolved by the ideas expressed in the 1981 conference. So I therefore commend to you that earlier record. Either buy or borrow a copy of it and read the article by my associate, Lawrence Aten, called "Planning the Preservation of Archeological Sites." I think it's very, very prescient.

During the past two days, I've heard mentioned four basic, fairly fundamental approaches to funding rescue archeology. I'd like to hit the highlights of those four approaches and then offer a possible fifth, which I don't think any of us is using.

First, you can fund a program. You can get your legislative assembly to appropriate money to your National Park Service or your National Museum or your National Institute, and that organization can then establish a program to rescue endangered archeological resources. I think that that kind of program is essential in any national effort, in any nationwide approach to rescue archeology. But you can predict that such a program will be instantly overwhelmed. It will confront a far greater work load than it can ever execute. So just be prepared for that when you undertake the funding of a rescue archeology program.

Second, you can find a way to get your legislative assembly to fund projects completely, for example, using the approach Raymond Thompson just described concerning the Corps of Engineers and other federal agencies in the United States. Let's be certain that when we fund a development project, we also arrange for funding needed to remove or at least mitigate the adverse effects to important prehistoric and historic properties that might be caused by that project. Basically, that *is* the device that is providing most of the money for rescue archeology in the United States today. And I think it's a very valid device. You have to operate on the theory that not every new thing one wants to do is, without exception, desirable. Because there will always be some social costs, such as the displacement of people, that are paid when new things are done, we might as well take those realities into account and include those costs as part of the development project.

Both of these approaches require the concept in law—or at least in morality—that archeology is a public asset. That concept relates directly to the public education that we have been talking about. Fortunately for us in the United States, the public is very fond, particularly, of prehistoric archeology. Ours is such a young country, and such an amalgam of various cultures, that most Americans are fascinated by the antiquity that we do not have in our own contemporary American culture.

The third approach that has been mentioned is funding through private philanthropy. One can always find major donors or foundations, people who can afford to give away money to do good things such as rescue archeology. And some of that does occur. I personally believe that there's room for expansion in getting funding from private philanthropy, at least in the United States, and I think that would be true on an international scale as well.

The fourth approach is to try to fund rescue archeology through market sources and through the profit motive. Try to find a way for someone who's in business to make a living, to make a profit. Try to find a way to make archeology attractive to that private sector profit motive. It's important for private companies to look good as conservationists, whether they're conserving endangered species or whether they're conserving information and sites that are five or ten thousand years old. They can make money by advertising how responsible they've been as they've gone about their development. And I think that that is an area in which much remains to be done. We ought to be doing more.

As a matter of fact, the fifth suggestion I would like to make is closely allied to this. I personally believe that you can identify some individual investor, someone with money who is about to spend it on a project, whether in the private or in the public sector. The closer you can get to the person who has the motivation to do the development project, the more likely it is that you will be able to fund the rescue archeology that might be required in that very project. I would like to suggest that you investigate the use of tax incentives. Because if an individual investor can realize a tax benefit, can reduce the amount of taxes payable to the national authority through income or property taxes or some other device, then that person can factor the cost of rescue archeology right into the profit and loss column.

Here in the United States we have a very successful tax incentive program that rehabilitates historic properties. Buildings listed in the National Register of Historic Places are eligible for a 25 percent investment tax credit if the person rehabilitating that property does so according to standards that are approved by the National Park Service. I would not have dreamed a few years ago that I would ever see a program of this magnitude. But as a matter of fact, in the past three years alone, that program has overseen the rehabilitation of about 7,500 certified historic structures in the United States. And the value of that rehabilitation—which I believe would not have occurred without the tax incentive—is over $5 billion. The tax incentives are very attractive, and during the recent economic recession, about two or three years ago when people could get little money to invest in ordinary development projects, there were people running around with bags of money looking for rehabilitation projects in which to invest. So, as you can understand, this program is attractive.

It's a given that we don't rehabilitate archeological sites. Sometimes we save them for research in the future, and often we rescue the data they contain. But there are ways we can use tax incentives for archeology. Even under the present tax code of the United States, which is very inadequate for this purpose, we have a provision in which an individual who owns an archeological property can take a tax benefit on his federal income tax return if he donates to a conservation organization a partial interest in the land, one that will lead to the conservation of the archeological resource. For example, if a developer is building new houses in the suburbs of Dallas and encounters an archeological site, he would build them around the site. He could go to the courthouse and register a covenant on the deed to his property promising to relinquish forever his right to develop that property. He could put that in the form of a covenant to a conservation organization such as the Archeological Conservancy or Southern Methodist University—many organizations would qualify. Then he could assess the value of his gift in terms of the value of the land with the archeology preserved, as opposed to the value of the land that he would have had had he developed. And then he could use the value of that gift in his federal income tax returns just as he would if he had given the same amount of money to the Red Cross or the March of Dimes or some other charitable organization. Well, that plan has had very limited use thus far, but I think it is worthwhile to keep in mind.

There have to be other ways to use tax incentives for rescue archeology. But first, let me caution you about one defect in this system. These conservation easements have to be in perpetuity. And perpetuity is altogether too long. I think we would be much wiser to allow a person to take that deduction if he grants an easement for a finite number of years, perhaps as few as thirty years. Certainly fifty years is a reasonable period of time, or even the more conventional ninety-nine years, which is really quite a long time to give up development rights. That would allow archeologists ample time to rescue the data, even if the site could not be preserved forever.

Let's think about other ways. Let's take another look at our architectural incentives. The state of Oregon, in the United States, has a state tax incentive that encourages the rehabilitation of historic buildings. If a person in Oregon rehabilitates a certified historic structure and has the approval of the State Historic Preservation Officer in that rehabilitation, the state agrees to a ten-year freeze on the assessed value of the property for property taxation purposes. So for ten years the owner can be confident that the tax appraiser or the tax assessor won't come around to tell him that his property is worth more this year than it was last year and that therefore his property taxes are going up. That approach is particularly attractive in times of inflation; several times during this conference I've heard people talk about economies that suffer from inflation. So that's a very attractive incentive. Why not grant a developer or a property owner a ten-year freeze on an assessed value of land if he sponsors rescue archeology during the course of his privately funded development project? Why not allow the owner or the developer to deduct the cost of rescue archeology from property tax assessments or even from taxes for a period of ten years or twenty years or whatever period of time one might find appropriate? In tax systems such as ours in the United States—where depreciation of commercial property, or any kind of property, is a factor in the amount of taxes one pays—why not allow the owner or the developer to add the cost of rescue archeology to the depreciable value of the property so that the individual would have a larger amount of money on which he could apply the normal depreciation scales and therefore enjoy a better income tax situation?

Any system of tax incentives will probably require oversight by some type of government agency. The question is how much oversight could one afford to perform, how much could one practicably perform? I can only tell you that the National Park Service certifies the rehabilitation of the historic buildings I referred to earlier. Last year, with the help of State Historic Preservation Officers in every state, we were able to certify 3,200 rehabilitation projects, and we did it with approximately forty-six federal employees and with our friends in the states helping out. Those forty-six federal employees ultimately certified work worth

$2.1 million in a single year. So actually, that's a pretty far-reaching accomplishment for a very small number of people.

RAYMOND H. THOMPSON
We also have with us another representative of the United States government, Ward Weakly. Dr. Weakly is Historic Preservation Officer for the Bureau of Reclamation, U.S. Department of the Interior, which is involved in a variety of water-related projects in this country. Dr. Weakly supervises a great deal of archeological work that is done in advance of water resource development. He will explain to us how that kind of activity is funded through his agency.

WARD F. WEAKLY—Panelist
I want to start by giving you a brief sketch of how we got where we are. The first archeological work that the Bureau of Reclamation was involved in was in 1935–36. We published articles on the archeology being done in the Hoover Dam (or Boulder Dam, as some of you will recall) Project. This was followed in 1939 by a greater involvement at Grand Coulee Dam in Washington State, where the archeology that was undertaken was not funded by the government but by a $100 bequest from the Inland Empire Indian Relic Association of Spokane, Washington. The government loaned a pickup truck. Actually, a great deal was accomplished that year, and several names very prominent in American archeology took part. This was the situation until the conclusion of the Second World War, when finally the government of the United States began to recognize that it had some responsibility for archeology in large development projects. What with the great expansion of public works construction in the United States—particularly dams and reservoirs—Congress began to authorize expenditures for salvage archeology. Money was very limited, and the work was usually carried out for the Bureau of Reclamation by other agencies, usually the National Park Service or the Smithsonian Institution. But this was a major step in the funding of salvage archeology, what we now think of as rescue archeology.
I won't enumerate the several laws and regulations that have been effected since that time, but the last major step was taken in 1974 with the enactment of the Archeological and Historic Preservation Act. This law authorized responsible federal agencies for the first time to expend monies for data recovery in projects they were conducting, licensing, or permitting. They no longer needed to have specific authorization for each project. The largest project that we have under construction at the

present time is a $3.4 billion project in the state of Arizona, called the Central Arizona Project, which consists of a system of canals, reservoirs, and delivery systems planned to bring Colorado River water into the central and southern portions of Arizona. I'd like to look at that just briefly in terms of the one percent of that amount we are authorized to spend for archeology. It sounds like a lot of money, and it is a lot of money, but properly managed we won't need to spend all of it for rescue archeology. The Granite Reef Aqueduct, the first segment of that project, brings water from the Colorado River to Phoenix, Arizona. This cost some $600 million to build, but the total cost of the archeology on the project was less than $500,000, or less than one-half of one percent. It took very close oversight, knowing the resource we were working with, supervision of our contractors, and a great deal of administrative time and effort, but I think we did more than an adequate job. The publication is available to anyone who would like to have it through Arizona State University. By contrast, the next segment of the main water delivery system, the Salt-Gila Aqueduct, which runs from Phoenix past Florence, Arizona, has cost us almost $2 million. We were presented with a slightly different situation. The archeology along the Granite Reef Aqueduct was mostly lithic scatters, sleeping circles—very minimal type material. When we built the Salt-Gila Aqueduct, we ran into the heartland of the Hohokam culture and encountered some twenty-five archeological sites, all of them village sites. We did not excavate every one of them, but we did some creative financing. We spent one percent of the project cost and persuaded the University of Arizona to cost-share the mitigation work. So the state of Arizona actually contributed funding to that project. It was a cooperative federal-state venture to accomplish what we felt needed to be done. It does take time, money, and effort to administer this type of research.

We have also encountered situations in which the authorization of the law is not sufficient. Our Dolores Project in southwestern Colorado is an irrigation project. We built close to Mesa Verde National Park, a mistake on our part from an archeological point of view, because Mesa Verde is one of the most archeologically sensitive areas of the United States. We have identified within the boundaries of the reservoir about fifteen hundred archeological sites, most of them Anasazi. We found it necessary in that case to exceed the one percent of project cost authorized by law. We had to return to the Congress and request authorization to expend up to four percent of project cost for archeological data recovery. We were successful, and the project is now essentially completed. One of the problems we encountered was that nobody wanted all the material we had recovered. At last estimate, we had six thousand cubic feet of material.

Funding for development projects in the United States is adequate. What we need now is the administrative capability, the management capability, and some creative thinking to implement our projects with the funding that's available.

RAYMOND H. THOMPSON

Up to this time, we have been focusing on procedures for financing archeological projects of primarily a governmental nature, although I think you recognize that Jerry Rogers's comments about tax incentives certainly involve the private sector right down to the individual investor. I wonder, therefore, if it might not be appropriate for us to stop briefly now and ask if there are any comments or questions either from the panel or from the audience concerning the governmental funding of archeological projects, before we turn to some discussion of systems of funding that come primarily through the private sector.

GEORGE GUMERMAN

I would like to address my comments to the more effective use of government funding. I'm aware of and understand the difficulty many nations have in getting *any* monies for rescue archeology, and so my comments to these developing nations who are having difficulty getting funding would be that I hope you can learn something about what not to do or how maybe to do it better from what we have done and misdone in this country. My appreciation is directed to the government agencies, both land managers and developing agencies, and to the U.S. research foundations. My remarks deal with how better to use the vast amount of money that is available for rescue archeology in the United States. My suggestion is to remove the *I* from archeology. When I say *I*, I'm referring to the individual, to the agencies, and to the institutions involved.

Let me cite some examples of what I'm thinking of. In some areas of the southwestern United States, millions and millions of dollars are being spent on archeology in some relatively small areas and on particular cultures. I know of instances in which archeologists from different institutions essentially ignore one another and refuse to cooperate with one another. In one case, two major southwestern institutions bid on two separate but short sections of an interstate highway. There was virtually no cooperation indicated in their proposals. What the peer review panel and the contracting people did was insist that they develop a third document showing how indeed they would cooperate, share information, and write their reports together. This they agreed to with some reluctance. But once the contracts were signed, both essentially ignored their agreement to cooperate. In this example, each was spending over a million dollars, and their cooperation or failure to cooperate could profoundly affect the interpretation of the archeology.

In this same area were three federal agencies, each spending millions of dollars. My suggestion to them was that for a tiny fraction of the money they were spending, they could invest in the salary of one or two people for a year or so to bring this material together, to look at the individual projects not as entities in and of themselves, but as entities that were part of a whole area, especially since the whole area was already being looked at, even though the work was being sponsored by different agencies. To say the least, this was met with a very, very lukewarm reception. And yet, can you imagine the amount of information that could be gotten by one or two individuals looking at the entire area as the capstone of that research? It could have provided some incredible results.

Let me switch now to another area completely: Micronesia. Archeologists are pragmatic people. We take money where we can get it to get the job done. In Palau we have been able to get money from numerous sources with great help from many people in different aspects of the government, enabling us to look at the archeology of this island nation. There are many small projects. What is needed, of course, is to sit down, to bring everything together, to figure out how the sum can be greater than the whole. In discussing this with the program director for anthropology in the National Science Foundation, he said: "Well, there is nothing wrong with your applying for a grant for this purpose. And technically there's nothing wrong. But I do have to warn you that the panel does not generally look favorably on a project that has been funded by other sources in order to bring this information together for the final interpretation." And yet, what better way could money be spent than to do a capstone study of that kind in a highly labor-intensive and expensive operation like archeology? Here's a way to insure results.

So what I'm saying is, I think we have to remove that *I* from archeology if we are going to use most effectively the archeological funds that we get. In short, I find what has happened in anthropology ironic—that the concept of culture area is no longer really considered, although it is intellectually a very viable concept. What we *have* done in archeology is build our own culture areas, the culture area of the individual, the culture area of the institution, and the culture area of the agency. To use our dollars effectively, we have to break down those culture areas.

MICHAEL J. SNARSKIS

I enjoyed Jerry Rogers's comments on the tax incentives, tax breaks, and so on, that are available in the United States. It seems to me, though, that you spoke primarily of U.S. cases. In Costa Rica, for historical and political reasons, the collection of taxes is less than efficient. Most people, in fact, do not seek out such opportunities—even though some do exist—because it is simply so much easier to avoid paying part of your taxes in other ways. I wish we had the sort of thing you mentioned. It strikes me as a very viable way to go about it. But I think it would be difficult to implement such a scheme in Costa Rica and probably in many other Latin American countries as well.

DANIEL WOLFMAN

Part of what I have to say is a followup to what George Gumerman said, in the sense that I also believe the project-by-project basis of federal funding for rescue archeology has certain problems.

I was a little surprised to hear Ward Weakly say that there *is* adequate funding. Maybe in some sense there is adequate funding on a project-by-project basis, but for some problems that require broader consideration there does not seem to be. George mentioned cases of projects right next to each other in which the archeologists were not collaborating. Another area that requires a perspective broader than the project-by-project view is that of archeometric analysis, i.e., the application of the natural sciences to archeology. In the United States, and probably throughout the hemisphere, archeologists have found that although there are a variety of new techniques and methodologies—i.e., methodologies and techniques borrowed from the natural sciences, whether they be dating methods, methods of chemical characterizations such as neutron activation to study trade routes, or studies of natural material to provide information about prehistoric diet or climate—these methodologies are not being adequately used in rescue archeology situations. This is partly because of the great increase in rescue archeology in the United States during recent years. Our existing facilities are being taxed beyond their ability to produce results for all. In other cases, laboratories simply do not exist for some of these experimental types of analysis. And although methods may have been developed by a few scientists, these scientists have absolutely no interest in running samples over and over again for archeologists. So my question is, where within the system does one find the budget for these laboratories and for these types of analyses?

RAYMOND H. THOMPSON
There is no easy answer of course. The question I'm sure that agencies and corporations and governments involved in development must ask at this point is, how far does their responsibility extend in financing the archeological research and development costs that provide the capabilities of the archeologists to respond to the individual projects? I think that's the question that we can expect from the other side of the fence.

DANIEL WOLFMAN
Over the last ten years in the United States there has been considerable discussion about the quality of rescue archeology. And if anything important has happened during the last generation in American archeology it is, perhaps, the shift in focus from a cultural-historical approach to a processual approach. I think that a lot of operationalizing of ideas that were thrown around in the 1960s and 1970s is precisely what is going to come from the archeometric analyses. If rescue archeology is to achieve the high standards we should expect of it, it must include these analyses. A second point that I might make is that if such an approach is to be implemented, it should not be limited to the United States but should involve international collaboration. Laboratories need not be established only in the United States and funded only by U.S. agencies. I suspect that in most cases we're not talking about the development of new methods, although refinements do occur in the day-to-day application of the methods I'm specifically talking about. Some methods such as archeomagnetic dating, which is now used on a limited scale, can yield very precise results in certain situations, whereas other dating methods cannot. Yet the number of archeometric laboratories is extremely limited, and few people are working in them because there has been little funding support for them.

DONALD LATHRAP
Because there has been less call recently on the high-tech labs at some universities for things like the space program, physicists, chemists, and other hard scientists have begun reaching out to the archeologists and vice versa, and cooperative programs have been set up within universities. This has certainly been the case at Berkeley with the Laurence Radiation Lab. We have developed a consortium of laboratories at the

University of Illinois in which there is a good deal of cooperation among labs already funded. These organizations will probably request funding support from the National Science Foundation for further lab development and for specific research projects. I think that in many cases it's been a matter of the archeologist not approaching the physicist or vice versa.

JAMES J. HESTER

As I understand it, the approach to funding that we've been hearing about relates primarily to funding of archeological excavations or of renovation of historic structures, that sort of thing. I have a specific question for anyone from a Latin American country, a question that concerns a very specific funding problem. What is to be done about the *huaqueros*? It seems to me that if you are going to take away their livelihood, there needs to be an alternative program either in education or in offering legal employment that would reduce the *huaquerismo*. So my question is, is there any such program already in effect?

PRESLEY NORTON

I think that anywhere *huaquerismo* exists, most people directly involved with archeology or conservation agree that such a program is the only approach to a solution. Unfortunately, as far as I know there is no program of this nature that is being implemented in any country in South America. And if there is nothing happening in my country, Ecuador, I'm sure there is nothing happening in Peru. We all recognize the problem. But it doesn't go beyond that, unfortunately.

STEVE BAKER

Over the years American archeology has begun more and more to recognize historical archeology, particularly as differentiated from the Amerind studies or from a prehistoric cultural context. In the eastern United States, it has become commonplace for historic sites, particularly early American sites, to be included in rescue archeology programs.

The great black eye, one of the great ones in the United States today, is the way we have systematically gone about destroying the historic resource base of the western United States, particularly in the Rocky Mountain states. As coordinator for the Society for Historical Archaeology newsletter, I can attest to the fact that it is hard to find a project in historical archeology today in that region. In fact, some agencies have begun to use oral documentary history as their mitigation technique.

My point is simply that because of the lack of time depth in the Euro-American history of the western United States, in most areas, with the exception of the Spanish Colonial area, we have overlooked a very important resource that represents one of the few chances in American archeology in which we can use both the oral and documentary history and the archeology in front of us to document cultural change and to understand patterning. We give a lot of lip service to it, but for the first time in the history of the United States and the world we have all the tools at our disposal to study these sites, and I would like to see the bureaucrats allow us to do it.

MICHAEL J. SNARSKIS

On the looting question, several years ago *huaqueros* in Costa Rica attempted to form a labor union. In fact they did so, and it was legally constituted. Only later, when someone in government got wind of what was really going on and of who these people really were, did it fall through. In many of our projects we have used *huaqueros* or former *huaqueros* as laborers with great success.

I think there's no answer to this problem in Latin America at present. It is simply too large, too dispersed, and too hard to grasp. I think that most countries probably feel that the way to tackle the problem is not by dealing with the *huaqueros* themselves, directly, but by cracking down on the middlemen and the smugglers who buy from them. If this is done effectively, the market where *huaqueros* can sell their pieces diminishes slowly enough that the *huaqueros* can easily get into other things. In Costa Rica, at least, most are already legally employed.

RAYMOND H. THOMPSON

At the risk of sounding facetious, I would like to suggest that there might be an interesting development project with respect to *huaquerismo*. It seems to me that with economic development of the region in which many peasants are depending upon the selling of antiquities to provide alternative employment, new industries in the area may well appeal to an international banking organization. Using the model of the United States, I'm sure that if we really get concerned about what we call "pot hunters" in this country, rather than punishing them and fining them and putting them in jail, we might do the same thing that we do for unemployed steel workers. We might develop a federal program to retrain pot hunters for some more lucrative contribution to the economy. I know that it sounds like a facetious idea; nevertheless, it addresses the root of the problem. And it addresses mechanisms that already exist in the multinational and governmental areas.

We've had a very good exchange on this topic, and I would like now to shift to our colleague Presley Norton for some more of his good comments. He is the Executive Director of the Program for New World Archeology in Ecuador, and I think he can contribute some ideas about how to fund rescue archeology in a Latin American country.

PRESLEY NORTON—Panelist

As I was listening to George Hasseman's description of the situation in his area, I found myself nodding vigorously and thinking that at last here's somebody who's speaking my language. And suddenly I realized that he was saying, very well, exactly what I had intended to talk about.

We have heard the very interesting remarks by Jerry Rogers and Ward Weakly, who discussed the various interesting and, shall we call it, "massive" alternatives for funding rescue archeology that are available in the United States. In my case we have to look at the other side of the coin. Most of the republics of South America are popularly called developing countries. But in the last couple of years, unfortunately, we have been developing backwards. We have to approach the problems of rescuing the national patrimonies of these countries from a pragmatic point of view. Many have said that rescue archeology is essentially a political problem, and in financing rescue and conservation the public's response has to be part of an entire picture. Unfortunately, the entire picture—we'll talk about Ecuador—includes the very real problems of health, housing, basic nutrition, education, and other problems; there's a great deal that *has* to be done, but there isn't enough money to do *any* of it.

So when we go to our legislatures with our very legitimate concerns about preserving archeological sites, rescuing certain monuments, etc., etc.—to the legislatures that set out guidelines and create programs for rescue on a continental, regional, or national basis—it is extremely important that we be realistic and keep in mind that in most of the South American republics our efforts are not going to go very far beyond the rhetoric stage. I'd just like to mention that in my own experience, while it's been very important to develop programs in the public sector and to give them as much support as possible, we have found an alternate solution, at least on a very small scale, to some problems of rescue and conservation.

In our particular case, we started a private research foundation in Ecuador. Once we had set our overall goals and program, we simply went to anybody from whom we could possibly get money. We got very good responses from the Central Bank of Ecuador, from private banks, and from some industries. But we didn't limit ourselves to banks and industries. We went to foreign foundations, international bodies—really, anybody who'd listen—and were able to raise enough money to implement a program in which we have been working on a sustained basis, in an area approximately 1,200 kilometers long, on a long-term archeological program that has many rescue components. Hearing recently about billions of dollars being spent for rescue archeology virtually made my mouth water. But in South America we are able to get a great deal of mileage for our buck. My program right now sustains a year-round archeological effort in which we have anywhere from fifteen to thirty people permanently employed. We manage to operate on about $45,000 a year. I don't think $45,000 would go nearly as far someplace else. So I'm simply saying that our kind of alternative does exist. If it hasn't been tried or if the public sector simply is not responding to the needs of rescue archeology and conservation, it may be possible to use our approach.

RAYMOND H. THOMPSON

We would now like to turn to the private sector and hear from John Driskill. Mr. Driskill is with Las Colinas Corporation, a real estate development group, here in Texas. He is an engineer by training and in fact had a long and distinguished career in the Corps of Engineers before he entered the private sector. I think that we now need to round out these approaches to funding by hearing from someone in the private sector, which keeps popping up as the final solution to all of our funding problems. We've saved you until last, Mr. Driskill, so that we can all go away with the secret funding mechanisms that you are going to tell us about fresh in our minds.

JOHN DRISKILL—Panelist

I wish it were that easy. I appreciate the opportunity of participating in your conference. As Raymond Thompson has indicated, I'm one of those long-time engineers who have had relatively limited involvement with archeologists and archeological matters.

My twenty-seven years of public service have been followed by five in the private sector. I'm basically responsible for the land development aspects of a large real estate development between the western side of Dallas and the Dallas–Fort Worth Airport. Here we are taking what once was farmland or ranchland and, by putting in streets and utilities, turning it into land that can be developed for office or apartment uses or for single-family residences. Our project is about ten years old and about 30 to 40 percent complete; if things go as we think they will, we project that Las Colinas will probably be completed by about the year 2000.

To this point, our involvement in archeological matters has been limited, primarily because our lands have not yet yielded anything of any significance. But I'm optimistic that if we were to have such an encounter, we could deal with it in a positive way that each side of this equation could be proud of. I'm confident because we are basically a very conservative development, one that tries to conserve the beauty of the lands that exist in Las Colinas—the woodlands, the lakes, and the streams.

But I'm sure you didn't invite me here to talk about Las Colinas; I'm sure you'd rather hear some of my views about the private financing for rescue archeology that we've talked about here. Jerry Rogers helped me out considerably, but I would use just a little bit different language. The first thing that everyone needs to keep in mind when they look to the private sector as the panacea for this problem is that the private sector doesn't have the luxury of deficit financing. If we don't make a profit, we don't exist. That's the first cardinal rule. Now I would agree completely with Jerry that there are two basic ways for the private sector to participate. One is via the outright gift, one that comes from the people who've been very successful—the individuals or corporations who've been very successful in making a profit and who want to contribute in some humanitarian way to making the world a better place to live. That's the first—and I think a very lucrative—source of funding because all the peoples of North, South, and Central America, I think, have an interest in preserving their historical heritage. It is a very popular cause and a lucrative one for private funding.

Now we use different words, but the other mechanism has to make business sense for the private sector. That gets back to being able to make a profit or at least not to lose anything. I'll try to put this in the context that we would use when developing land here in Texas, which will reinforce a lot of things Jerry said.

We recognize that we're still in the land of open spaces, but real estate development is essentially changing the land use to a normal use and, to some, a higher and better use. So if we're out looking for lands to develop, we wouldn't knowingly buy one with an important archeological site on it. In other words, there's still a lot of room for us to do what we want to do; we don't want to get into an argument about whether the land use we propose is better or worse than the existing land use. That's the first thing.

Now I recognize that we're in a very fortunate position, which is not the case in many places in the world. If an important archeological site was discovered after the purchase, we would do just what Jerry suggested. We would donate it to some guardian who could protect, develop, or study that resource, and we would recoup through the tax system a portion of our investment. We would not wait; indeed, the budgets that are developed for the process wouldn't permit the time to wait. So we would dispose of the property by donating it.

I think there is potential in the fourth approach that Jerry brought up, the profit motive. But one must recognize that there are apt to be complications in that process. And unless the developer starts out with title to that archeological site, it may be in public ownership already. I've been in the public sector long enough to know that it would be awfully hard for that developer to bring those two things together so as to enhance the archeological resource and tie it to something that will make a profit for him. I'm not saying it's impossible. I'm just saying that it's difficult.

I don't really have any magic solutions from the private sector. I think that assistance to the Central and South American countries will have to come as private gifts either from individuals or corporations.

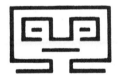

General Discussion

LEE PATTERSON
In all of these financing methods—some complex, some straightforward—I haven't heard much discussion about the role of the

serious, qualified amateur. I'd like to point out a self-truth: amateurs come for free, especially in Texas. If you would convert the equivalent contributions of amateurs from all over the state, it would total thousands of dollars per year: for transportation, digging, writeups, and many other things. I think that any place in the world where you could organize amateurs, you will get your money's worth.

MICHAEL J. SNARSKIS

In the last three years, a group of us in Costa Rica—both Costa Ricans and foreigners, mostly North Americans—have formed what we call the Archeological Association of Costa Rica. We work strictly on a one-to-one basis, or on a face-to-face basis. We have no organized support as of yet, although we're working on it. During this time we've raised about $25,000, which, as someone said before, in any Latin American country goes a long way. We've begun to distribute it in the form of student fellowships and small donations for projects already underway. We're now pursuing some larger grant support. So I'd just like to say that we have had some success with our fundraising efforts and we plan to keep it up.

During my ten years in Costa Rica, I've repeatedly gone to the American Embassy and have spoken with ambassadors and others. And I ask why, when the United States is giving so much money to Costa Rica, is no part of it ever earmarked for archeology? I'm repeatedly rebuffed. They explain that archeology is a very low priority item in Costa Rica and that their instructions come from Washington. Therefore, they are unable to do anything about it. I'd like to know whom I should talk to or write to in Washington about this sort of thing. There is a tremendous amount of U.S. money coming into the country now, and it appears that in the future there will be large road-building projects started. There's an oil pipeline project being talked about now, but never is there any mention of archeology.

JERRY L. ROGERS

Governments are made of many, many agencies. And the United States Embassy, of whom you're asking the questions and from whom you're getting the answer, is an entity of the Department of State. And so I would recommend that the State Department should be the point of contact. There are areas within the Department that are very deeply involved in cultural resource matters, including tangible things, not just the fine arts. There are many friends of archeology and of other forms of cultural conservation in the Department of State, and they might very well listen.

RAYMOND H. THOMPSON
I wonder if we may not have a responsibility (by *we* I mean those of us who are citizens of the United States) to urge our representatives in Congress to expand the recognition that Ward Weakly mentioned, i.e., that it is immoral for our government to use its powers to destroy the heritage of this nation and immoral for our government to use its powers, whether by money or other actions, to destroy the heritage of fellow republics in the New World. I think we have already discovered that in a great many cases we can be much more successful working with our elected representatives in developing long-term policy through the passing of laws than we can be in dealing with the representatives of individual agencies during individual administrations.

PRESLEY NORTON
To answer some of those specific questions we could talk it over, but there is a possibility at the Agency for International Development (AID), and there's a Latin American program at the National Science Foundation, the Endowment for the Humanities, and the Endowment for the Arts. At least they will listen to you. And in any World Bank financing of a major program or project there's a built-in rescue clause. I understand that by *law* most American money that goes into a project abroad, where archeological sites are endangered, has to include some sort of a rescue element.

MICHAEL J. SNARSKIS
I was aware of the NSF program and the AID program. In fact, they have given some help in the past with a long-term salvage project in Costa Rica. But what I'm getting at is the recent influx of U.S. money into Costa Rica.

GLORIA LOYOLA-BLACK
I wish to address two matters touched upon in this afternoon's meeting. The first concerns the overall issue of the financing of our work. I believe that experience has shown us that the OAS is not a funding agency but a technical cooperation agency. The regular financial channels for the region are the Inter-American Development Bank, the World Bank, and to some extent, the Caribbean Development Bank.

When we talk about financing, we have to look at where our archeological rescue work fits into the social and economic fields. Unfortunately, neither our work nor our discipline has yet been clearly acknowledged or, as Iraida Vargas said, "legitimized." The truth is that we appear only sporadically in some development projects. We are not normally taken into account when major infrastructure projects are undertaken in the hemisphere, whether in Central or South America or in the Caribbean. Since there has been discussion of issues arising from this fact, it is important for this meeting to bring them together into a recommendation: to stress or demand, once more, that the environment and rescue archeology be taken into account as factors to be considered in development planning.

Much is being said about the cultural dimension of development, but the terms are vague and no specific action has been defined. Michael Snarskis referred to AID assistance. My own experience, living and working in Washington, D.C., has been that the Agency for International Development does not currently support or consider archeology as a part of development programs. AID does understand other facets of cultural work but still does not consider archeology to be essential or to have a valid reason for being included in development efforts.

I should like to use these final moments to make an observation to the people attending this conference and to the organizers, especially the invited senior government officials from Latin America and the Caribbean, and to those from the Ministries of Planning and Public Works. The United States is represented by participants from the private sector who are interested in our work. That is not the case in Latin America. Even our public sectors failed to understand why they were invited to attend an interdisciplinary meeting to discuss "development as it affects archeological rescue operations." Thus, the response was not encouraging, and we have with us only Esther Kirkland, representing the Ministry of Public Works of Panama. Regrettably, the rest of the hemisphere failed to respond. It would seem that this problem is viewed quite differently south of the Rio Grande.

These efforts in South America are directly related to our identity; therefore, though it is a hard and difficult task, it is one we cannot relinquish. We must embark upon it facing many obstacles in both the private and public sectors. Such is not the case in the United States, where there is support from the public sector and the private sector, as well as from the armed forces and the education sector. I wish to stress this, because it is important that in the discussions among professionals from the North and the South, we be very clear that the Latin Americans are making immense efforts to change this situation. It is therefore necessary that our colleagues in the United States let those working in the area of U.S. foreign policy know that we in Latin America and the Caribbean have a vastly different attitude toward the problem and that it is our firm desire to know who we are, where we are, and why.

GEORGE HASSEMAN
Back to the specific question that started with Michael Snarskis. There is, in fact, a federal law in the United States that does address the kind of circumstance Presley Norton mentioned. It is Public Law 96-515, the 1980 amendment to the National Historic Preservation Act of 1966. In Section 402 it specifically discusses this point and states that something should be done when U.S. funds are used in foreign countries. So if U.S. funds are being used in Costa Rica, there is a law that provides for rescue archeology at the expense of the United States. In fact, the law led to an Army regulation this year that says very much the same thing. The regulation specifically refers to the U.S. Army Corps of Engineers, which does a lot of the construction for other agencies, so that Corps activities outside the United States will comply with the historic preservation requirements of the host country.

As Raymond Thompson mentioned, it is not always easy to implement this sort of thing, and it is sometimes necessary to work through our representatives in the Congress. Over the last several months I have been involved in such a situation. I have worked in Honduras on several specific projects. As many of you know, a great deal of U.S. money has been spent in Honduras during the last four years. And in those cases, U.S. funds were *not* used for rescue archeology, although U.S. funds were used to construct air bases. Representatives in Congress have written letters, and we hope the matter will be handled in the proper fashion.

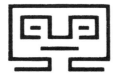

PART V

A Critique of Rescue Archeology in the New World

George Gumerman, Moderator

GEORGE GUMERMAN
This session is entitled "A Critique of Rescue Archeology in the New World." We expect it to be a relatively long and comment-filled session because we will be dealing with problems. And it's a lot more fun to discuss what's wrong than to discuss what's right. We all have a catalogue of things that go wrong, but I ask you all to keep in mind that occasionally things do go right.

Fortunately, we have a group of panelists from a diversity of nations and with a wide range of viewpoints. I think it is very important that we keep in mind the perspective from which a panelist speaks, in order to keep those comments in perspective. The speakers also represent very diverse aspects of the archeological profession and speak with a greater or lesser representation of the profession in their countries. For example, our representative from Canada, Jacques Cinq-Mars, represents the federal perspective in a country where provincial or regional archeologists are often more influential in rescue archeology than those at the federal level. U.S. archeologists, of course, can speak with less confidence as individuals about the state of the profession because each of us represents a miniscule portion of the total. For example, when you hear me speak, you must keep in mind that I represent perhaps one six-thousandth of the viewpoint of U.S. archeologists.

While Jorge Marcos speaks for the entire continent of South America, he represents at the same time a much smaller or a much larger aspect of professional archeologists in South America. So we represent proportionately different parts and different aspects of our profession.

In addition, people like George Aarons and Jorge Marcos have to take on many roles as spokesmen for archeology, while archeologists in the United States have more narrowly defined roles. For example, Lee Patterson will speak from the point of view of an archeologist employed by a large multinational corporation, and Ruthann Knudson will talk about problems in rescue archeology from the viewpoint of one working in a large environmental analysis firm. So please keep these differences in mind as we speak.

The first speakers will represent those nations that, unfortunately, have problems obtaining funds for rescue archeology even though the countries have various degrees of enabling legislation—some very fine, some very poor, some very old. These speakers will address their problems from their points of view. After that, we will deal with Canada and the United States, where we have better enabling legislation and funding but nevertheless have run into a number of problems. Perhaps these two countries can offer some examples of what not to do. So we will start with Jorge Marcos from Ecuador. He will discuss the problems of lack of planning and enabling legislation and of ineffective legislation on rescue archeology in South America.

Now, before Jorge speaks, let me say this. I told you earlier we were going to try a different version of the round table, but the surprise is I didn't tell you what the version was going to be. We are going to try to have the audience comments directed toward the speaker's comments, and so we will have questions immediately after each speaker. Please ask your questions of or direct your comments to the speaker; make sure they are well honed and brief. Otherwise I will have to be the ogre. So with that, let me turn the microphone over to Jorge Marcos.

JORGE G. MARCOS—Panelist
Let me say at the outset that I will be speaking officially for the national patrimony of Ecuador, not for myself. The National Patrimony laws of Ecuador became effective in 1925. Most of the South American legislation on antiquities was written in the 1940s. In Ecuador today, unlike in most other South American countries, we now have a set of bylaws by which the antiquities laws can be enforced. They were signed by the President of Ecuador just before he was retired from office by the new

administration. We have, however, several problems—some very grave ones—but we do also have some examples of rescue archeology going in the right direction. One of our problems is that because of the long period in which we had no appropriate way of doing rescue archeology, the concept of rescue archeology in Ecuador has been varied and sometimes bizarre.

Ecuadorian law in general reads like most South American legislation. The state owns all archeological remains, whether in the ground or on your bookshelves. Although all collections belong to the state, the government does recognize private curation. In fact, the government allows deductions of private collections from taxes if curated properly. If you don't take proper care of a collection, the government will take it away. That's what the law says. The law also forbids the purchase of artifacts, considering contraband all artifacts that are bought or that have been excavated without a permit from the national patrimony. If you buy an antiquity from somebody, you're actually corrupting that person and assisting in the commission of a crime. In a way, this law is very good. But, on the other hand, the law also says that if a construction firm, for example, finds something archeological, the firm must immediately get on the telephone—of course there aren't any in the field—and call in an archeologist to conduct salvage while everything is stopped until salvage has been completed. We also have contracts, for instance ones made between granting agencies and the Ecuadorian government, by which salvage archeology is supposed to be done before a project gets underway. Now all of this is more or less what the law says, but between what the law says and what really happens is a rather large difference.

I would like to go backwards in a sense and tell you what really happens. In one case, an agency received a large grant of money and had to do salvage archeology before moving a great amount of dirt. Well, the agency found an elderly and prominent archeologist and said, "We will pay you to write a book about the region." And with that they felt they had salvaged the archeology. From the old man's standpoint, it was a very nice arrangement because he actually wrote a very good book. On the other hand, the provision in the law that says that you have to stop whenever you make a find is a legal requirement that is very, very old and is common to all the South American countries.

In another example of what really happens, an international agency sent an expert to Ecuador to give advice on how to modernize the National Patrimony laws. Now it was very simple for him to come in with a Mexican law under his arm, spend a few days in Quito, and copy, more or less, the Mexican law, which of course was rather old for that particular purpose. So nothing about advance planning or rescue archeology was incorporated into the new ruling.

Before getting back to an earlier point, I want to talk now about some of the good things we have been able to do. There has been an increasing awareness on the part of some government agencies (and also of some private citizens) of the need for doing rescue archeology. One reason is that since 1980 we have been training Ecuadorian archeologists. So nowadays, no one can say that there isn't an archeologist to do the job. Of course, the archeologists must get into the field immediately whenever an emergency arises. But two institutions have responded very well to rescue archeology. One is the Ministry of Natural Resources and Energy, which actually asked us to help them draft a set of regulations by which they would contract out portions of the land and would conduct rescue archeology every time the land was going to be used by third parties (or by themselves). These regulations have worked with shrimping and oil companies. Speaking of oil companies, an excellent example is an Ecuadorian company, the National Oil Company, which has been financing a rather large rescue archeology project for the past three and a half years.

But to us in South America rescue archeology is not only salvaging the threatened artifacts or the sites, but also salvaging a way of life. We have people living on sites who have a long history and who have systems of agriculture that they have been using for a long time. In such cases, when there is an impending danger of an area being destroyed or modified in some way, we will do salvage archeology. It is not the kind of salvage archeology in which artifacts are removed; instead, it is a type of salvage archeology in which we begin to look at the processes by which people produce and at the ways these systems have served the people's economic needs.

Finally, I would like to discuss another threat to archeology. Some institutions in Ecuador still think very much like turn-of-the-century antiquarians. They think that salvage archeology means going into an area, quickly removing all the artifacts from the endangered sites, and locking them up somewhere. Then there are others who, since they don't have the capability to actually go into the field, will pay good prices to *huaqueros* to salvage antiquities for private collections. We made a study that showed that for every artifact bought by one of the museums, nine other artifacts go to private parties. For every artifact of high quality bought by the museums, two others typically go to international dealers who sit on the verandas of their houses near the rich sites and pay natives to bring artifacts to them. In that way, private dealers finance the whole process. They buy the artifacts before they're taken to the museums. The other artifacts go either to the cities, where they end up in the hands of dealers or private collectors, or to tourist shops, where they are sold to tourists who take them home.

I am very pleased that the Italian government and the Ecuadorian government were able to reach an agreement allowing an enormous collection of artifacts to be returned to Ecuador. But it is also very good to understand that the national institutions and the upstanding citizens of Ecuador were honestly thinking that they were salvaging archeology by spending huge amounts of money to buy things from the illegal *huaqueros*; otherwise, possibly none of these artifacts, at least not such a large quantity, would have ever left the country.

THOMAS F. KING
You point out that much of the depredation that results from purchases from *huaqueros* would not occur if the populace didn't see their work as a form of salvage archeology. What can you do, or what are you doing, to try to change the minds of the population as to what really is proper salvage?

JORGE G. MARCOS
Thank you for reminding me about that. We're doing several things, one of which is to try to reach the people. For instance, the oil company that gave us money to do salvage archeology also gave us money to reach people all over the country. We made two movies: one to show the reconstruction of the history of the area—what we found through the archeological survey—and the other to show exactly what rescue archeology is. We were also given the money to build a regional museum in the area of impact, in which everything we have found is going to be shown. In addition, the grant will allow us to write and publish on our different researches in the archeology of the area. I think that what we are doing is a most effective way of stopping or discouraging pillaging.

PRESLEY NORTON
I think Jorge was being very diplomatic when he discussed institutions in Ecuador that purchased antiquities. But if this conference is really going to have any concrete results, I think I might as well stick out my neck and take off the gloves and talk very specifically about this particu-

lar situation. Jorge was referring to the museums of the Central Bank of Ecuador, which over the last decade and a half have purchased more than two hundred thousand artifacts from *huaqueros*. Now the volume of money that this has produced has in effect created and subsidized *huaquerismo* as an industry. The museums' excuse for this practice was that if the antiquities had not been purchased by the museums, the antiquities would have been spirited out of the country and would have fallen into the hands of nasty foreigners.

In the first place, if the museums hadn't started this practice, the market would never have been created. For several years now Jorge has been doing everything he could to stop this practice. I think I've supported him a bit in this. There is now a new management at the Central Bank, which I think is very sympathetic to the concept of stopping these purchases. Instead of investing huge sums of money to subsidize the pillaging of archeological sites, the Bank could spend a bit more of that money to subsidize rescue and legitimate field archeology.

GEORGE GUMERMAN
This may be something for the Resolutions Committee to take into consideration.

JORGE G. MARCOS
Now that somebody has taken the gloves off, I want to give you some facts. Take into consideration the Bank's contributions to archeology. During the past ten years, the Bank has spent forty million sucres. Because of the inflation of the sucre, that amount translates to about one hundred thousand U.S. dollars. At the moment, that includes fifty thousand dollars because it was a joint grant; fifty thousand dollars from the National Science Foundation went to Rio Alto. That's what the Bank spent in research. During the same ten-year period, the Bank spent four times as much to buy archeological artifacts.

GEORGE GUMERMAN
Our next speaker is George A. Aarons. He is the archeologist in charge of the Port Royal Project, and he's Technical Director of Archeology at the Archeological Division of the Jamaican National Trust. George's concern today is underwater archeology in the Western Hemisphere and the problem of treasure hunters of underwater cultural resources, something that so far has not been a topic of discussion in this conference.

GEORGE A. AARONS—Panelist
There are basically two types of field archeologists: those who work on land and those who work under the water. Perhaps at some point there will also be archeologists who work in outer space, so some day we may have a third category.

I am privileged to be one of those who work both on land and underwater. When Rex Wilson invited me to come here and speak, I thought for some time about a proper topic. Then I looked at the list of people who would be here and decided that in all probability, if I didn't make a statement about the subdiscipline of underwater archeology, no one would. I also looked back at the precursors of this conference. In 1978 a conference was held in Panama, sponsored by the Organization of American States and other organizations, which devoted a session to rescue archeology, including some discussion on underwater archeology. As many of you know, in the Quito meeting three years ago, J. Barto Arnold III, from Texas, talked on underwater archeology and highlighted some of the ways it could be done and some of the problems it involved. I actually read his paper after arriving in Dallas and discovered that many of the problems he spoke of are still very much in evidence. So I feel justified in delivering a paper that is polemic, rhetorical, and pragmatic— "Rescue Archeology Underwater in the Hemisphere: Utopia Turned on its Head." First, the ranting and raving.

For most of this century, the business of shipwreck salvage and treasure hunting has been a feature of Caribbean life from Florida to Brazil and the Guyanas and from Bermuda to Trinidad, but in the last quarter of a century the incidence of this activity, both legal and illegal, has increased in both frequency and quantity until it has attained proportions that are little short of alarming. Shipwreck after shipwreck has been dynamited and pried apart—utilizing methods equivalent to those of an excavator on land—so that salvors and treasure hunters can better enrich themselves from what has virtually become an underwater "Bank of Spain." Never has the "Beard of the Spaniard" been so comprehensively singed as by these twentieth-century pirates and commercial salvors who have often camouflaged themselves as "underwater archeologists" and who have sold their professional integrity and code for the immediate and often immense returns from the salvaged species, objets d'art, and artifacts. In some countries in the area are commercial concerns, some given official governmental approval and some of long standing, who are able to cloak this destruction of the Caribbean underwater heritage with respectability. Shipwrecks are not the only underwater sites that have suffered; the list includes also submerged cities and ports, ceremonial wells, and underground caverns not only under the sea but also under rivers and lakes. All in all, the picture is one of almost unadulterated gloom for those concerned with the preservation and research of the Caribbean nations' underwater cultural heritage.

Shipwrecks, sunken cities and ports, ceremonial wells, and underground caverns are incredible time capsules. The sites usually occur as the result of a single dramatic, catastrophic, and usually climatic event. At very specific times, these sites can provide a closely datable archeological context. Oftentimes, they become silted over and covered with coral so rapidly that their state of preservation is sometimes better than in terrestrial contexts. Properly studied, excavated, and interpreted, they can shed incredible light on various aspects of the Caribbean maritime heritage as well as on Caribbean life in general at various periods, for example, the Port Royal underwater city, the Brown's Ferry ship, the Mexican Ceremonial Wells, and the Florida Mineral Springs sites.

When the sites have been treated to the attention of the treasure hunters and commercial salvors, the result has been almost without exception the typical archeologist's, conservator's, and curator's nightmare: a large collection of objects, many damaged during retrieval and almost entirely without provenience, uninventoried, unconserved, unpreserved, unrestored, unrecorded photographically or graphically, uninterpreted, and unpublished. In the case of the shipwrecks themselves, hardly, if ever, are the hulls or parts thereof photographed, drawn, recorded, or even retrieved or studied. As such, the shipwrecks provide no data for naval architectural analysis. In addition, the treasure hunters and commercial salvors usually have an *idée fixe:* they are after one particular shipwreck or a series of shipwrecks, or one particular part of a submerged city, i.e., the treasury. In consequence, several submerged sites may be damaged before the one sought is located. All around this hemisphere in the Atlantic and in the Pacific are mounds of objects so retrieved in public sector and private sector collections. The objects are often the focus of litigation that will in the end benefit the host countries not one iota and that will forever remain as a reminder of what might have been learned if the proper procedures had been followed.

Perhaps the most revealing case concerns the shipwrecks of caravels in the hemisphere. Probably the most revolutionary type of ship in all history, the caravel was the vehicle by which the Spanish and Portuguese voyages of the late fifteenth and early sixteenth centuries, notably those under the command of Christopher Columbus (whose quincentennial we will shortly be celebrating) and Vasco da Gama among others, were able to reestablish contact between the New World and the Old World on the one hand and between the Old World and Africa, the East, and the Far East on the other. These contacts resulted in the founding of the modern world as we know it today, in the peopling of the New World by the peoples of Africa, Europe, and Asia at a rate unprecedented in all history, and in the opening up of an immense new trade network across the globe. Experiencing its heyday in the middle of the second quarter of the sixteenth century, the caravel was gradually replaced by the merchant galleons and smaller vessels of various types. By 1600, very few caravels were on the stocks and in use. Although these vessels had been a familiar sight all around the hemisphere for at least forty years, their actual design and construction, probably learned and adapted from North African prototypes, were kept secret by the Spaniards and Portuguese lest any Lutheran rivals, through adoption of the design, enlarge and enrich rival empires.

With the plans and specifications for the caravel kept hidden and obscure, if not destroyed, contemporary naval architects are left with only a few models—small line illustrations in portolans—and with precious few detailed designs from which to replicate a caravel of the sixteenth century. All modern models, full scale or scaled down, are thus the best possible replicas based on available data. They all have serious technical problems because educated conjecture had to be used in place of hard data. Also, very few treatises of sixteenth- and early seventeenth-century naval architecture deal substantially with the construction of caravels, and unfortunately, these few are written in the obscure Spanish, Portuguese, Italian, or Latin of the medieval period, characterized by colloquialisms and strange conjugations and syntax. And they are often written in spidery characters on fading and poorly preserved parchment, making them not only incomplete but also difficult to read. Admiral Paris, Nicolas Guillen, R. C. Anderson, Jose Martinez-Hidalgo, William Baker, and Dick Steffy of this century have needed raw data to complete the picture of the caravel, raw data that can be provided only by the actual timbers of a caravel itself. As exemplified by the Niña and many others of her class, the caravel sailed so well that many made several round trips from the Old World to the New and from the Old World to the Far East in the contrariest of weather, in the roughest of seas, and often in record time. Unfortunately, however, until the early 1970s every single caravel discovered in the New or Old World had been salvaged by treasure hunters and commercial salvors to such an extent that by the time the ships came under the purview of the underwater archeologists and the naval architects, very little was left either of the ships themselves or of their contents that could add appreciably to our store of knowledge.

The ongoing excavation of the Basque whaler in Red Bay, the Labrador in Canada, the Mollasses Reef Caravel in the Turks and Caicos Islands, and the Padre Island ships off the coast of Texas, as well as the continuing search for the 1503–04 and 1519 caravels of Christopher Columbus and Pedro de Valdivia in Jamaica, promise to reverse this trend because we expect that sufficient raw data will be unearthed to justify the careful investigations being done. What holds true for the caravels is also relevant to the case of the galleons of the sixteenth to the eighteenth centuries and to all other ship types that, through the centuries, have ended up wrecked on reefs and harbor bottoms in this hemisphere. An immense amount of information and material culture has already been lost, both to the professional researcher and to the general public. Fortunately, however, many wrecks and other submerged sites still lie undamaged and undiscovered.

Apart from the growing number of underwater archeological excavations being accomplished, the other glimmer of hope lies in the growing interest of the general public in the hemisphere in the conduct of archeology in general and in underwater archeology in particular. There is an increasing awareness of the importance of going about archeology in the right way and an increasing revulsion at the carnage that has hitherto been the order of the day; in consequence, we can lessen the stranglehold of the treasure hunters and the commercial salvors and ultimately, like Sir Henry Morgan in his later years, drive these "modern-day pirates" from the hemisphere.

It is clear, based on the evidence of the last thirty years or so, that lamenting this destruction is as adequate a solution as trying to disinter Columbus's ghost. It is also clear that archeologists' attempts over the last two decades to work in the field with treasure hunters and commercial treasure salvors have also failed. Trying to mix the former's expertise with the latter's investment capital has resulted only in making it impossible for the archeologists to conduct their work in its proper methodological context. In other words, the treasure hunter is essentially in a business funded by investors who want a return on their capital within a certain time, and as such, the treasure hunter's methods are guided by the best results achievable in the most expeditious way possible. The commercial salvor's practices are the antithesis of the slow, careful, methodical approach of the archeologist. The celebrated cases of the Atocha and the Margarita off Florida, of the Concepción, the Guadalupe, and the Conde Tolosa off the Dominican Republic, and most recently of the HMS Thunderer on the Formigas Bank between Cuba and Jamaica and Haiti, are notable examples of the incompatability of these two very different rationales. It is now possible, based on these experiences, to enunciate a law that treasure hunters or commercial salvors cannot be used by archeologists to fund underwater archeology. These strategies having failed, we must address ourselves to a campaign and program that can—and must—work if we are to leave for posterity any aspect of this hemispheric maritime heritage. This assault must involve the following:

1) Education. Legislators and politicians, in particular, need to learn about the importance of this hemisphere's maritime heritage, about its research and study, and about the aims and objectives of archeology in general and underwater archeology in particular. Education programs should be presented in such a way as to make it clear that archeological methods are the only means by which our maritime heritage can be interpreted and preserved.

2) Legislation. Many of the political entities of the hemisphere lack comprehensive, or even particular, legislation dealing with the maritime heritage, its preservation, or its study. This legislation is linked in particular with national and regional legislation on territorial waters, contiguous zones, economic zones, the seabed itself, international waters and their definitions, and the ongoing Law of the Sea. Formulae for comprehensive national regulations and for regional and bi- or multi-lateral conventions must be worked out on the level of the Law of the Sea, bi- or multi-laterally and nationally, so that the body of law that emerges truly protects what it seeks to protect, effectively prohibits action against the law, establishes appropriate and effective monitoring systems, and encourages bi- and multi-lateral cooperation and international concerted response. The legislation should also include tax and other incentives for individuals and organizations, encouraging participation in an appropriate medium.

3) Training. At present in the Western Hemisphere, only two universities (Texas A&M and East Carolina State) offer formal training in underwater archeology at a postgraduate level. These programs must be strengthened, and additional training programs of various durations and intent must be established in the hemisphere to train nationals in the

discipline of underwater archeology and its variants. Training should be available in the related fields of artifact conservation, preservation and restoration, naval architecture, ship reconstruction, maritime history, diving, etc. An effort in this area is the field school run by the GOJ/Texas A&M University (TAMU)/Institute of Nautical Archeology—at Port Royal, each summer since 1981—for Jamaican, American, Canadian, Caribbean, and European students. The program can be expanded on a more regional basis and is part of the postgraduate Nautical Archeology program at TAMU. Another effort is a proposed CARIMOS (Caribbean Monuments and Sites) Plan for Monuments and Sites in the Greater Caribbean Underwater Archeology Workshop, to be held in Cartagena or Bogota, Colombia, in the spring of 1985. This workshop will provide practical experience for Caribbean nationals in the discipline of underwater archeology for one month's duration. In Jamaica we plan to set up a regional institution, to teach both land and underwater archeology, which initially will be offered to midlevel people and ultimately will confer degrees. This institution will be funded, we hope, by both UNESCO and OAS. Universities and educational institutions in the hemisphere are urged to develop courses in underwater archeology. International, regional, and private sector funding agencies are urged to add such courses to their curricula so that ultimately a cadre of trained hemispheric nationals will be available to undertake research. Currently, many political entities are forced to contract the recovery of their underwater cultural heritage to commercial salvors, etc., because the alternative does not exist either nationally, regionally, or internationally.

4) Institutions. Already in the Caribbean, the governments of Jamaica, Mexico, the Dominican Republic, Colombia, and Cuba, as well as the state authorities of Florida and Texas, have established underwater archeology departments to undertake research for identifying, locating, and preserving sites. Soon the governments of Panama and Puerto Rico will follow suit. Other entities, such as the Cayman Islands and the Turks and Caicos Islands, have contracted for archeologists to conduct maritime heritage surveys in their territorial seas. The Archaeological Division of Jamaica, the GIS of the Dominican Republic, the DAS of Mexico, and other fledgling groups must be strengthened, supported, and expanded as other governments follow suit. Organizations like the Institute of Nautical Archaeology, the Council for Underwater Archeology, and the CARIMOS Working Group for Underwater Archaeology must also be supported, strengthened, and expanded. Strong regional bodies can be established for planning national and regional responses

to the problems of preserving hemispheric maritime heritage and for effectively disseminating information and learned academic and professional discussion. There must also be an expanded program of archival research on an international, regional, and national level to locate, research, and publish previously unavailable data on the maritime history of the hemisphere. Data on the naval architecture of the maritime cities, ports, and sites need to be made available so that interpretation of the excavated sites will be advanced. Finally, the political entities of the region must be encouraged to establish more museum centers, such as the proposed Museum of Underwater Archeology in Cartagena (CARIMOS Project for 1986–87) and the proposed Museum of Port Royal History in Jamaica. These centers will be designed to house, store, exhibit, and preserve the material culture and related movable and immovable property that embody our maritime cultural heritage.

As I have noted, the waters of this hemisphere contain conditions eminently suitable for the propitious preservation of submerged sites. Clarity and warmth are such that in most instances it is often as easy to work underwater as on land. A true heritage Utopia has been "turned on its head" by the trepidations of the modern-day pirates and Philistines. I have suggested a formula that, if carefully followed and regionally adhered to, may result in the maritime heritage of the hemisphere becoming a real part of the living, visible heritage: Utopia will slowly return to its original status quo. With the near advent of the Columbus Quincentennial there could not be a better time.

GEORGE GUMERMAN
Thank you for that very eloquent statement. We have the unusual situation here of hearing not only the statement of a problem but also the proposal of a solution. I hope that representatives of the Resolutions Committee are on hand and heard George's statement.

HENRY CLEERE
Both Jorge Marcos and George Aarons have raised the problem of treasure hunting. Among the dubious importations we've had from the United States into the United Kingdom in the past few years—along with McDonald's and cruise missiles—has been the electronic metal detector. The effect of the metal detector on archeology in Britain has been horrendous! I estimate that there are probably a half million of these infernal machines around Britain. That's not to say that all of them are being used every day or every weekend on archeological sites. Many

of them are hung up in garages because people didn't make their fortunes within the first month. But nevertheless, these metal detectors have created a climate of opinion that is inimical to the best interests of archeology. In Britain we archeologists find ourselves under threat from this "alternative archeology," because this is the way fortune hunters are promoting themselves in Britain at the present time. I read an article not long ago, in a very reputable English weekly magazine, by a treasure hunter who had informed himself on the government subventions towards rescue archeology—some five and a half million pounds. He pointed out that for a mere fraction of the cost, the treasure hunters could produce equally good results. And there the article was in this, to my mind, hitherto respectable magazine.

In my opinion, our problem is not going to be solved by the imposition of more and more stringent legislation. Of course we need legislation, but I believe the answer lies in our hands. I said earlier that I believe our greatest problem in the next years is one of education: education on two levels. First of all, we must make every effort to insinuate an awareness of the objectives and the techniques of archeology into the public consciousness through formal education, mainly primary and high school education. Above all else, we need to educate the next generation in what we are trying to do. We must also educate those who matter at the present time. And we must educate the media. My organization subscribes to a press clipping service. Twice a week a bundle of clippings arrives on my desk, about half of them referring to treasure finds. The newspapers are fired by the fact that somebody has found a handful of Celtic pieces or Anglo-Saxon silver pennies. The real developments in archeology, our achievements, get no kind of publicity.

We have got to learn to become better publicists of what we're doing. We've got to get the message over to our legislators and to our administrators of what we are trying to do. And another of our problems is our inability to get this message over in clear language. We have got to demystify what we are doing. There are very few archeologists, that I know of, who are capable of writing in such a way that the public can understand why we're doing what we're doing and how we do it, and who can convince the public that this is a worthwhile means of spending public money.

By all means, let us go for international conventions, recommendations, legislation, what have you. But that's not going to work unless we, in the words of Prince Philip, pull our fingers out and get our message over.

BENNIE C. KEEL

Legislation has been introduced in the last two sessions of the U.S. Congress to change the way we deal with shipwrecks, but unfortunately it died in this session of Congress. The same or similar legislation will probably be reintroduced in the next session. There was a tremendous effort on the part of the treasure salvors to defeat this legislation and a tremendous amount of pressure from what we refer to in this country as "hobby divers." The legislation that has been proposed does not interfere with their hobby diving in the usual sense, but we have not gotten that message across to them.

GEORGE GUMERMAN

Our next speaker is Jacques Cinq-Mars, head of the Archaeological Resource Management System at the Archaeological Survey of Canada, the National Museum of Man. He will be discussing the problems of rescue archeology on the federal level in Canada.

JACQUES CINQ-MARS—Panelist

Merci bien, George. I'll switch to English so there won't be any panic in the simultaneous translation booth. I said I'd use my time to talk about underwater archeology. While Canada has a lengthy maritime history, the country is also part of the northernmost portion of the maritime industry. There are tremendous problems regarding the cost of underwater archeology, as seen by the Red Bay case mentioned earlier. In another example, further work in this area by Parks Canada (the outfit that has the expertise to do underwater archeology in a systematic fashion) led to the location of a number of other shipwrecks last summer. Plans for a wharf just a few kilometers from Red Bay have allowed one of the museum investigators to uncover a very lengthy and very sizable bass-like deposit, a whaling type of site, with the good possibility of more of the same in the waters nearby. The main question we have to ask ourselves is, how much can we pay for? Underwater archeology in Canada is very, very expensive and *cold*.

Mention has been made of treasure hunting over and over again. There is a new type of treasure hunter in Canada—the prestige hunter. Underwater archeology brings a flavor of prestige and sells very well in the media. People become famous and make additional money in order to keep doing this kind of work, to indulge themselves in their very expensive hobby.

Let me tell you about some of the problems we are confronted with in Canada. For those of you who don't know, the jurisdictional situation in Canada is very different from that of the United States. The United States has fairly powerful provincial governments and a federal government that oversees matters of federal concern. Canadian provinces have developed over the last fifteen years a more or less coherent set of legislation regarding resource management. Various institutes have developed, with capabilities to carry out archeological research on a more or less systematic basis. Yet the federal government has yet to develop a coherent, cohesive series of mechanisms to deal with archeological research and management in areas of federal jurisdiction. Such areas comprise about 50 percent of the Canadian landscape, much of it in the Northwest and Yukon territories and the Arctic Archipelago. We have managed to do some archeology in Canada over the years, but rescue archeology has been done in a very ad hoc fashion using various sources of funding. The work has been done mostly through the National Museum of Canada, or more specifically, the Archaeological Survey of Canada, which is the organization I work for. The situation is very much like what has been described for Ecuador, for example, in which tidbits of legislation relating to environmental protection are scattered here and there.

In recent years we have managed to put together a series of packages making use of the archeology that happened to have been written into these various bits of legislation, specifically those acts that deal with environmental protection at large, land use regulation and what not, plus a number of lower-level regulations. Recently we have received a fair bit of support that results from our discussions and negotiations with various agencies, agencies that curiously enough are not involved in cultural matters but are involved in environmental protection for the most part. And a large program was designed to deal with northern concerns, especially those relating to oil and gas allotments.

We were able to plug archeology into the program. In the course of our negotiations we were asked by the government analysts whether we had a solid mandate that would allow us to do the kind of work that we were promising we would be doing. The only thing we could say was, "No, we have absolutely no formal mandate; we are just squeezing our way into this, hoping for the best in the long run."

They were fair enough to say, "Well, we will support you with funding, provided that you include as part of your program an analysis and recommendations for the development of a formal policy for archeology at the federal level." These recommendations will eventually lead, we hope, to at least internal regulations, then to more comprehensive regulations, and eventually to legislation.

In Canada there is a strong attempt on the part of various people to deregulate things. It is clear that the only thing we'll be able to work with will be a formal policy. A very Canadian way of handling matters is to use precedents to create a low-level policy that may develop a higher profile and eventually become legislation.

One interesting aspect of our work can be viewed as fairly positive. Since we have been working in an almost complete vacuum, with just tidbits of legislation and regulations, we have had the opportunity to develop a series of mechanisms that may enable us to carry out rescue archeology in northern Canada, which is in almost pristine condition from the viewpoint of archeology. The positive aspect is that by looking at what has been done in the States and other countries (this is part of the work that involves analysis for policy development), we can avoid mistakes that have been made elsewhere. One thing in particular I can mention is that the policy development we're involved in is carried out. This is a historical accident mind you; it was not planned out ahead of time, parallel to extensive, ongoing land claims negotiations with the major native groups that occupy the Yukon and Northwest territories, that is, the Inuit on the Arctic Islands and on the coast of the Northwest Territories and on the Yukon, and the major Athabascan groups—especially the Council for Yukon Indians and the Déné nations—in the Northwest Territories. Because of this historical accident, we have no choice but to integrate into the development of our archeological research program a long-term research and management policy. So far as I know, the views of major interest groups (including those of the natives), at least for the northern portion of the hemisphere, have not been sought in most instances in the past in developments such as this one.

Another thing that we have been giving a lot of thought to is the danger involved in playing this kind of game: we're dealing with the North, which is viewed in Canada as well as other places as the last frontier. Because the last frontier has nasty connotations for a number of people, we would like to avoid carrying out last frontier archeology in northern Canada. Pioneering archeology, yes, but in a scientific sense that allows us to say that since so little work has been done, very few people have actually been involved in working up there. And very few people are *interested* in working up there, I think in most cases for bio-physical reasons. We are trying to ensure that the research-management continuum will be kept alive in the minds of most people. For example, we are trying to avoid as much as possible the massive influx of consultant firms that have no experience whatsoever in northern regions and that would just be sucked into this vacuum the day development starts just because there is some archeological work to be done. The major benefit in a paradoxical negative-positive situation like the program we're trying to put together is that it is a preventive archeology program. In other words, the government has given us a mandate to study the situation so that when science-specific plans are implemented (and they are currently being reviewed), we will be able to identify some of the major problems that may be encountered in the process of land use planning in the North, and so that the archeology will be carried out according to clear standards. We're also working on better definitions of these standards; because of our close relationship with the major interest groups, it has been more or less a cooperative venture.

We have no choice but to try to ensure that the archeology we do will be translatable, not translated but translatable. I think it is critical that the information resulting from our work serve various interests: the native groups who have very special needs, the local Euro-Canadian population in the Yukon, the scientific community, and the international community.

RAYMOND H. THOMPSON
In September I had the privilege of attending the First World Conference on Cultural Parks, which was held at Mesa Verde National Park. It involved representatives from some forty nations around the world, in effect covering the entire world rather than the New World as our conference does. One of the very distinct impressions that all of us non-Canadians gathered from that meeting was the enormous success with which our Canadian colleagues are addressing the problems of relating environmental and archeological work in this vast northern region to the needs of the native peoples. Individuals from places as diverse as African nations, Indonesia, and China not only were impressed with the Canadian experience but also plan to use it as a model for their own efforts to keep the concerns of native peoples and the national needs of the development of these regions running on parallel tracks. I'd like to offer that very positive statement in the face of Jacques Cinq-Mars's possible positive-negative approach to this matter. I think our Canadian colleagues deserve a great deal of credit for those accomplishments.

JACQUES CINQ-MARS
I forgot to mention something important, having to do with Parks

Canada. Parks Canada is also a federal agency that is equipped to deal with archeology, except that its mandate is restricted to parks. So it is concerned with a very small portion of federal lands. I should also mention that because of its mandate, although it has fairly extensive capabilities it is restricted essentially to the very visible built environment. They handle some prehistoric archeology, but for interpretive purposes and in parks only. So there are definite problems with that arrangement. The federal agency that I am with is working in all areas *outside* of parks. Another thing regarding conservation—and this is the approach we've taken since we probably will be unable to have legislation soon—is to ensure that archeology will be recognized as an equal partner in conservation policies and environmental protection policies. At the present time, this seems to be the most positive aspect of our work.

GEORGE GUMERMAN
I think it should be pointed out that Jacques has noted several problems on the federal level. Some of the Canadian provinces have extremely effective provincial rescue archeology systems that are backed with excellent legislation, are well funded, and can be models for many areas of the world.

Our next speaker is Thomas F. King, Director of the Office of Cultural Resource Preservation of the Advisory Council on Historic Preservation. He has had a hand in an incredible variety of aspects of rescue archeology in the United States and Micronesia. Consequently, he is in a unique position to discuss what *not* to do in the development of a national archeological program.

THOMAS F. KING—Panelist
I hope that most of my observations on what not to do can't be attributed to my own mistakes.

Last year I was fortunate enough to be asked to review the proceedings of the First New World Conference on Rescue Archeology for *American Antiquity*, the journal of the Society for American Archaeology. In reviewing *Rescue Archeology*, it became clear to me that among the nations south of Mexico there are a variety of recurrent problems. In brief, it appears that most of the Latin American nations have laws that purport to prohibit absolutely the disturbance of archeological sites and artifacts. Usually, however, these laws don't apply in any effective way to agencies of the national government, to subdivisions of the national government, or to entities that are licensed by the national government; therefore, they provide no basis for rescue archeology. It also appears that these laws usually aren't enforced anyway. And finally, in many of the Latin American nations it's clear there's no effective national archeological rescue program that can attempt to make the laws work. As a result, archeological sites are often not even identified in advance of land-disturbing activities, and they are typically destroyed without any rescue excavation. We have received a very similar message in the last few days from the representatives from Chile, Argentina, Venezuela, Costa Rica, and other nations. In the United States, by contrast, we have quite specific legislation and regulations that require archeology be built into project planning. We have a substantial national archeological program. Archeologists in amazing numbers are firmly imbedded in government bureaus and in private industry, which is regulated by the federal government and therefore must comply with the archeological laws. Surveys are typically conducted in advance of construction projects. Many archeological sites are preserved in place for future generations. Rescue archeology is often, if not always, conducted in advance of construction projects with funds provided by the government agency or other entity that's responsible for the destruction. In the United States the taxpayers, rate payers, and private firms spend anywhere from one hundred million dollars to three hundred million dollars on archeology each year. Yet despite all this we are not happy. Why? Why are we not happy?

I think that those nations struggling to start programs in rescue archeology and to get past the immediate economic and social impediments to the development of such programs, may wish to learn some of the reasons for discontent among archeologists and about archeology in the United States, so that these nations will be able to avoid, to get beyond, the immediate economic and social problems and will be able to avoid some of the mistakes of the United States. So, based on the U.S. experience, I want to examine a few things that I believe a nation developing a rescue archeology program should *not* do in building such a program.

First, I suggest that it's extremely important for a nation to avoid the creation of multiple national entities responsible for rescue archeology. In the United States we have two primary agencies responsible for the coordination of rescue archeology. One, the Department of the Interior, is charged by law with providing leadership, regulations, guidelines, training, and coordination in archeology and historic preservation. The Department is charged with providing reports to the President and Congress. It's charged with working with agencies to identify, protect, and salvage archeological sites, among other things. The other agency is the Advisory Council on Historic Preservation, for which I work. The Council is an independent federal agency that is also charged by law with providing leadership, regulations, guidelines, training, coordination, and reports to the President and Congress and is charged with reviewing agency projects and programs that affect archeological sites and historic properties.

Now competition is inevitable between two entities that are so similarly structured and that are given such similar missions. Without commenting on which agency is right or wrong—though I obviously have my opinions—a great deal of time is wasted in argumentation and difficulties between myself and Bennie Keel, between the Advisory Council and the Department of the Interior.

On the other hand, there are obvious problems and obvious dangers in creating a single federal agency to be responsible for archeology. For example, there's the potential for the emergency of an archeological dictatorship, which could stultify creativity and, in fact, lead to the mindless destruction of archeological sites. But I believe it is possible to establish checks and balances to ensure that such a situation does not develop. I'm very attracted by the model of the Arkansas Archeological Survey in the state of Arkansas in the United States, in which the professional body, the Survey, is at least theoretically overseen by the Arkansas Archeological Society, an avocational group that attempts to represent the interests of the public at large in matters of archeology.

Second, I suggest that a nation should be careful about establishing its rescue archeology agency in a government agency that has competing missions. The U.S. Department of the Interior is a park development and land-managing agency. It also is involved in mineral exploitation and in regulating public use of the land, as well as in many activities that are fundamentally destructive to archeological resources. The interests behind these functions typically have a great deal more political clout than those that are concerned about archeology. Further, because such an agency has so many conflicts to resolve within itself, it naturally develops a large, cumbersome, and very slow-moving bureaucracy, which tends to impede its effectiveness.

Third, a nation should avoid a failure similar to that of the United States to link rescue archeology and historic preservation with the assessment and alleviation of impacts on contemporary indigenous communities. Obviously, we who study the past of indigenous peoples have the obligation to be responsible for their contemporary interests and their future. And besides, the concern for local welfare, as it's been repeatedly mentioned here in the last few days, builds a constituency that archeology desperately needs. But in the United States this linkage has characteristically not been made. Social impact assessments on major federal and federally regulated projects are conducted by economists and sociologists, occasionally by cultural or social anthropologists, with no reference made to the archeological side of the equation. The archeologists, meanwhile, go their way recording and dealing with archeological sites, giving little attention to the contemporary communities that may have vested interests in such sites. Only within the last few years have we begun to blend archeology with social and cultural assessments in the alleviation of impacts. We have a great deal to learn from the kinds of programs being discussed—yesterday by Leopoldo José Bartolomé from Peru, today by Jorge Marcos from Ecuador, and of course, by some of the Canadian participants.

Fourth, a nation should be very cautious in its establishment of a national register to record and inventory archeological sites. Clearly, an inventory is vital. You have to know where things are before you can figure out how to deal with them. But in the United States we have mixed up the need for a basic planning inventory with a variety of other requirements. Each is appropriate, each is important, but each is different and generates needs different from those needs appropriate to archeology. As a result, we have a single National Register of Historic Places, which simultaneously tries to be a comprehensive list of all important properties of all kinds for purposes of planning, and an honorific device to designate sites that are important to archeology and historic preservation. But the two purposes are often contradictory. The person who sees the National Register as enshrining his old building may not understand when precisely the same criterion is applied to a prehistoric shell midden. Further, the paperwork that's necessary for providing things like tax relief to a historic building owner may simply not be necessary for an archeological inventory. The result is confusion, unnecessary arguments, unnecessary delay, and paperwork that may be relevant to some purposes but irrelevant to others. So, I simply say that a nation should carefully consider the purposes that it wishes its National Register to serve and should consider whether it really wants a single National Register or several registers that serve different purposes and different functions.

Fifth, and very important, a nation should consider how it is going to obtain the archeological services that it needs to carry out the functions that its archeological laws require. In the United States ten years ago, the question was frequently raised as to just where we were going to find the archeologists to serve the needs that were being generated by our new laws. We've heard similar questions from a few nations here during the last few days. Being a nation that believes strongly in the free market system, we in the United States concluded that market dynamics would create the supply to fill the demand by the time the demand reached substantial proportions. Well, market dynamics did just that, and the results have been fairly dismaying. We now have thousands of institutional and noninstitutional archeological contractors. Some certainly are excellent; a few, or perhaps even many, are unqualified; some are dishonest; I think rather a good many are categorically unethical. The very fact that there must be competition between contractors for contracts leads to the perception that archeologists can't agree on anything. We've heard that view a lot in the last few days. And I think it's true, in part as a fundamental fact of archeological life, but it's also true in substantial part because in the United States we are engaged in a highly competitive business system. The competitive contract situation also contributes to the perception that archeologists are in the field for the money. This perception, of course, is extremely damaging to our entire program. The contract archeological approach has tended to shut out qualified and interested amateurs and has discouraged the involvement of the avocational community in archeology.

Finally, the very fact that we deal with individual contracts—one contract for this project, another contract for that project—leads to a failure of coordination. The archeologist on this side of the hill is not necessarily performing in a manner compatible with the archeologist on the other side of the hill working under a different contract. Hence we have noncomparable results, with no real synthesis in the comparison of those results, and of course, it is synthesis and comparison that's vital to productive archeological research. The National Park Service in particular tries to provide for such synthesis and comparison through the preparation of overviews and state and regional designs and plans. But these are not integral parts of our contracting system. These aspects have relatively low priority for funding; they're mere bandages slapped on the problem, not fundamental cures. So I think it's necessary for a nation beginning a national rescue archeology program to think very hard about how to procure archeological services in a way that minimizes fragmentation and encourages coordination and synthesis.

I want you to consider one strong point of our program in the United

States that's been little mentioned over the last few days. In the various states and territories of this nation we have fifty-seven State Historic Preservation Officers and one formal government office in each state that is responsible for coordinating historic preservation and archeology. Each SHPO has at least one archeologist on staff; some of them, like the Texas SHPO, have quite a number of archeologists on staff and have very vital, vigorous archeological programs. We also have many local historic preservation programs. There are now over six hundred cities and towns in the United States with historic preservation commissions and at least ten major cities with archeological programs. These programs work in partnership with the federal government, receiving funding and assistance from the feds and providing the basic coordinative services that archeology and historic preservation need. The state and local programs are steadily evolving toward greater sophistication and greater importance in the system, with the federal government increasingly returning to a position of providing oversight and guidance to the local and state programs.

England, Canada, Australia, and some of the Eastern Block nations, such as the People's Republic of China, have carried this approach to greater extremes than we—and typically, with excellent results. I think it's very important to look at these models as well as at the U.S. model in thinking about the development of a national archeological program. You must, of course, face the inevitability of competition among these levels. In the United States today there's rather fierce competition between the states and the federal government for dominance in the national program for archeology and historic preservation. But I believe that we can cope with it through consultation and negotiation.

My conclusion, then, is that while the rescue archeology program in the United States is very big, it is not necessarily very good. If Latin American nations are successful in overcoming current economic and social impediments to growth in rescue archeology, they should be very careful in the application of the U.S. models; they should analyze them very carefully, consider our mistakes, and examine other models that may be more effective for their particular interests and needs.

BENNIE C. KEEL
Tom King has given us food for thought and, I think, good clear advice for our Latin American neighbors to consider. I do, however, want to make a couple of other comments.

I often find myself totally discouraged in carrying out the role I've been given when I hear only the negatives about rescue archeology—allegations of all the unethical, crooked, and incompetent work that goes on in the academic, private, and governmental sectors. We all have imperfect people in our organizations. But if you will take the time to look at the publications we have produced recently, you will agree that these represent some major contributions to American archeology and are as competently written, as thorough, as inventive, and as creative as you will find anywhere. And I want to assure you that without our rescue archeology program, we just wouldn't have much. One rescue archeology project that I am very pleased to have had a small part in was put together by the Federal Highway Administration and the Illinois Department of Transportation across one of the most important archeological properties in the world, one recently placed on the World Heritage List. There are many projects I could mention that we have good reason to be proud of. So I hope you will look at some of the good things we've done rather than always bringing up the negative.

THOMAS F. KING
Bennie, you didn't identify the project. It was the American Bottoms Project and certainly a model of its kind. And I would not disagree with Bennie for a moment that there have been some excellent rescue archeology projects and programs in the United States. But I don't think they have addressed the fundamental negative characteristics of our overall program.

SALLY GREISER
The comments of Tom King and Bennie Keel prompt me to suggest a remedy for some of the problems we have in controlling the quality of archeological reporting. I want to commend the Corps of Engineers. I believe they require their contractors to publish results in a regional or national journal. If that policy could be standardized for all agencies and could be followed through, and if high quality work resulted, then those contractors should continue to get contracts.

BARRY G. ROUGHT
In response to Tom King, I think that the competition we see is very good and that the end result of competition is a higher-quality product. I certainly do not want to see a single agency or single czar over archeology. I think the very fact that this conference was put together to bring archeologists and planners and engineers together, that we're able to bring in the Bureau of Reclamation, the National Park Service,

the Corps of Engineers, and a number of private enterprises like Brown and Root and Woodward-Clyde, is an example of how competition can bring together a high-quality group and provide the interchange that results in a better product in the long run. I like competition. I think that it's good for the country.

GEORGE GUMERMAN
Our next speaker is Mark Raab, who is the Director of the Northridge Center for Public Archeology at the State University of California at Northridge.

L. MARK RAAB—Panelist
I think that over the past two days we have gotten a somewhat unrepresentative picture of archeological work in the United States. We do have a great deal to be proud of in a relatively well-endowed archeological program, but I think we still face some rather severe challenges for the future. In fact, I think that in a paradoxical way the very abundance of resources and of social and political commitments that we have to archeology in this country may be provoking a kind of crisis of expectations with regard to archeological planning. Let me try very briefly to put archeological planning into a political and professional context to give you an idea of a crisis that we may be facing in the United States.

We're well aware that over the past twenty years or so several laws have come into existence that generously support rescue archeology in the United States. We've seen that American archeologists have recently had adequate—actually unprecedented—levels of funding for rescue archeology. And there is evident interest on the part of the general public and commitment by public agencies to carry out rescue archeology. Archeology in this country has, in effect, been invited *into* the national process of development and has been given an opportunity to contribute to that process. We have been invited to integrate our scientific and scholarly objectives *into* the broader goals of national development, of environmental and economic planning. The burden has been put upon us to carry out our role effectively. But when archeologists become participants in the inner workings of large development programs they accept the risk of intense criticism if they cannot produce in accordance with expectations. There are some significant problems with regard to planning in the United States today; a look at them may provide some lessons for those of us who may need to do some planning for rescue archeology.

So what are the problems? For nearly twenty years we have witnessed the development of archeology and historic preservation plans at the state level. But if we look at the plans that have been developed to date, we will see that they do not address themselves very well to the real world needs of planners. Archeologists have a tendency to organize their information in ways that are meaningful to them but not necessarily meaningful to planners. What we often find is that archeologists tend to see an archeological planning situation as an opportunity to do the things that they especially want to do and not what the planners need to have done.

GEORGE GUMERMAN

It's unfortunate that there's a general feeling among professional archeologists and those dealing with archeology that there has to be a division between managing archeological resources and research. For several years Canadian archeologists have been telling us that the discipline of ecology has quite successfully melded management and research, so that the two are compatible and mutually supportive. I think we must learn to accept management and research as complementary forces in the archeological rescue system.

RUTHANN KNUDSON

I sometimes thought I was privileged and sometimes thought I was insane, but I've been a participant during the last two years in a relatively, I think, innovative management planning program for the Army that might be useful for some of you to review. Our group coordinated about twenty institutions around the United States. We've been responsible for developing overviews and management plans for seventy-five Army bases, ranging in size from a one-acre cemetery to the whole White Sands Missile Range as part of the DARCOM Project. These overviews are all being done according to a nationally applicable work plan that won't work for all kinds of projects but is working well for those that we have completed. We've completed about 60 to 70 percent of the project, and the rest will be finished within the next couple of months. We've been able to shape the management recommendations to the needs of the Army so that the Army can fund and program the work that will follow. It's a first start, and it's been a very different and very pragmatic approach to using old dirt analyses of geomorphology and land forms to develop research priorities and to put them into language that somebody else can understand.

LARRY D. BANKS

A really critical need in planning that may not have been introduced here concerns funding. Whether this is in the Corps of Engineers or in any other agency, if you've got a plan that's tied into the budget process, you present management with something in writing and you say that this particular phase of archeological investigation needs to be carried out because it is part of a plan that has been previously agreed upon. In the Corps of Engineers we call these "Feature Design Memos," in which we lay out what's going to be done on a project. You don't have to rejustify over and over and over why you're doing a particular element. It's tied to the planning document and tied into the budgetary process, and it really does make a big difference in how well the program goes in terms of the perspective of the managers themselves.

GEORGE GUMERMAN

Our next speaker is Ruthann Knudson, who is the Director of Cultural Resources for Woodward-Clyde Consultants, which is a large, international, geotechnical, engineering and environmental services firm. The recipient of many awards, including the prestigious Margaret Mead Award, Ruthann Knudson is in a unique position to discuss issues regarding the public nature of rescue archeology.

RUTHANN KNUDSON—Panelist

I think that in a conference like this, where we've been talking about things and values that many of us share, by the time we get to this point in the program I, and probably Lee, feel like we're not going to say a single thing that's new.

I would like to talk about what I think is the value system that all of us operate within, either in part or wholly, or that we need to operate within as part of implementing all the rescue archeology programs. It's interesting that in the last two or three days we have never really gotten into any discussion about the techniques of doing archeology. Nobody has gotten into the nitty-gritty of grid systems vs. remote sensing vs. some of the other things, because we've been talking exclusively about the social and political and economic contexts in which we are trying to carry out these things. So my comments will be more of a summary than something specific.

I'd also like to say that my perspective reflects a somewhat different career path that I've taken over the last few years, one I'd never envisioned before and one that not too many archeologists take. In the United States today we have large numbers of archeologically trained professionals who serve as members of the regulatory community. They're in the state and federal agencies, where they develop rules and regulations and handle quality control. We have an archeological professional community that does the archeology for contract firms and universities; there is a whole series of different options. I find myself in a unique situation in that I work for a private industry and am, in the long run, speaking most frequently in behalf of the developer. I am an archeologist and enjoy doing archeology some of the time, but I have taken on as my role being the spokesperson for the developer. That's a very different kind of role, and I find that what I'm doing is being an anthropologist in ways that I never understood in the university. So what I'd like to do is just briefly summarize the ways I think archeologists need to perform and behave within a broader context.

I will say, by the way, that there's nothing like consistently having to explain in two minutes to a vice president of Exxon why you're doing all of this and then going back home and having the archeologist ask you why Exxon wants to do it in such a hurry. That sort of thing gives you a good perspective.

The one issue that we talk about a lot is the public nature of the archeological resource. We have a very difficult time as individual scientists and scholars, whether our funds come from the National Science Foundation or from Shell or Exxon, dealing with the concept of the public nature of the resource base, because in the long run, it's *my* resource base, it's what I make my living off of, it's what I get my thrill studying. I want to study Paleo-Indian lithic artifacts from the High Plains. At the same time, the public may not want to have that particular site dug right now. They may want it locked up. They may want to have the really crummy-looking little lithic scatter or the Spanish Colonial Aqueduct that's in the way of a dam dealt with first.

We have cultural resources all around the world that have a very public nature. We have public laws that deal with them, we have public funds to look into them, and even though in the United States we have a concept of private land ownership, we have never dealt very well with the private land container, in which what we usually think of as the publicly valued artifacts reside. We always have to understand that it's really the twenty people down the block—and what they care about and what they want from the research values or the esthetic values of the sites—that we're responsible for dealing with.

What I'd like to do is go through some ideas and identify a problem and then talk about the asset and the reality and the opportunities that we can create out of it—because it's more fun to do it that way. One of the problems that we have clearly identified in the United States is the whole issue of traditional, indigenous community values, whether in terms of burials or the artifacts themselves. And we do have a problem, as Jacques Cinq-Mars pointed out, of having developed a legal system to protect our archeological resources that has for all practical purposes never involved the community that is responsible for the creation of these resources. We have, however, assets for dealing with this situation. For example, in the Pacific Northwest for the last twenty years we have had memoranda of agreement between the archeological community and the Native American community for the management of traditional values and burials within that context. The state of Iowa has a recently developed program that will handle these issues, giving each site a chance to speak. I do not have a copy yet, but I understand that in the last few months the state of Idaho has codified a state reburial policy that was developed by the Native American community in collaboration with the professional archeological community. It seems to me that we have to deal with reality. The Native American community has an interest; they have political sophistication; they are real brokers in the game. As I believe one Native American told the Park Service and Air Force the other day, if we as archeologists don't deal with the Native American value systems, they have cheaper, quicker solutions to the reburial issue than we do, and we will have to play in their ball game. That's one of the realities.

There is another issue concerning how we deal with the public nature of these resources, and that is dealing with professional archeological collectors. Whether we call these people avocational, paraprofessional, or amateur archeologists, they are a concerned community that has a lack of involvement, that sees the artifacts from the projects stored away in museums, unaccessible to the public. In one case I know of, a dam is being built and seven or eight million dollars is going into a data recovery treatment program that will deal with only about 10 percent of the archeological materials behind the dam. And yet, we have a policeman standing there, not allowing any of the amateurs to come in and dig, while the water is covering the 90 percent of archeological materials left behind. And people understandably ask, "Hey, where do we fit in there? Why can't we have access?" I don't have an answer. But I do believe the question has some validity.

We also have a problem in this country that we archeologists have created for ourselves. We created a national law known as the Archeological Resources Protection Act, which views a relatively low threshold of destruction to an archeological site as a felony. We had a case in Oregon recently in which a jury was not about to argue that the pot hunting of a one-meter hole in a relatively unrecorded site warranted a felony conviction. As archeologists, we have to look at the public value, the professional value, of a resource base to see where we want to draw lines and assess penalties.

A third area that needs a little more attention is that we as archeologists are having some real trouble accepting the responsibility to participate in the general environmental review and planning and decision-making process in which we want to conduct our research. I mentioned this before, and we need to think about it. In the past year I've reviewed a couple of National Science Foundation proposals for what I thought were exciting research projects in areas where there is a tremendous impact from oil and coal development. I questioned whether the monies would not be better spent in some threatened and endangered areas than in areas that are going to last for another thousand years. I think we as archeologists are beginning to understand the environmental review process better. The reality is that we have to consider it, and we have to comply with it, and we have to prioritize some of our research interests within that structure.

A fourth area, a real one and one that I do find quite unpleasant to deal with, is the question of legal responsibility as we are participating in some of these economic development projects. We are an increasingly litigious society in the United States; we can create more and employ more and feed more lawyers than Pandora could open out of the box. We have not yet come to the question of a large major developer suing the archeologists because a project has been held up, but frankly, I think that that's a possibility. Professional liability is becoming an increasingly sizable issue. As a member of a large professional firm where the largest item in our overhead, greater than the rent, is the insurance that we carry for professional liability, I'm much more aware of it. We're seeing legal questions come up in arguments between archeologists as to who could do what when, at the same time that we're seeing projects completed halfway a couple of times around. Frankly, we'll have to deal with this as a legal issue somewhere down the line. The good point about this is that most of our delays so far haven't been very costly; it's cheaper to throw money at the archeology and to get it done than to delay the project. We do get the archeology done, but I think that as we learn to be better contract managers we'll be able to solve that issue. Again, the reality is that archeology is just one element of a very complex economic and political development. We're not very expensive, but we do take time. And time sometimes is the commodity at greatest risk in these development projects.

The other question that's been mentioned here is the cost of archeology, the cost of doing underwater archeology in a cold environment, the cost of saving twenty-nine tipi rings in a coal mining area that we have to evaluate. We've talked about that enough.

It seems to me that these are all areas in which we need to think about our value system and about how we participate within the broader public community; we *do* think about these aspects now, but we need to do it more consistently. And I think we need to do it more self-consciously. And when we do that, it seems to me we will create a tremendous number of opportunities for our own interests. If we recognize the multiple objectives and the public nature of the resource, the resource will get more consideration—in education programs, in decision making, and in planning as Mark Raab talked about. If we recognize this when we're developing state plans, we'll find it's probably more effective and appropriate to use planning district guidelines that some planner developed in 1966 rather than to lay A. L. Kroeber's culture areas over it. We also need to use and understand the language of the decision makers and to begin thinking of ourselves more self-consciously as anthropologists. After all, most of us have a good portion of our training in anthropology. There's a structure, there's a function, and there's a language peculiar to the Corps of Engineers and to the Section 106 compliance and to the construction engineer who is telling you how he plans to build his pipeline. And we need to use that language, not just the language we prefer, if we want to be effective in the decision-making process. It's called co-opting the system, and we don't usually think about it in those terms. We think of it as a "no-no."

Overall, I think we have to be very firm, but not shrill, about the research values of our archeological resource base. It's our professional responsibility to study the resource so that we can provide information to the public. But the more we participate in the other subcultures—from the built environment architects to the Corps of Engineers, from the manager who has to make a decision about funding allotments to the Native American community—the better off we'll be.

LARRY D. BANKS
The topic of money is a very critical part of this conference. And we really haven't dealt with it much. In articles that have come out in the

Dallas newspapers during the conference, we've pointed out that we spend something on the order of three hundred million dollars a year on archeology in the United States. But when you look at the amount of money being spent for archeology in this country in comparison with the development that occasioned the archeological work, it doesn't seem like so much. For example, between 1974, when the Corps of Engineers was first given the authority to expend funds for major archeological excavations, to the present day, we have averaged only four- to five-tenths of one percent of development costs over that entire period. If I'm not mistaken, there have been only five Corps projects nationwide in which we've had to spend all of our one percent limitation.

When we look at the amount of time we're talking about, or the amount being spent on archeology in comparison to everything else, it's a relatively minor percentage of that total cost, whatever the project is. I suspect that the same is true whether the archeology is being done with private funds or with public money. One person asked me during the conference how much it cost to put the conference on. I told him that it was roughly one-tenth of what it would cost to go see a Cowboys football game on Sunday. In terms of the money being spent for archeology itself, to separate the cost of archeology from other considerations in the projects, is a little bit misleading. I think that's something for us to keep in mind.

JACQUES CINQ-MARS

With regard to the cost of archeology, something that was mentioned by our South American colleagues that is confronting us more and more in Canada is the actual cost of followup on the archeological work. I have the impression that what people have been talking about is the cost of carrying out rescue archeology but not the cost for disposing of collections, for analyses, and for the curation and conservation of collections. A tremendous amount of money is being burned through this kind of activity—especially as we become more successful in developing our various rescue archeology programs—probably more than the costs of carrying out the fieldwork itself or of conducting the basic initial analyses and reporting. The long-term costs of curating and conserving collections and using them for interpretative purposes have to be taken into consideration.

PAUL F. DONAHUE

Jacques is quite right on the costs of long-term conservation and curation. And I think one thing that should be given attention here—something we do in Canada both nationally and provincially—is to make the state of legal jurisdiction responsible for long-term curation. This burden is not imposed on the developer; it is not imposed on the consultant. In the Province of Alberta, all archeology is paid for by the developer; the Archaeological Survey of Alberta doesn't pay one penny toward it. The developer is seen to be taking the cultural heritage. The province owns that heritage, so the developer has to pay for the right to destroy that heritage. We have heard arguments from some developers about the high cost of archeology in terms of dollars and in terms of time. We work very closely with the developers, and we get in quite early, and I think I can honestly say that we have never delayed a major project. And we have never imposed unfair responsibilities upon the developers.

Recently, however, we were attacked by a housing lobby group in the province, actually a federal lobby group. (We're undergoing a process of deregulation in the Province of Alberta.) They said we were proposing rather draconian measures upon them in terms of costs of doing archeology and in terms of delays. It was my responsibility to respond to their allegations. A little homework proved that I was dealing with a housing industry. Some more homework showed me that between 1979 and 1980 the average cost of housing in the two major centers in Alberta was $99,900 per house. Now these are very good government of Canada and United States government figures, very solid. I then checked around with the archeologists who were doing the work on various projects in these two major metropolitan areas. We don't know what the archeologists charge; it's private sector stuff. They work with the developer. Anyway, we got several figures from them, enough to be statistically valid. We found that the cost of archeology per house in Edmonton and Calgary was $8.14. Percentagewise, that's .00818 percent of the total cost of housing, or $32.00 per acre. Development and building profits totaled 17 percent. We have had numerous meetings with developers of transmission lines, major oil projects, and the like, and they have never once complained about the cost of archeology in terms of actual dollars. Their biggest concern is—"Don't hold us up! Don't come in at the eleventh hour!"—which we can do with our legislation. We cooperate with them in the planning process, and it has worked out very, very well.

ROBERT J. BURTON
Something that is pertinent to the costs and talk of planning is the fact that if you get early identification and early incorporation into the plan-

ning process, you can often avoid the large cost of archeological curation simply by leaving the materials in the ground. This does have the
added problem that it's not enough to preserve by merely avoiding, but
there is a necessity for an active process of ensuring that preservation.
On our Corps of Engineers projects we commonly put aside some of
the archeological sites that are only going to be inundated or are going
to receive minimal impact, and we save part of our mitigation costs. Part
of our preservation is ensuring that those sites are going to be preserved
for future generations to study.

GEORGE GUMERMAN

Our next speaker is Lee Patterson, who is the manager of Environmental Affairs, including cultural resource management, with Tenneco, Incorporated. He can—and I trust will—speak with authority on the
problems U.S. industry has with cultural resource regulations.

LEE PATTERSON—Panelist

There have been in existence for a number of years, laws and regulations
for the protection of cultural resources. For U.S. industry, however, significant concern for cultural resource regulations started in the early 1970s,
with the development of environmental regulations for new construction projects. In general, industry must comply with cultural resource
regulations for projects involving public lands or for projects on private
lands requiring federal permits. Small industrial projects on private lands
are usually not impacted by this type of regulation. The general issue
of addressing cultural resources on private lands in the United States
has never been adequately addressed; it remains the most important issue
concerning preservation of cultural resources in this country.

Compliance with cultural resource regulations by industry has become a fairly routine part of the overall environmental protection process. The existence of experienced personnel in regulatory agencies and
the availability of competent contract archeologists have tended to minimize compliance problems of industrial projects. There are still enough
problems in this area encountered by individual projects, however, to
warrant some further discussion. In some cases, unjustified problems
with cultural resource regulations can be significant in terms of mitigation costs or, more often, project delay costs.

I have heard few complaints from industrial managers concerning
compliance with regulations in which significant cultural resources were
actually involved. Most complaints involve unjustified work that has been

caused by either regulatory officials or contract archeologists. It should be noted that in the majority of industrial projects, mitigation costs are minimal. Generally, surveys do not find significant cultural resources, or significant sites can be avoided. Most problems are caused from excessive requirements by regulatory people for survey work or by excessive work performed by contract archeologists to obtain higher profits. It should be remembered that the public ultimately pays for cultural resource management by industry in costs passed on to the consumer.

Cultural resource laws and regulations are difficult to interpret due to their general nature. Few good definitions exist on how to interpret the significance, or value, of specific cultural resources. Therefore, regulatory requirements by various government agencies can be very subjective. For example, a small lithic scatter or a few potsherds will seem significant to one regulatory group but not to another. Problems in interpretation occur most frequently when inexperienced regulatory personnel are involved, those who tend to believe that all cultural resource materials are significant, to the same extent.

A few examples of problems in industry with regulations are (1) requirements for surveys well beyond the area of construction impact; (2) requirements for additional testing of sites that have marginal significance; (3) requirements for formal excavations in disturbed plowzone areas; (4) excessive survey requirements due to failure to develop and use predictive models; and (5) the lack of uniform interpretation of regulations, that is, the same regulations for different geographic areas. In construction projects, costs caused by delays due to regulatory actions are often more important than the direct costs of regulatory compliance. At times, managers will submit to excessive regulatory requirements to maintain a project schedule rather than take time to appeal a regulatory decision. In some cases, this practically amounts to blackmail by the regulatory agency. Due to the diffuse nature of the administrative structure of agencies concerned with cultural resource management, it is often difficult to find a higher level of administration that will act promptly on a complaint from industry. The Bureau of Land Management's organization of resource management areas is a good example: appeals of regulatory decisions are difficult to make, as each group tends to act rather autonomously.

Work for compliance with cultural resource regulations by industry is generally done by contract archeologists for purposes of third party credibility and because very few industrial firms employ their own archeological staffs. At the present time, there is good availability of qualified people to do this work. Hiring contract archeologists is not much different from hiring other types of consultants to aid in work on compliance with environmental regulations, such as biologists or air pollution engineers. In all cases, the scope of work must be approved by the industrial project manager so that unjustified work is not performed by the consultant simply to gain a higher profit. Problems usually result when the industrial project manager simply accepts the contract archeologist's definition of scope of work. For example, on a large synthetic fuels project in the Midwest, contract archeologists saturated an extensive site with a large number of text excavation pits, even though none of the initial or subsequent test pits yielded any artifacts. Industrial firms seldom rehire a contract archeologist who has not given satisfactory performance, which aids in correcting continued poor practice by contract archeologists.

Unfortunately, neither the regulatory officials nor the contract archeologists have any real incentive to see that cultural resource work is performed in the most cost-efficient manner. In the majority of cases, the competitive nature of proposals and the integrity of contract archeologists and regulatory officials usually serve to maintain costs at a reasonable level for the industrial project. It is still fairly common, however, to see industrial cultural resource projects with an unjustified scope of work, but, I might add, it is becoming less frequent.

Underwater archeology on the Outer Continental Shelf (OCS) offers a good example of what I believe is unjustified cultural resource management regulations, regulations that are associated with oil and gas production in federally controlled waters. Currently, administration is done by the Minerals Management Service of the Department of the Interior. The area involved is basically over three miles from the coastline, in deep water. The value of cultural resource regulations for this type of location is not well demonstrated. Currently, these regulations address the subjects of historic shipwrecks and prehistoric submerged sites.

Originally, regulations for the OCS were mainly concerned with historic shipwrecks. This type of object can be detected by remote sensing devices, such as the magnetometer and side-scan sonar. Regulations cover only the detection and avoidance of shipwrecks. Oil and gas producers have no specific requirements to do any underwater archeology for shipwrecks. Costs of surveys for underwater shipwrecks are not high, as this work can be combined with work for marine hazards surveys. The incremental cost of shipwreck detection studies usually involves only the interpretation of data from remote sensing equipment.

It should be noted that the efficiency of detection of underwater shipwrecks is largely undetermined for the Outer Continental Shelf that I'm addressing. In most cases, industrial projects simply avoid detected physical anomalies on the sea bottom. In many cases, it is not known if significant cultural resources are involved or not. Under current regulations, there are no requirements that certain areas in the Gulf of Mexico be surveyed for underwater prehistoric sites. In actual practice, this means that the grid density for surveys for remote sensing equipment is doubled, increasing survey costs by approximately 30 percent. The yearly cost to Tenneco for compliance with regulations related to prehistoric underwater archeology is roughly one hundred thousand dollars. If all companies operating in the Gulf of Mexico are considered, this level of expenditure for compliance work could easily involve a cost of several million dollars per year.

In my opinion, the incremental costs for survey work concerning underwater prehistoric sites on the OCS are not justified. No proven detection methods or reliable predictive models exist that can justify survey work of this type. The increased scope of survey work now being required for studies related to underwater prehistoric sites provides more details of the physical structure of the sea bottom but does not give any direct detection of prehistoric sites. Archeologists of the Minerals Management Service claim that this more detailed geological data might have *future* value in developing predictive models. The fact remains, however, that industry must spend money to perform survey work that has no demonstrated direct usefulness. Remote sensing devices now in use, such as side-scan sonar, are not capable of detecting underwater prehistoric sites.

Only one predictive model for underwater prehistoric sites in the Gulf of Mexico has been developed. It involves the identification of the properties of culturally related shell middens. There are major problems with the application of this specific model. Its use is dependent on core samples. Core samples involve very small areas, so that there is a low probability of finding sites with this sampling strategy. Another important consideration is that the early Indians who inhabited land areas that are now submerged may not have made extensive use of shellfish, so that culturally related shell middens may not be an important type of archeological feature on the OCS. Regulatory abuses such as this example for underwater prehistoric archeology contribute a negative image of the value of archeology in general, as viewed by industry and the general public.

To summarize, I believe that, in general, industry has come to re-

gard cultural resource regulations as a routine part of the overall environmental regulatory process. There are few complaints concerning
compliance when significant cultural resources are actually involved.
There is room for improvement in the cost effectiveness of the implementation of cultural resource regulations. Justifications for the large yearly
expenditures for compliance with cultural resource regulations in the
United States are not always clear.

GEORGE A. AARONS
We recently had some remote sensing done in Jamaica in the form of
side scans and sub-bottom sonar—which is, I think, pretty much state
of the art—and we were able to pick up objects as small as a brick. I
think that remote sensing is undergoing rapid sophistication. In a few
years it will probably be so sophisticated that some of the problems Lee
Patterson mentioned will be taken care of.

THOMAS F. KING
I just can't resist adding to that rejoinder a little bit. First, to defend a
sister agency, you should be aware, Lee, that the Minerals Management
Service is conducting extensive studies at this very moment to test the
applicability of a predictive model for the Outer Continental Shelf in
the Gulf of Mexico with direct fieldwork. I'm cheered to hear that industry does not object to the conduct of archeological work when truly
significant resources are found or truly exist. I can hardly imagine a more
significant archeological resource than a Paleo-Indian site on the Outer
Continental Shelf. It is unquestionable that Paleo-Indians were all over
the Outer Continental Shelf. And it is hard to believe that Paleo-Indians
didn't eat shellfish. It's also very difficult for me to see how the industry is going to carry out its acknowledged responsibilities toward those
significant sites if it doesn't make some effort to find them.

LEE PATTERSON
Our main objection is that the methods are incapable of finding sites.
I don't think you can defend the protection of a site when it's not known
whether the site is there or not. This is a practical sort of thing, we do
not see spending money on methods that are incapable. But when the
time comes that there are methods and proven models, then that's a
new ball game.

THOMAS F. KING
Without meaning to belabor the matter, the methods that are being ap-

plied are used to identify, with some precision, high-probability land forms on which it is very likely that prehistoric sites occur, not to identify prehistoric sites themselves. High-probability land forms are then avoided in the exploitation process.

GEORGE A. AARONS
Perhaps industry and the agencies that are involved in this particular problem should get together to develop a system for dealing with this particular problem inasmuch as both have vested interests. I cannot believe that with all the good minds involved, more sophisticated predictive models cannot be developed now.

DONALD LATHRAP
I'd like to mention a letter, written almost forty years ago, that bears on this whole session and not just on the last paper. It's very pointed, and I fear it could have been written yesterday.

In 1945 the Rockefeller Foundation sent the late, great cultural geographer, Carl O. Sauer, down to Latin America to investigate why U.S. funds for improving Latin American science weren't as effective as they should have been. Sauer wrote back about the most remarkable of all Latin American archeologists, Julio C. Teyo. Although Teyo was a highland-born Indian, he became one of the most remarkable scientists and politicians of all time while keeping very busy as a practicing M.D. with a Harvard degree—a pretty good record for a highland Indian.

Sauer rightly notes that in 1945 Teyo was the outstanding archeologist working in the New World. Sauer went on to record that Teyo had built a tremendously effective infrastructure and that Teyo was not just an archeologist but was the most effective person in all of social developmental science in Peru. And because Teyo was the first full-blood Indian in the Peruvian Senate, he was referred to as El Indio. Sauer also pointed out in his letter to the Rockefeller Foundation that the Andean Institute, which had been set up to help the development of archeology and other kinds of studies in the Central Andes, had given a great deal of money to itself and relatively little to Teyo, whose program could have used the money far more effectively and could have made real strides in developing social science in Peru and in South America.

Generally, Sauer found fault with the Andean Institute. He didn't name the three persons involved, but because all three are dead, I will: William Duncan Strong, Wendell Clark Bennett, and Alfred Kidder.

Looking back, the only view one can take of their behavior is racist. Bennett, in particular, was despicable in the way he claimed Teyo's findings and published them as his own. This situation split the U.S. archeological establishment at the time, with A. L. Kroeber and S. K. Lothrop totally on the side of Teyo. It even split the Viru Valley Project while it was in operation. Donald Collier was the one North American archeologist who spent a good deal of time in the field with Teyo, but there was one other member of the Viru Valley Project who was most vociferous and outspoken in defense of El Indio and in support of the best archeologists in Latin America. Not surprisingly, this was the late Clifford Evans.

GEORGE GUMERMAN
Because several questions have been addressed to our Canadian colleagues about their role with the World Heritage List, I will give them an opportunity to discuss the World Heritage List in relationship to Canada.

JACQUES CINQ-MARS
I'm not really in a position to talk much about that, but apparently the most important and most visible thing that is happening in Canada right now is what is going on in Alberta with the "Heads Smashed In" site, which is, as you know, a very important Plains Indian site. It represents a fairly long sequence of prehistory and is being developed by the Provincial Government of Alberta.

PAUL F. DONAHUE
It's hard to say just a few words about "Heads Smashed In." Canada has seven World Heritage sites scattered throughout the country. "Heads Smashed In Buffalo Jump" is one of those seven, and it's located in southwestern Alberta.

The province of Alberta has put into place a master plan for the development of prehistoric and historic resources. There will be ten such themes developed within the master plan. "Heads Smashed In" was declared a World Heritage site by UNESCO in 1981. We had started a concept plan for the site in 1979: Could this site be developed? Would it be worthwhile to develop? Would soft data develop? We knew a bit about the site as archeologists, but we weren't too knowledgable about tourism, potential visitor impact, or the site's interpretive merits. The concept plan indicated that yes, it would be worthwhile, and we started the different phases of the planning process. The site will be open to the public by 1987.

"Heads Smashed In Buffalo Jump" covers approximately thirty-six square kilometers and is largely intact. Drive lanes behind the site, which faces east, go back about six miles. The site is quite deep, and the jump itself is about eighteen hundred meters long. It's very, very extensive.

PART VI

Summary of Conference Accomplishments

José Luis Lorenzo, Moderator

JOSE LUIS LORENZO

Henry Cleere could not be with us this afternoon because he had to fly to Paris. Hugo Ludeña will take his place. Also, General Robert Dacey could not be with us; Barry Rought will take his place

In many ways our meeting here in Dallas has not differed greatly from our Quito meeting. But there is one fundamental difference. This time, we have listened to those on the other side of the problem. For the first time, many of us have heard from those who apparently confront us, who have expressed reality in unfamiliar terms. I say apparently because there appears to be some antagonism between development and conservation. In my view, that antagonism is not real. It is absurd. There is a necessary correlation between development and conservation, and the two must be integrated.

Now, finally, we are together, face to face, explaining our problems, our positions, and our realities to each other. I have been involved with what we call rescue archeology for twenty years. I have had terrible dissensions with engineers, builders, and contractors. But suddenly the path is clear. We have a real base on which to build; we have found a way to communicate with each other, and it benefits all of us.

I will summarize what has been said at the conference. I have been given cards that indicate concrete, specific points. But rather than become lost in specifics, we should be thinking in generalities. We want to end the conference with proposals for broad and significant changes. For example, we have talked about creating local, regional committees, which would group together those interested in our work. The unexpressed premise, as I understand it, is that these committees are to be formed by parties that might otherwise be in conflict. The committees should take care to include representatives from outside the community of archeologists.

By now it must be clear to everyone that we ought to raise the consciousness of our people, on all levels, to the value of archeology as a fundamental instrument in establishing a people's cultural identity, a national identity. If this is to happen, the archeologist must share the knowledge he has gained in various ways and at various levels. Our first consideration, of course, is the scientific report, the archeological monograph or research paper. It is absolutely necessary, but only for the use of scientists. It is the method of communication within the profession. Generally speaking, however, it is entirely too abstract for public consumption. We speak a language and use a terminology with which we are perfectly comfortable. We understand each other, but much of our professional language is unintelligible or unclear to the average person. Yet there are other categories of communication that we cannot afford to overlook or ignore.

We must start with the high authorities in each of our countries, authorities who, although seemingly having nothing to do with our work, are important to us and to archeology. Because we have this tie with the past, there is also a critical need for effective jurisprudence, for real laws, for laws that can be brought to bear on the problems we have been discussing. This is a fundamental realization for me. Our duty is not to convince the lawmakers but rather to inform them of our particular concerns; they should be convinced by themselves. We face a difficult situation, considering the different political constitutions of each of our countries.

In Mexico we have no problems. According to the law, the project that disturbs an archeological context must pay the cost of rescue archeology. Everything that is archeological is automatically included in the national patrimony and is therefore untouchable. But our constitution is structured in such a way that the possession of the soil is nothing more than usufruct. The territory, the soil, and the subsoil belong to the state. It is not the same in the United States. Thus, we could go from one country to another and find important differences in each. I am convinced that the laws that protect the national patrimony must be concordant with the constitutions of those countries and must be derived from those constitutions.

Among the general population, we cannot afford to overlook or ignore the educated, cultural public—people who are neither archeologists nor anthropologists, but professionals interested in and supportive of our work. For them, another level of divulgence is possible, one that is cultured, sophisticated, but straightforward.

There is a third kind of communication, one that is not necessarily unsophisticated but that is popular, with broad public appeal. We have an obligation to use this communication to reach another segment of the population. These people, too, can be motivated to support archeology.

Finally, there are the museums—and not just the great museums. I give you the case of our Museum of Anthropology, that architectural wonder in Mexico City. We need to create other, smaller places, more closely related to the locale, where people can identify with what we have done. If our museum is not to reach all cultural levels of the society, why are we here? This is the big question that many of us, at some time in our professional lives, have asked ourselves: Why am I doing this and for whom? We have got to keep these things firmly in mind.

Something else occurred to me while reading the notes I was given. To teach those who need to learn the value of a people's cultural patrimony, we first have to teach the teachers. We cannot enjoy their confidence, because they are not trained, and they will not have access to our world if they are not taught.

I found the position of the Navajo representative very interesting. Ladies and gentlemen, there is something we have to keep very much in mind: a life ideal that is not ours. Because this ideal exists, it is absolutely and necessarily respectable. We have to accept that our way of facing life, our philosophy of life, is not the same as everywhere else and is not for all people. It is necessary to respect others in order for us to be respected.

Another point we should consider with great care is archeological tourism, i.e., archeology viewed as tourist promotion. To begin with, UNESCO has suggested that archeological tourism is destructive in itself. The same thing is happening to the national parks in the United States. The visitor destroys, not because he wants to but because of the frequency of his visits. Something we have to suffer in Mexico is doing archeology in order to prepare a site for tourism. It is an outrage that, for political reasons, we have had to confront several times in Mexico. A site should be prepared for tourist visits only after several years of work. These sites should be previously investigated. We do not have to create scenarios; this is not theatre. It has more depth.

During our meeting, I realized that there was an important point not being addressed. My colleagues talked about not having economic means for carrying out archeological fieldwork. We also need money for analyses, study, and publication of the results. If we don't address those needs—if, at the same time that we appropriate funds for fieldwork, we do not receive monies to finish a publication—then I have to ask myself: What purpose do we serve? Is our purpose to store the specimens that are recovered? Should we store the field data, the materials, and the rest indefinitely? Dear friends, for that there is no need to do rescue archeology because nothing is rescued. If the results are not published, there is no need to have done the fieldwork.

Another thing we should keep in mind is community participation—rural, aboriginal, and urban communities. In our work, it is always necessary to depend on them, but it is their responsibility to defend what is theirs. The communities are the best defenders. We cannot be at all the sites and be aware of everything. They have to be the ones to inform us of anything that may be in danger. What has to be done, then, is to create a bond between our work and their activity.

Another point: We have to discourage certain entities, such as banks and museums, from purchasing archeological pieces that have been looted. Purchase of an archeological item, called *rescue*, is really the basis for and perpetuates looting. But the rescue of an item itself has nothing to do with our problem. The concept of purchasing an item so that it does not disappear, or does not go on the world market, is false. What these entities should do is support major scientific rescue archeology projects, not spend so much money in collecting, because in reality, these entities are simply collecting. They are not helping anything. On the contrary, their practice contributes to an increase in looting.

Regarding information on the destruction of certain historic and archeological contexts that have occurred because of national or foreign military activities, it is requested that in all cases the international recommendations for the defense of cultural patrimony be followed. We have specific cases, which I should not mention and do not want to mention, but the cases exist. This is a very serious matter.

Another series of proposals we have received may be summarized as follows:

1) Create work groups with professional training that would participate in the defense of the cultural patrimony both on the inter-American and the national level.

2) Maintain, from one meeting to another, some kind of unity among

ourselves that will have an effective capacity for action. In other words, the problem we face is that every two or three years, more or less, the same people meet, with some new faces, depending on political changes in each country. Between meetings, however, there is no action. Of course, on an individual basis, some of us do communicate with one another. But I think we need to begin something specific that will include all who are directly interested in this problem, so that something is done between meetings.

3) Share data among practicing archeologists in order to achieve homogeneous and basic shared models. There is a reality in this. Archeology varies from country to country. There may be valid differences on the local level that cannot be generalized. But, in any case, we must try to know each other better, to see what is useful regarding what one does in one place and another does in another place.

4) Use a part of the funds for development from international organizations for rescue archeology. All development is concerned with and creates modifications of the landscape. Therefore, by obligation, a part of the budget of these development processes ought to be devoted to the defense of the national patrimony, of the cultural heritage.

There were other proposals regarding subject matter and organization, modifications, and enlargements. But it is our opinion that these should be considered in organizing the next meeting.

Now, an important contribution that comes from those of us south of the Rio Bravo, or the Rio Grande, concerns the techniques and analytical systems of archeological research. Those that are routine in North America are not practicable in other countries because of the absence of infrastructure and economic resources. For those of us from the South, it is magnificent to see all the gadgets, all the things that are used in the United States and Canada. Magnificent! We know how they function, we know their potential, but we do not have them. In other words, you may use bulldozers to lift a pile of boxes; I have thirty *peónes* with picks and shovels. But that does not discourage us. What we have to do is precisely what is within our possibilities. We have to do the best possible and not give up thinking and dreaming; we cannot refuse to do it because we do not have a proton magnetometer. Although we do not have such equipment, we manage to conduct our explorations with some kind of manual apparatus.

Before my colleagues speak, I would like to acknowledge and extend our thanks to Fred, Larry, Rex, Gloria, and all the rest for the opportunity to get together, for the wonderful experiences we have had, and for the way everything has been run. If something important comes from all of this, it will undoubtedly be due to their efforts. And last but not least, our thanks to the translators.

GEORGE GUMERMAN—Panelist
José Luis Lorenzo pretty much summed up the conference. My abiding impression of this meeting is essentially the same as my impression of our conference in Quito three years ago. I'm sure we've all been struck by a sense of incredible diversity and frustration. Some of us are talking about our millions of dollars and whining that we can't have more. Others are talking about using thirty men with picks and shovels instead of a bulldozer.

But our first and greatest need is the public, and as José Luis has noted, not only the public in the big urban areas, the middle class, but also the general public. In particular, we need the public's support of the law. If we don't have laws that people can understand, respect, and live with, we could have antiquities legislation that is no more effective than prohibition was in the United States.

Second, we need archeological spokespersons, that is, people who are willing to get out of the trenches, to spend the time organizing meetings such as this, to be "Doctor Archeology" for local communities, to serve on committees, to speak to legislators, to invest time and energy doing thankless tasks. Such people are almost never shown the appreciation they deserve from those who have benefitted most from their efforts—the professional archeologists.

Third, we must resist the temptation to emphasize the role of the contract archeologist over that of the traditional academic researcher. Because by doing so, we are likely to save only the spectacular or old sites. It is the researcher who helps us to understand the importance of the less spectacular site. It should be obvious that we need contract archeologists and we need the university researchers. And we need them to work together.

Finally, we need that much-maligned manager of archeological resources, the person who must enforce the legislation, who must work through the problems of permitting, who, on occasion, must say, "No, you can't do that because it's not good enough archeology." This person, at least in the United States, is often maligned and criticized, but he's an essential and valuable cog in the archeology business.

Our success or failure in carrying out rescue archeology programs depends on how well these roles are filled.

JOSE LUIS LORENZO

Thank you, George. I will not presume to respond on behalf of my colleagues; in fact, no response is really necessary. Each of us has his own ideas on what the conference has accomplished here in Dallas and on where it should be headed in the future. Now Hugo Ludeña has something to say.

HUGO LUDEÑA—Panelist

I have nothing to add to these concluding remarks, but I have been asked to report for Henry Cleere and to summarize the work of the round table he moderated, the group that dealt with the social and political realities of rescue archeology. Here are their main conclusions.

First, the long-term acceptance of the importance of rescue archeology can best be assured by the introduction of archeology into primary and secondary education, thereby ensuring the emergence of a generation that is aware of the importance of the subject and is informed about archeology's objectives and techniques.

Second, in the short term, archeologists must recognize the overriding need to make their results known to the wider general public in terms that are immediately comprehensible to the public, choosing every medium available to them: exhibitions, museums, displays, handbooks, radio, television, and the press. Whenever possible, and within the constraints imposed by security considerations, members of the general public should be invited to visit excavations where the objectives and results must be explained to them in nontechnical language.

Third, archeologists carrying out recent excavations financed by public funds must accept the fact that their accountability to the public, the ultimate source of funds, is as great as to their fellow professionals and to the discipline of archeology.

Fourth, cultural resources such as archeological monuments and sites are primary expressions and manifestations of cultural identity. Their exploration, conservation, and protection should be seen as an essential component in the establishment and identification of cultural identity. General policies for the management of cultural resources in this line are urgently required, policies that are adaptable to the different governmental and legislative structures, political systems, and cultural and historical traditions of different countries.

Fifth, the development of such policies will be immeasurably aided by the establishment of inventories, registers of cultural property, in every country to avoid unnecessary expenditures of time and money in the formulation of guidelines for inventories in countries that do not yet possess them. There is an urgent need for cooperative action involving the participation of those countries with well-established inventory systems and policies.

Sixth, in evaluating the feasibility of rescue archeology projects that form part of major world programs, the social impacts of such projects must be assessed and the wishes of communities must be respected— especially in the case of those indigenous communities that have long historical links to the land and that have cultural traditions distinct from those of the prevalent society.

JOSE LUIS LORENZO
The next moderator with a summation is Raymond H. Thompson.

RAYMOND H. THOMPSON—Panelist
Fortunately, I don't have to summarize very much, because everyone has done such a good job of it. The group that I moderated dealt primarily with the funding of rescue archeology. We saw that there were no magic formulae but rather various sources of funds, some of which have not yet been adequately exploited by archeologists or by the international community.

I should like to offer an impression, however, of the conference, in fact, of both conferences. I believe that we now need to move to an entirely different level of sophistication in this conference, a truly international level. We have been, both in Quito and here in Dallas, talking a little bit too much to each other. North Americans have shared North American problems with one another, without making the problems relevant to our Latin American colleagues, and to a lesser extent, Latin Americans have shared problems with one another that we North Americans have not fully understood. This is a very natural kind of thing. And it is necessary for a group of human beings to go through this kind of process in order to rise to a truly international level. But I fervently hope that as we think ahead to future conferences on New World Rescue Archeology, we will all strive very hard to provide that fully international perspective that is needed in order to make our deliberations effective in the social and political arenas that we've been talking about.

JOSE LUIS LORENZO
Our next speaker is Barry Rought of the U.S. Army Corps of Engineers.

BARRY G. ROUGHT—Panelist
Before summarizing the round table I was with, I want to introduce Colonel Ronald Kelsey, who is Assistant Director of the Civil Works for Environmental Programs of the Army Corps of Engineers in Washington. In addition, he is the Historic Preservation Officer for Civil Works in the Corps of Engineers.

RONALD KELSEY
I just want to say again we regret that Major General Wall could not be here, although he very much wanted to be.

I'd like to share a few observations about the conference from the Corps perspective in Washington. I've been impressed by the people I've met here, by their talents and their expertise. I've been enlightened in the areas of what's happening in rescue archeology in the hemisphere: rescue archeologists working closely with engineers, the recognition of the social and political realities of rescue archeology, and the mixing of archeology, engineering, and development.

I was impressed with Mario Sanoja's concluding remarks yesterday morning. For me, this conference has been very productive, and I think it's been a productive one for the Corps of Engineers.

BARRY G. ROUGHT
On behalf of the round table I took part in, I have several points to make. For the Corps of Engineers—and for the other federal agencies that have presented themselves during this conference and for those that haven't—environmental design, including cultural and archeological work, is firmly imbedded in the planning, design, construct, and operate mode. General Dacey's panel tried to present this idea. Judging from several of the discussions, it seems apparent that environmental impact analyses, including cultural and archeological assessments, should be expanded to include social assessments and the impacts of projects on society itself.

Another topic that was touched on lightly is the matter of curation. We believe there are two facets of the problem. First, there is not enough use of the material that is already being curated. This is especially true in the United States, where we have extensive collections the federal agencies have accumulated that the archeologists can use to research and publish. The second facet is curation of the new material being collected; we are having trouble finding a place to put it.

The large number of Corps archeologists here demonstrates our commitment to the field and the importance we attach to archeology. But the real essence of our session, and of subsequent ones, was the great value of good, cross-disciplinary communication among developers, engineers, archeologists, planners, and financiers.

JOSE LUIS LORENZO
I have here a document that Mario Sanoja wishes to present. I think it should be read in its entirety, although in some aspects it is repetitious with regard to the conclusions we have reached.

MARIO SANOJA
The Second New World Conference on Rescue Archeology in Dallas, Texas, on November 15–17 states as follows:

WHEREAS cultural properties, as they are defined in the 1970 UNESCO Convention, constitute one of the fundamentals of the national and cultural identity of nations, and their true value is greatly diminished without information concerning their origin and historical context;

WHEREAS cultural properties of many nations of Latin America are in imminent danger of destruction, due to the development of public and private engineering works that have an impact on our cultural heritage but take no account of the importance of preserving this heritage for the future;

WHEREAS the rescue and conservation of cultural properties of these countries require that the people be made aware of the meaning and significance of their cultural heritage; and

WHEREAS the Organization of American States (OAS) is a regional body which is responsible for the coordination of cultural and scientific policies at a hemispheric level;

The Second New World Conference on Rescue Archeology in its meeting held in Dallas, Texas, from November 15–17, 1984, now therefore urges:

1) THAT the Secretary General of the OAS express concern over this loss of our cultural heritage and the imminent destruction of cultural properties in many Latin American countries as a consequence of accelerated economic development, and that he introduce a resolution at the next meeting of the General Assembly of the OAS urging the Member States to adopt the necessary measures for the rescue and conservation of their cultural heritage;

2) THAT the Member States of the OAS review their existing laws on archeological resources both on land and under water, update the language of these laws, revise and expand the authority for action suitable for today's world, require full participation by qualified archeologists in development projects, and make all agencies of government responsible for protecting and preserving the cultural resources impacted by their actions;

3) THAT the Member States should prepare a national inventory of important public and private cultural properties, both on land and under water, in order that the destruction and loss of our cultural heritage might be reduced;

4) THAT the Member States satisfy the urgent need to promote the development of scientific, cultural, and technical institutions (archeological, anthropological, and historical schools and institutions for restoration and conservation, educational museums, laboratories, libraries, workshops, etc.) required for the training of the qualified people needed for the protection of cultural property;

5) THAT the history or social science taught in primary and secondary schools introduce the concepts of cultural property, cultural heritage, and cultural identity as a means of contributing to the efforts of the people of the Americas to define their cultural, ethnic, and national heritage, and to preserve that heritage for future generations;

6) THAT the aboriginal populations' ways of life also constitute an important part of our cultural heritage and that, therefore, ethnic groups should have the right to conserve their ways of life in the manner that they deem proper to the interests of their communities;

7) THAT the Member States of the OAS that have not yet done so should sign and ratify the UNESCO and San Salvador Conventions prohibiting the import and export of cultural heritage properties;

8) THAT the OAS establish an Inter-American Committee which will facilitate the proper supervision and coordination of measures for the rescue and protection of cultural heritage property at a hemispheric level as follows:

a. to work with the host nation to organize the Third New World Conference on Rescue Archeology;

b. to define the common archeological principles shared by all Member States of the OAS and to draft a statement of organizational principles and policies for presentation to the Third New World Conference;

   c. to suggest ways of implementing those principles in the differ-
   ing social and political environments of the hemisphere;
   d. to determine how best to accomplish the goals set forth at the
   First and Second New World Conferences on Rescue Archeology.
   In addition, the Conference:
   9) Is concerned that the efforts of public and private organizations
to preserve archeological objects by purchasing looted materials may
be contributing significantly to the market demands for the products
of illicit excavations that are so destructive of the archeological record;
   10) Urges that the international development organizations, both
governmental and private, follow the lead of the World Bank in requiring and funding inventory and evaluation of cultural resources as well
as mitigation of the impact on those resources in all development projects
they sponsor;
   11) Urges prompt and full enforcement of the existing laws and regulations of the United States concerning the protection of archeological
resources impacted by international development projects, especially
in Latin America;
   12) Urges that all indigenous people affected by development
projects and rescue archeology efforts be included in the planning and
decision-making process;
   13) Urges that the value of archeology to tourism be recognized by
closer cooperation among government agencies in planning development projects;
   14) Urges that educational programs in engineering, finance, and
archeology be modified to include training which will reflect the interaction of these disciplines in the proper conduct of rescue archeology;
and finally
   15) The participants in the Second New World Conference on Rescue Archeology held in Dallas, Texas, November 15 to 17, 1984, extend
their sincere thanks to Southern Methodist University and the Southwestern Division of the U.S. Army Corps of Engineers for hosting the
conference; to the Organization of American States, Southern Methodist University, the U.S. National Science Foundation, Corps of Engineers, Bureau of Reclamation, Department of Transportation, and National Park Service for their sponsorship of the conference; and to the
Smithsonian Institution, the Owens Foundation, the Gilmore Foundation, Woodward-Clyde Consultants, the National Trust for Historic
Preservation, and the Advisory Council on Historic Preservation for their
financial support;

16) The participants especially thank Fred Wendorf, Larry Banks and the Organizing Committee, and Daphne Derven, Jim Bruseth and the Local Arrangements Committee for making the conference an intellectual and social success; and Gloria Loyola Black and Rex Wilson for providing the energy and effort that carried the spirit of Quito to Dallas;

17) The participants are grateful to their archeological colleagues in Texas from the Dallas Chapter of the Archaeological Institute of America, the Archaeology Research Program of Southern Methodist University, the Texas Archaeological Society, and the Council of Texas Archaeologists for their many volunteer contributions to the success of the conference; and

18) The participants thank President Donald Shields of Southern Methodist University for making it possible for Dr. Galo Plaza to share with them his seminal comments on the archeological heritage of the hemisphere, thereby greatly enriching the conference.

JOSE LUIS LORENZO

Our colleague Mario Sanoja has presented a resolution that brings together the background of this meeting with regard to Latin America. Perhaps in the case of the United States and Canada, the lines to be drawn should be different. But for Latin America, these are the ones we should follow. May I have comments from the audience?

MARIO SANOJA

I simply wish to propose this document as a formal motion to the conference to be approved and then placed in the hands of the Secretary General of the Organization of American States with the request that it be discussed officially in the next General Assembly. I therefore submit it for consideration as a formal proposal or motion.

CARLOS G. ZEA-FLORES

As a representative of Guatemala, I approve and congratulate my colleague Mario Sanoja and ask that in addition to sending it to the Secretariat of the OAS, it be sent to all of the countries.

RAYMOND H. THOMPSON

I believe that our colleague from Venezuela has summarized the necessary principles of the New World Conference on Rescue Archeology and that it is our duty to approve his proposal as a resolution of this conference.

JOSE LUIS LORENZO

I believe the applause is a positive reaction to Mario Sanoja's motion. So I declare the motion approved by the conference and direct that it be given to the appropriate persons to be delivered to the pertinent national organizations.

I wish that Fred Wendorf would take my place, because I believe he has something to say.

FRED WENDORF

Thank you very much, Dr. Lorenzo, for your very good words. I agree with what you had to say. This conference has been a very interesting experience. I also want to acknowledge the splendid help we have had from the Dallas Archaeological Society, which contributed so much to the success of this conference. Finally, it gives me great pleasure to announce that the Third New World Conference on Rescue Archeology will be held in Venezuela in November 1987. I hope you all will plan to attend.

HUGO LUDEÑA

I would like to take this opportunity to express my appreciation on behalf of the Peruvian delegation. We have four representatives here. We are most happy to have been invited and are pleased to have been able to express our concerns for the endangered archeological values in our country.

I also think this is the proper time to recognize the institutions responsible for underwriting the costs of this conference: the National Science Foundation; the Organization of American States; Southern Methodist University; the U.S. Army Corps of Engineers; the U.S. Bureau of Reclamation; the U.S. Department of Transportation (Federal Highway Administration); the U.S. National Park Service; the Smithsonian Institution; the Owens Foundation; Woodward-Clyde Consultants; the Gilmore Foundation; the Advisory Council on Historic Preservation; and the National Trust for Historic Preservation.

We are pleased that the next New World Conference on Rescue Archeology will be held in Venezuela, and we trust that we shall again have the support of some of these prestigious organizations.

MARIO SANOJA

I also want to take advantage of this moment. First, to express my appreciation that our country has been designated as the seat of the Third

New World Conference on Rescue Archeology. I sincerely hope to see you all in Venezuela in three years, and I look forward to working with you as we move to another stage in the business of rescue archeology. We should all exert our best efforts during the next three years to ensure that we will be adequately prepared for the meeting in Venezuela.

FRED WENDORF
If there are no further comments from the audience, I declare this conference closed.

PART VII

Contributed Papers

Archeology on the Cheap

by James J. Hester

As the result of intensive activity by the majority of American archeologists over the last decade, we now have in place a system of archeological site identification, recordation, and mitigation, or protection and preservation. This system has been sanctioned by historic preservation legislation and regulations and is enforced by a well-established state and federal bureaucracy. Termed "Cultural Resource Management," the system and those working within it have the responsibility of acting in the public interest. This assignment includes compliance with existing legislation and regulations—most specifically Section 106 of the National Historic Preservation Act of 1966 as amended—implementation of the Archaeological Resource Protection Act (PL 96-95), compliance with state and federal procurement regulations, adherence to a set of professional standards and ethics in the conduct of archeological investigations most specifically promulgated by the Society of Professional Archeologists, and a need to expend wisely the public monies available for these purposes.

We are now at a point where we can ask, how well is the system working? Federal and state agencies have dramatically increased their archeological staffing to meet the work load. Innumerable private archeological contracting firms have been established. In addition, in the late 1970s and early 1980s such firms have flourished and, subsequent to the 1982–1983 recession, gone bankrupt as well. With the worldwide glut of oil beginning in 1981, and the resulting decrease in energy development since that date, archeological contracting has fallen on hard times. A significant associated aspect has been an increased emphasis on projects being awarded to the lowest bidder.

Increasingly, archeological contractors are becoming aware that if they are to survive and remain in business they must shave their bids to unrealistically low levels. This situation is reflected in a number of ways. Disappointed bidders who are priced out of the market claim that low bids result in a low number of sites being identified. Whereas this is at the level of hearsay, it is a common theme that is stated by different contractors with reference to different projects on which they bid and have specific knowledge concerning the conditions of the Request for Proposal and the archeology of the project area. Such an allegation can be refuted only by resurveying the project area.

A second concern is that only underqualified or minimally qualified people are selected for CRM projects because they are willing to work more cheaply. The concern here is not just with federally funded projects but even more critically those projects that are funded by private industry. In industry the concern is to produce a product at the lowest possible price in order to compete in the marketplace. No matter whether the product is gas, oil, uranium, or irrigation water, the producer views the associated archeological costs as a detriment in the competitive market. If we may assume that such cost cutting is a reality in CRM, then what are its negative effects?

One of the first items to be eliminated is employee fringe benefits. Archeologists are, quote, "temporary employees" working on short-term contracts and are not eligible for employee benefit packages; the nonpayment of such benefits, therefore, represents a cost saving to the employer and ultimately the client. However, the temporary jobs so created and their continued sanction by low bids doom the archeological practitioner to a career as an itinerant worker similar to that of a lettuce picker. Whereas many young and single individuals enjoy the field experiences associated with doing archeology and may at age twenty-five not particularly mind temporary employment, as the individuals age and acquire spouses, children, and mortgages they may find that archeology as a permanent career has little to offer. Here we can ask, does a profession which does not provide a permanent future career for its practitioners constitute a true profession? As things stand at the moment, archeology does not provide the employee benefits one expects of a true profession. The payment of unemployment insurance is viewed as a burden rather than protection for the employee. The employee often has no medical plan, sick leave, or other routine fringe benefits. Finally, the low contract amounts provide no financial cushion for the firm to exist on between contracts. In fact, if the firm has a pension plan for employees, it often must be cashed in in order to bridge the gap between contracts. This line of reasoning documents the need for higher contract amounts rather than the lower amounts resulting from underbidding.

Where else can we detect the unfortunate effects of cost cutting? When clients buy the cheapest product they are probably willing to hire anyone who promises to deliver the product. When selection is applied in terms of price, the first to be eliminated are those who are the most qualified and therefore the most expensive, i.e., those with the best professional credentials. This certainly was the case during the summer of 1984. Tenured university professors with long experience in CRM were idle while their own graduate students were fully employed. Another manifestation is that when layoffs were initiated in private consulting firms the highest paid staff members were laid off first. One such person in Colorado was the former State Archeologist, which suggests that salary level was a more likely causal factor for his release than a lack of credentials.

Another factor concerns the nature of the bidding process itself. When a fixed contract amount is specified, the bidder who promises the most gets the contract. At a later date the successful bidder may not produce the promised product or may renegotiate a higher contract price. An outstanding example concerns the Piñon Canyon expansion area of the Ft. Carson Army base. The initial review identified one proposal as superior to all others in scientific design. Approximately a year and a half later, after two field seasons, the winning principal investigator was removed from the project and not replaced, and the contract amount was increased from $566,576 to $1,513,369. Whereas this is a very complex situation and many factors are involved that are not relevant to this paper, it does provide food for thought.

On another project, the best scientific proposal was considered too expensive and was disqualified. By the time the field season was underway, the winning bidder had subcontracted with the person who had written that "best" proposal as a means to enhance the scientific quality of the work being done. Here we have the first bidder being placed in double jeopardy, being officially disqualified but unofficially recognized as most competent, responsible for the scientific quality of the report, but not in charge of the budget.

Other horror stories illustrate other aspects of the problem. A Forest Service survey in the Olympic National Forest was estimated to cost $1.5 million but the successful bid was $125,000. In this case the winning bidder simply did not realize that the area was covered with impenetrable rain forest. However, the agency accepted the bid.

Another case concerns a Forest Service contract requiring the excavation of twenty-five one-meter-square test pits. The winning low bid was equal to the per diem costs for the crew. Because the contractor was operating an archeological field school, he simply extended the term of the field school without paying the crew. All equipment belonged to the university that sanctioned the field school.

At Mesa Verde National Park, a contract-winning proposal promised to accurately locate and map nine hundred sites for $40,000, which equals $44.44 per site. At $5 per hour, only nine hours would be spent per site. Another contract required the recording of the plaster in six hundred cliff dwellings for $19,000, or $31.67 per site. If we assume one worker at $5 per hour and a supervisor at $10 per hour, then two hours could be spent on each site. If we assume logistical costs would be 40 percent of the budget, then the time per site is reduced to 1.2 hours. Assuming a round trip time of one hour for access to each cliff dwelling, we are left with .2 hours per site for the actual recording time.

We may define underbidding as a deliberate attempt to secure a contract by means of systematically underestimating the true costs of a project. The reasons for such underbidding are several. They provide a means of minimal level employment, which is an alternative to no employment at all, a situation that Raab (1982) states even extends into the area of academic-based archeologists. Another purpose is to eliminate the competition. When the contracting agency controls the funding, a low bid saves the agency money. The means by which projects are underbid include (1) promising to do more than can be done with the funds available; (2) hiring less well-qualified personnel; (3) producing a minimal product; (4) utilizing borrowed equipment and/or volunteer labor; and (5) providing no employee benefits. The results of underbidding are an inadequate product; a request for additional funding; or a requirement that the job be done over again.

An example of the latter fiasco concerns a large energy company developing a plant site in a western state. Their original contract for survey testing and mitigation of all sites within the one-square-mile tract was bid in at $200,000 by a PI prior to the conduct of any fieldwork. When the federal agency managing the lands rejected the survey report, it became clear that the PI had no field notes to substantiate the claim that minimal archeological remains were present. Faced with the agency's rejection of the original work, the client had to rebid the project. The resurvey documented almost continuing lithic scatters and burned rock; testing revealed the sites to be multicomponent with a depth of 1.5 meters. The new bids on the mitigation alone were between $600,000 and $1.2 million.

Here we have a case where the original underbidding caused the client to pay for the same product twice. Further, due to the delay, the second bidder had only a month to prepare a three-hundred-page research design and the client had to pay overtime to get the job done on schedule. Undoubtedly, another major result was the creation of much ill will toward archeology.

An additional problem concerns what may become a double standard. When industry is footing the bill and a federal agency must review and approve the work, it is possible to require high standards at a corresponding cost. When the agency funds its own projects, the agency simply states that it is paying $1.70 per acre, or some other unrealistically low figure. It is possible to put dots on a map for that amount but not much more. Can we honestly term such a practice Cultural Resource *Management*?

The solution to these problems would seem to lie within the purview of the State Archeologists and State Historic Preservation Officers. If these officials stand firm, require high standards of performance, and reject all work not up to those standards, then underbidding will cease to be the serious problem that it is today.

There is a growing literature expressing concern over the methods used and the results of cultural resource studies. Criticisms include a lack of problem definition, inadequate sampling, undue reliance on weak predictive models, the desire to identify areas of low site density, inadequate reporting of site information, lack of compliance with CRM laws and regulations, lack of publication of project results, use of volunteer labor, and absence of a peer review system. These critical comments have been made by King (1983, 1984a), Berry (1984), Brose (1984), Klesert (1984), Spencer (1984), Wendorf (1981?), Frison (1984), and Ambler (1984). There is also a growing literature defending some of these practices: King (1984b), Plog (1984), Hester (1984), and Brose (1984).

The reasons for these criticisms include more than underbidding; they include the desire to avoid sites (King 1983:147) and to write off areas of low site density (Berry 1984:851), the transfer of regulatory authority from federal to state agencies (Niquette 1984:834), the meeting of the needs of the client (Raab, Klinger, Schiffer, and Goodyear 1980), etc. We may thus perceive that the saving of inventory and mitigation costs is not the only reason for the conduct of inadequate cultural resource research. However, in all too many instances *cost cutting is achieved* by the implementation of these other self-reinforcing motives, and the loss of cultural resource information is the result.

We may conclude that the practice of underbidding directly contradicts the basic principles of archeological resource management as outlined by the Society for American Archaeology (Knudson 1982: 165-66):

    I. Archaeological materials and sites are unrenewable resources of significant value to our society as well as to the rest of the world, and merit affirmative protective management....

    II. Society should assure the wise use of these valuable resources to the best manner possible insofar as is compatible with other social needs (e.g., energy, food, shelter)....

    III. The United States Government, acting as and for the people of the nation, should assure the wise use of these resources as outlined in (II) on all properties and projects under federal control.

    IV. The United States Government, acting as and for the people of the nation, should join with other nations to assure the conservation and wise use of archaeological resources throughout the world and to suppress the illegal traffic in antiquities that threatens a world heritage base.

Viewed in this context, we thus perceive that underbidding consists of unethical behavior which directly violates the SOPA code of ethics (Davis 1982:161).[1] As a word of caution then, archeological resources will not be protected by the passage of legislative acts and regulations but by their implementation by professional archeologists guided by a strict code of ethics and standards.

Note

1. As stated in Davis (1982:161):
    1.2 An archeologist shall not:
        (a) Engage in any illegal or unethical conduct involving archeological matters or knowingly permit the use of her/his name in support of any illegal or unethical activity involving archeological matters;
        (b) Give a professional opinion, make a public report, or give legal testimony involving archeological matters without

being as thoroughly informed as might reasonably be expected;
(c) Engage in conduct involving dishonesty, fraud, deceit, or misrepresentation about archeological matters;
(d) Undertake any research that affects the archeological resource base for which he/she is not qualified.

References

Ambler, J. Richard
    1984   The Use and Abuse of Predictive Modeling in Cultural Resource Management. *American Archeology*, Vol. 4, No. 2, pp. 140–46.

Berry, Michael S.
    1984   Sampling and Predictive Modeling on Federal Lands in the West. *American Antiquity*, Vol. 49, No. 4, pp. 842–53.

Brose, David S.
    1984   The Modern Modal Model Muddle, or Some Comments on the King and Plog Explication. *American Archeology*, Vol. 4, No. 2, pp. 96–97.

Davis, Hester A.
    1982   Professionalism in Archaeology. *American Antiquity*, Vol. 47, No. 1, pp. 158–63.

Frison, George C.
    1984   The Carter/Kerr-McGee Paleoindian Site: Cultural Resource Management and Archaeological Research. *American Antiquity*, Vol. 49, No. 2, pp. 288–314.

Hester, James J.
    1984   Response to King's "Has Conservation Really Helped?" SAA Plenary Session on Conservation Archeology. SAA 49th Annual Meeting, Portland, Oregon.

King, Thomas F.
    1983   Professional Responsibility in Public Archaeology. *Annual Review of Anthropology*, Vol. 12, pp. 143–64.
    1984a   Has Conservation Really Helped? Paper presented at the SAA 49th Annual Meeting, Portland, Oregon.
    1984b   The OSMPMOA is Coming. *American Archeology*, Vol. 4, No. 2, pp. 83–88.

Klesert, Anthony L.
  1984   Federal Coal Mine Archeology and the Radicalization
          of a Moderate: A Reply to Plog and King. *American Ar-
          cheology,* Vol. 4, No. 2, pp. 102–5.
Knudson, Ruthann
  1982   Basic Principles of Archaeological Resource Manage-
          ment. *American Antiquity,* Vol. 47, No. 1, pp. 163–66.
Niquette, Charles M.
  1984   Lands Unsuitable for Mining: A Kentucky Example.
          American Antiquity, Vol. 49, No. 4, pp. 834–41.
Plog, Fred
  1984   The McKinley Mine and the Predictive Model Limited
          Survey Approach: The Archeology of Red Herrings.
          American Archeology, Vol. 4, No. 2, pp. 89–95.
Raab, L. Mark
  1982   Cultural Resource Management in the University: Get-
          ting What We Deserve. *Journal of Field Archeology,* Vol.
          9, pp. 126–28.
Raab, L. Mark, Timothy C. Klinger, Michael B. Schiffer, and Albert C.
Goodyear
  1980   Clients, Contracts and Profits: Conflicts in Public Ar-
          chaeology. *American Antiquity,* Vol. 82, No. 3, pp. 539–51.
Spencer, Jean
  1984   Another Fieldworker's Perspective. *American Archeology,*
          Vol. 4, No. 2, p. 160.
Wendorf, Fred
  1981(?) A Report to the United States Army Corps of Engineers
          in Fulfillment of Contract No. DACW63-81-AS-M-0481.
          7 pp.

The Collaborative Approach to Rescue and Conservation: The Case of Salango

by Presley Norton

The section of the Central Ecuadorian Coast between Puerto Cayo and Ayampe, including the islands of Salango and La Plata, has been the subject of study by members of the Salango Research Centre since 1978. Their work has revealed that this area has been inhabited by man more or less continuously since at least 3500 B.C. and that until the populations' obliteration by the diseases introduced by the Spaniards in the early part of the sixteenth century A.D., the cultural development followed what would appear to be a smooth continuum.

The earliest radiocarbon dates so far obtained at Salango are associated with the Valdivia III phase (2700 B.C.). At that time, the populations lived in scattered permanent or semipermanent nuclear settlements, on river estuaries or on spurs overlooking alluvial floodplains. Throughout the preconquest period, such locations were favored for settlement and primary ritual centers. The relative paucity of suitable sites contributed to the continual reuse of existing sites, which has resulted in the enormous depth of stratigraphy encountered by the Salango Research team in the course of its excavations (Norton *et al.* 1983). The prehistoric groups maintained an egalitarian social structure and subsisted almost entirely on hunting, fishing, gathering, and shifting cultivation.

Over the next five thousand years the populations developed into complex hierarchical mercantile chiefdoms whose wealthy elite depended primarily upon maritime trade in order to maintain their economy. The government of the incipient state, known to early Spanish chroniclers as Salangame, was centered on four urban complexes that existed between modern Machalilla in the North and Salango Village in the South. At the time of the Spanish Conquest this merchant elite of Salangame also controlled the Ecuadorian Coast from the Esmeraldas River to Ayampe (Norton 1984a).

201

Various stimuli led to the development of such societies:

1) Geographical position: the major settlements were situated in optimum locations for both maritime and inland trade as well as for good agricultural land.

2) The presence of balsa wood *(Ochroma lagopus)*, indigenous to the area: the wood's properties enabled the building of oceangoing sailing rafts with capacities of up to twenty-five tons and more (Norton 1984a). Using these vessels, the people could trade as far south as Chile and as far north as Acapulco (Estrada 1965; Heyerdahl 1955, 1961; Holm 1964, n.d.; Jijón y Caamaño 1954; Marcos 1977–78; Rostworowski de Diez Canseco 1970; Lothrop 1932; Lathrap 1973).

3) The local abundance of the *Spondylus princeps* and *Spondylus calcifer bivalves*: the shells were valued by successive civilizations from Mesoamerica to the Central Andes of Peru for esthetic and ritual purposes and as a means of exchange. Recent excavations indicate that La Plata Island and the section of the Coast from Puerto Cayo to Salango Village were important centers for the collection and initial working of *Spondylus* from at least 1500 B.C. (Norton 1981; Marcos and Norton 1979–81a; Norton and Marcos n.d.). This may have influenced the development of Salangame as a ceremonial center, with Salango Island, referred to in the chronicle of Samano (Samano 1842–95), as the focus.

Surveys and excavations carried out by the Salango Research Centre under the auspices of the Programa de Antropología para el Ecuador have revealed the four urban complexes of the Integration Period (800–1500 A.D.): ceremonial centers, elite cemeteries, a major *Spondylus* workshop, and numerous nuclear village settlements throughout the study area of twelve hundred square kilometers.

The main problems facing the work of the Centre are the destructive effects of natural phenomena, and of man, on the local archeological remains. Severe floods devastated much of the Ecuadorian Coast during 1982 and 1983. Many archeological sites were destroyed, those on alluvial flats and estuaries being particularly vulnerable to washout. Because the majority of prehistoric settlements were situated in such areas, the problem was critical, although rescue work was carried out wherever possible, and one major site (OMJPSL141C) was discovered after exposure by the deluge.

In addition to the direct effects of the flooding, many sites have been temporarily obscured by the sudden abundant increase of dense vegetation stimulated by the rains. While this has had the advantage of protecting sites from vandalization by treasure hunters, it has also severely impeded fieldwork and may do so for many years to come. During the

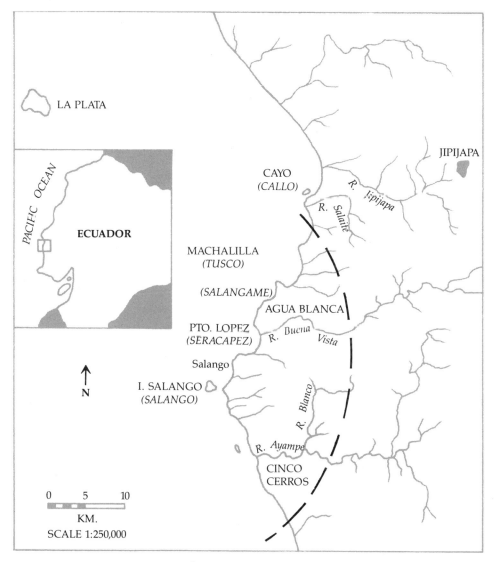

SEÑORIO DE SALANGAME

rather more prevalent and extensive dry periods, sites located in the scrub and arid savannah grassland (*secale*) ecozones are subject to aeolian erosion because the vegetation cover on light sandy soils is so thin that it affords little protection to underlying deposits.

The annual climatic cycle in the Salango area normally comprises two seasons, each of approximately six months duration. The dry season is characterized by intense insolation with intermittent squalls. The remaining half of the year is known as the *garúa* season, when atmospheric humidity is high and the coastline is shrouded in a bank of wet fog. Certain montmorillonitic clays, such as those on La Plata Island, have a tendency to swell and heave when wet and to shrink and crack when dry. The marked seasonal fluctuations of humidity to which these soils are exposed mean that this expansion and contraction occurs at least twice a year and can severely disturb deposits.

Ecuador lies on a major faultline, and earth tremors are relatively common, three of which affected the Coast of Ecuador, including Salango, between November 1983 and June 1984. Although a severe earthquake has not occurred since 1948, Ecuador is sufficiently prone to tremors to make the likelihood a problem for the conservation of archeological remains.

The effects of man on the archeological heritage of the Salango area have been less cataclysmic but possibly more damaging than the more spectacular natural disasters.

Salango Village is dominated by a fishmeal plant that is situated on deposits of stratified archeological material that reach depths of at least five meters. By agreement with the plant managers, a team from the Centre has excavated a six-square-meter trench (Site OMJPSL141A) to Valdivia levels within the yard of the plant and has opened up a larger area (Site OMJPSL141B) that it is proceeding to excavate using stratigraphic techniques. Site OMJPSL141B is scheduled for development as a warehouse extension to the existing plant, while OMJPSL141A was situated in what is now an access roadway. Excavations have revealed a ritual area containing adobe structures and elite burials, which would have been lost to posterity had not a team of archeologists, in conjunction with sympathetic management, been able to temporarily arrest development in order to rescue the artifacts and make a scientific recording of deposits.

Between Salango and Rio Chico, a distance of some five kilometers, the main coastal highway follows a contour that is also an ecozonal boundary. The contour appears to have been favored for settlement by prehistoric communities, as evidenced by modern road cuts through several occupation deposits. Because the road was constructed before the Salango Research Centre established itself in the area, it was not possible to save the entire sites. In addition, sites are constantly being lost as the road is widened or repaired after rains. However, remnants of exposed sites have been surveyed and mapped as thoroughly as possible by members of the project.

Most construction in the area occurs in the form of private housing or cooperative ventures by the various official groups, such as the new church being built in Salango Village. The structure overlies deposits dating to the Late Valdivia period. In some cases, it is possible to put in test pits prior to the commencement of building, but the Salango Research Centre is limited in both manpower and resources. Small construction projects are numerous, and the villagers do not always have the time, the funds, or the interest to await such events. Fortunately for long-term preservation, modern living structures tend to have shallow foundations, and archeological deposits may simply be obscured, not destroyed.

Unlike areas with intensive mechanized agricultural programs that employ deep ploughing techniques, the traditional methods of slash-and-burn cultivation practiced in the Salango area have, in themselves, little effect on subsurface deposits. However, vegetation clearance on slopes, particularly during extremes of either drought or heavy rain, can cause erosion or gullying that will contribute to the disturbance of archeological remains. This is especially true during periods of extended drought, when the demand for land increases, the period of fallow decreases, and the soil structure weakens. In recent times mechanization has been introduced by wealthier individuals who use machines primarily to clear larger tracts of land, and it is possible that such activity may scatter artifacts lying near the surface, thus distorting the record.

The most damaging of man's activities to the archeological heritage of Salango (and indeed of Latin America) is undoubtedly the willful and illegal destruction of the patrimony by treasure hunters or *huaqueros*. These people are highly skilled in the location of prehistoric sites from which they remove objects of maximum contemporary market value. The desecrated sites, usually tombs, are left as gaping holes, with the surrounding stratigraphy disturbed and relics considered to be of no intrinsic value tossed aside or broken. The *huaquero* is more often than not only the first in a long line of mercenaries who trade in artifacts solely for financial gain. The objects are sold on the black market to tourists or to connoisseurs, collectors, and even museums. Beginning with the pillaging by the Spanish in the sixteenth century, *huaquerismo* has resulted in the loss of unaccountably large amounts of priceless information regarding the pre-Columbian societies of Latin America. In the area of Ecuador covered by the Salango Research Centre, *huaquerismo* has long been a result of ignorance and poverty. The attraction of large sums of easy money to a people whose material standards of living are low, coupled with a lack of education regarding their national heritage, has resulted in a certain laissez faire attitude toward the numerous sites on their land. With the establishment of the Salango Research Centre by the Programa de Antropología para el Ecuador in 1978, it became apparent that the *in situ* archeology could be as valuable in its own way as the artifacts that were sold on the black market. Local people were also made fully aware of the illegality of *huaquerismo* by the presence of an official body of archeologists who actively discouraged such trade.

The Salango Research Centre, then, in addition to carrying out its own long-term research aims, pursues an active policy of rescue and conservation of the archeological patrimony of the Central Ecuadorian Coast. In addition to those aspects of its work mentioned above, the Centre carries out its policies in two principal ways:

I) *Information Retrieval*

By carrying out extensive survey and mapping exercises on the islands of La Plata and Salango and on the mainland between Machalilla and Ayampe, the majority of prehistoric sites in the vicinity have been recorded so that basic information on spatial patterning and settlement densities is available.

The highly accurate stratigraphic approach to excavation employed by the Centre (Harris 1979) is being used to establish the first reliable chronological sequence for pre-Columbian coastal deposits in central Ecuador. This, in addition to C14 and thermoluminescence, should help to date all similar artifacts, particularly ceramics, including those already in museum collections.

Every site excavated by competent specialists is a site rescued from possible oblivion. The Salango Research Centre acts as a base for the fieldwork of several excavation and survey teams. There is a permanent field staff at the Centre, which means that a greater amount of material can be collected per annum than is usual in field projects of this nature.

The installation of computer facilities at Salango will allow for the complete storage of the large body of scientific data that has been accumulated by the project over the past seven years.

II) *Education*

The role of education in rescue archeology is of major importance, especially in Latin America, where there are few field archeologists and fewer suitable facilities for student training. In recognition of this need, the Salango Research Centre will undertake a program designed to train students and volunteers of both North and South America in all aspects of practical field archeology appropriate to tropical prehistory, and plans are underway to develop the Centre into a field school. A number of local people are employed by the Centre as part of its work force and are included in the existing educational program.

Excavations are always open to interested parties, and frequent visits are paid by organized high school and college groups, which are given extensive guided tours by the Centre staff.

An exhibition entitled "*Cambio y Continuidad en Salango,*" incorporating all results of the work until June 1984, is at present in the Banco del Pacífico museum in Guayaquil. Together with associated publications (Norton 1984b, Norton *et al.* 1984), the exhibition focuses on the archeology of the area and not merely on the spoils and treasure troves of the past. After touring Ecuador, the exhibition will be housed permanently in a small museum to be built at the Centre in Salango.

In presenting for consideration what is being done at Salango, there is no attempt to set up a model. Every rescue problem is sui generis, and in almost every case a unique response is required. Salango is merely one situation where the collaborative approach seems to be working. In the United States or Canada it would slip by almost unnoticed. But in Latin America, where governments are doing practically nothing to stop the destruction of archeological sites, the Centre demonstrates that when there is no response in the *public* sector, an effective initiative can be generated from the *private* sector.

The institutional base for the rescue effort at Salango is the Programa de Antropología para el Ecuador, a private, research-oriented Ecuadorian foundation that runs the Salango Research Centre. The Programa de Antropología has no permanent endowment or fixed government subsidy. Its research is supported primarily through specific grants, contributions, and voluntary labor. Thus, a private Ecuadorian foundation serves as a catalyst in this particular case to pull together and marshall support derived from five different areas: the Ecuadorian public sector, the Ecuadorian private sector, an international body, non-Ecuadorian nonprofit foundations, and the labor of individual volunteers.

In the public sector, the Banco Central del Ecuador, through its archeological museums, has provided unprogrammed support during the past two decades for archeological fieldwork in Ecuador. From 40 to 50 percent of the Salango Research Centre's annual operating budgets have been covered by the Banco Central.

Two Ecuadorian private corporations have also made substantial contributions. The Banco del Pacífico, Ecuador's largest commercial bank, and Norlin International, a company that owned and operated breweries in Ecuador, underwrote specific aspects of the research.

On two occasions the Organization of American States has provided grants to support students in the field from its regional education funds. With the initiation of a formal field school, OAS support will be intensified and extended to technical consultancies.

Two nonprofit foundations have actively supported the Salango Research Centre's activities. Earthwatch of Belmont, Massachusetts, has supported the project financially since 1978; they have also sent teams of volunteers to work in the field for three-week stints. In 1982, the Centro de Studi Ligabue of Venice, Italy, made a generous, unearmarked grant to the project.

The constant participation of individual students and volunteers, for periods of up to one year, has enabled the research team at Salango to meet its objectives in spite of a relatively modest budget. In this category the work of a permanent staff can also be included, as salaries at Salango are little more than symbolic.

At Salango, long-term research, rescue and conservation, field training, and public education are being successfully combined thanks to a multi-tiered support structure that at times is a little reminiscent of "The Perils of Pauline." For those who would point out that the situation is far from ideal we at Salango can only answer that, though we are not quite sure how or why, it works.

References

Estrada, Emilio
    1965   Balsa and Dugout Navigation in Ecuador. *The American Neptune*, Vol. 40, No. 2.

Harris, E. C.
    1979   *Principles of Archaeological Stratigraphy*. New York: Academic Press.

Heyerdahl, Thor
    1955   The Balsa Raft in Aboriginal Navigation off Peru and Ecuador. *South Western Journal of Anthropology*, Vol. 2, No. 3, pp. 251–64.

1961 Archaeology in the Galapagos Islands. *California Academy of Science*, Vol. 44, pp. 45–51.

Holm, Olaf
1964 Las Islas Galápagos en la Prehistoria Ecuatoriana. *Casa de la Cultura Ecuatoriana*. Guayaquil.
n.d. La Navegación Precolombiana. (Análisis de una leyenda.)

Jijón y Caamaño, Jacinto
1954 Antropología Prehispánica del Ecuador. Quito.

Lathrap, Donald W.
1973 The Antiquity and Importance of Long-Distance Trade Relationships in the Moist Tropics of Pre-Columbian South America. *World Archaeology*, Vol. 5, No. 2, pp. 170–86.

Lothrop, Samuel K.
1932 Aboriginal Navigation off the West Coast of South America. *Journal of the Royal Anthropological Institute*, Vol. 62, pp. 266–99.

Marcos, Jorge G.
1977–78 Cruising to Acapulco and Back with the Thorny Oyster Set. *Journal of the Steward Anthropological Society*, Vol. 9, No. 1–2, pp. 99–132.

Marcos, Jorge G. and Presley Norton
1979–81a From the Yungas of Chinchay Suyo to Cuzco: The Role of La Plata Island in *Spondylus* Trade. 43rd International Congress of Americanists. Vancouver, Canada.
1979–81b Interpretación sobre la Arqueología de la Isla de La Plata. *Miscelánea Antropológica Ecuatoriana*, Vol. 1, pp. 136–54.

Norton, Presley
1981 Excavaciones en la Isla de La Plata. In *Ecuador Nubes y Selva*. Venice: Centro de Ricerce Ligabue.
1984a The Chiefdom of Salangame and the League of Merchants. In *New Models for the Political Economy of Pre-Columbian Politics*. Edited by P. Netherly and D. Freidel. New York: Academic Press.
1984b Salango en la Prehistoria. *Cromos*. Guayaquil.

Norton, Presley, R. Lunniss, and N. Nayling
1983 Salango, Informe de Progreso. *Miscelánea Antropológica Ecuatoriana*.
1984 Cambio y Continuidad en Salango. *Cromos*. Guayaquil.

Norton, Presley and Jorge G. Marcos

n.d.   La Plata, Informe Final.
Rostworowski de Diez Canseco, M.
    1970   Mercaderes del Valle de Chincha en la Epoca Prehis-
                tórica. *Revista Española de Antropología*, Vol. 5, pp. 135–77.
Samano, Juan
    1842–95   Relación Samano-Xerez (1525). In *Colección de Documen-
                tos Inéditos para la Historia de España*. Edited by Martín
                Fernández, *et al.*, Vol. 5, pp. 193–201.

Archeological Mitigation of the Darien, Georgia, Sewer System

by Martin F. Dickinson & Lucy B. Wayne

Archeological mitigation conducted in conjunction with construction of the new sewer system in Darien, Georgia, provides an example of many of the ideas discussed during the Dallas conference.

The Darien project is an excellent example of a set of conditions for which the federal cultural resource legislation and funding process was developed. Darien, Georgia, is an area containing significant archeological resources that will be impacted by development. But the community involved lacks the financial resources required to conduct even minimal archeological research. The community of contemporary Darien resides atop a historic, archeological record which is the property of the public at large. Darien, as the steward of this resource, cannot carry the burden within the limits of local resources. Thus, the federal laws that require cultural resource studies in conjunction with federally funded construction provide possibly the only opportunity to study, protect, and rescue the resources and information inherent in significant archeological properties.

The Darien project also points out the importance of the many factors impinging upon major construction activities using public funding. These factors include the following: 1) The need to prioritize the sites to be studied because of time and budget constraints. These priorities should be related to regional and national research interests in order to make maximal use of the available funds and of the effort to retrieve information, not available in any other way, that may contribute to an understanding of the history of the sites. 2) Since the project is publicly funded, it is vital to provide full information to the public. This will result in an increase of public awareness of the importance of the resources; a spirit of cooperation and a positive attitude on the part of the public; public contributions to the project in the form of oral/written history and, at times, volunteer participation; and a sense within the local citizenry that the basic goals of the program are worthwhile. 3) Education and involvement of the engineer and the contractor can lead to avoidance of delay or disruption of either archeological

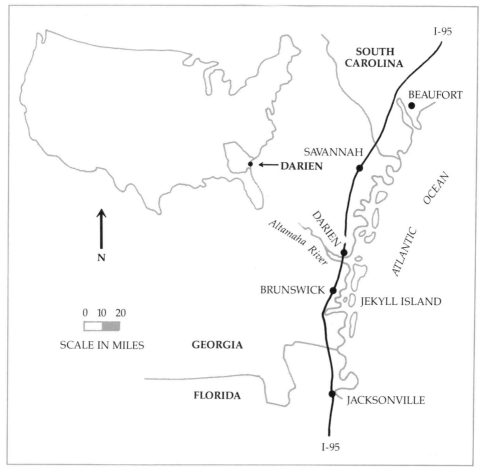

FIGURE 1. **General Location of Darien, Georgia**

studies or construction. In most projects, this involvement can also lead to protection of the resources through redesign or carefully planned construction techniques.

The Darien archeological project involved a three-phase program tied to the improvement of public utilities in a town of approximately 1,800 people. Darien serves as the county seat of McIntosh County (figure 1). This coastal county has one of the lowest income bases in Georgia with an economy based on commercial fishing and timber byproducts. It also happens to be situated in a spot that is historically and archeologically one of the richest portions of the Georgia coast.

In 1983, the town began the initial phases of the construction of its first municipal sewer system. This project will have a major impact on both the economy and the cultural resources of the area. The economic impacts include the cost of the project, which is largely funded through a combination of federal grants and loans by EPA and FHA; the availability of temporary jobs related to the construction activities; and the increased potential for future industrial/commercial development tied to the availability of a sewer system.

The cultural resource impacts consist of the potential destruction of those portions of the resources that lie within the sewer corridors; a major contribution to regional knowledge; and the potential for providing data that will enhance the area's attractiveness for development as the result of enhancement of knowledge of Darien's history as a community.

Because the sewer project is largely federally funded, existing legislation required the excavation and management of cultural resources as part of the project. This situation results in a certain amount of conflict between development and preservation interests regarding the expenditure of the rather limited funds available to the city. Archeological studies were conducted to make the most efficient use of these funds and to provide a major contribution to an understanding of the area's cultural history. This required close coordination with the design engineers, the city of Darien, and the construction contractor, as well as complete justification for each stage of the archeological project in terms of time restrictions and costs.

To understand the nature of the archeological project in Darien, a brief description of the environmental and cultural setting is necessary. Darien is located on the mainland proper of the Georgia coast (figure 1). To the east is an extensive area of tidal creeks, lagoons, marshes, barrier islands, and the Atlantic Ocean. The Altamaha and Darien rivers, with their associated wetlands, are located to the south. The mainland topography is characteristically low relict sand ridges. Darien is located at the southern end of one of these relict ridges. Natural vegetation consists of coastal pine and hardwood hammock with pockets of pine/palmetto flatwoods associated with poorly drained areas.

Potential human subsistence resources are substantial. The vast marine and estuarine systems to the south and east provide an abundance of fish and shellfish. These are supplemented by extensive upland resources (such as nuts, deer, small mammals, reptiles, and birds) to the north and west. These subsistence resources, the comparatively high elevation, and an access to a navigable waterway have made Darien a highly desirable location throughout prehistoric and historic periods.

There is archeological evidence of human occupation in the Darien area dating to the Late Archaic or Sapelo period about 4,500 years ago. Aboriginal occupation continued up through European contact. During the late sixteenth century, the Spanish mission of Tolomato was established at a Guale Indian village on the Darien Lower Bluff area. Spanish presence lasted until 1670 when English raids brought an end to the mission system in Georgia.

The English established Fort King George on the same Lower Bluff area in 1721; it was abandoned in 1727. The present town of Darien was established just to the west in 1736 by Scots Highlanders recruited by General James Oglethorpe. The town plan was provided by Oglethorpe and remains largely intact today.

By the early nineteenth century, Darien was a thriving port and commercial center for the rice and sugar plantations of the Altamaha delta. Although Darien contained the largest bank in the South during the 1830s, this prosperity dwindled during the 1840s to 1850s. The town was almost burned in 1863 during the Civil War. After the war, it was rebuilt with an economy based on the timber industry. The city was a major timber center and port until the end of the nineteenth century. A severe hurricane in 1898 coincided with a dwindling supply of timber, ending Darien's last boom period. Since that time, Darien has been a quiet town dependent on commercial fishing and timber byproducts.

The present town has no real civic center. Commercial activities are concentrated along the major transportation routes, US 17 and the Darien River. Only the main roads are paved. Since 1865, the town has been characterized by the lack of clear socioeconomic divisions; residential areas consist of mixed racial and economic groups with little definite clustering. The lack of development or significant change in the town layout provides a situation in which archeological resources are largely undisturbed.

An archeological assessment in the form of construction monitoring conducted during the 1977 to 1978 modernization of Darien's public water system identified a number of potentially significant archeological sites, potentially sensitive areas, and a National Register of Historic Places archeological district. This information provided the basis for the archeological studies conducted prior to the 1983–85 sewer construction (figure 2).

In the fall of 1983, after sewer construction had begun outside the previously identified sensitive areas, we began an intensive subsurface survey utilizing a 12½-inch power auger to place screened tests at staggered ten-meter intervals. Test lines were based on engineering drawings for the sewer project plus consultation with the general contractor. The survey confirmed the presence of archeological remains throughout the town.

Upon completion of the survey, assessments of National Register significance were completed and priorities were established for mitigation of individual sites. The mitigation sites ranged in time from 2500 B.C. to the late nineteenth century. These areas were identified on a map provided to the engineer and contractor.

Due to various bureaucratic delays, mitigation was not begun until very late in the sewer project contruction. This resulted in delays and inconvenience for the contractor as well as in a certain amount of pressure on the archeologists from local officials. In order to facilitate construction, an agreement was reached with the Georgia State Historic Preservation Office (SHPO) whereby the archeologists coordinated directly with the general contractor. As soon as mitigation field activities were completed, construction areas were released by the archeologist to the contractor for sewer construction.

In order to optimize use of archeological mitigation funds and time, our methodology was oriented toward extensive use of power equipment. The first step of mitigation was consultation and coordination with the contractor as to the exact location and extent of construction impacts (figure 3). The legally surveyed sewer corridors consisted of twenty-foot wide construction right-of-ways plus twenty-foot wide temporary easements. Within these corridors, sewer excavations ranged from ten to twenty feet wide and up to twenty feet deep. Obviously, excavations of this scale could be expected to destroy any archeological remains encountered.

Once the actual impact area was established, a road grader or front-end loader was utilized under the direct supervision of the archeologist to remove the overburden of recently altered strata characteristic of urban roadside areas. This scraping required close coordination with the local utilities in order to avoid cutting shallow underground telephone, gas, and water lines.

Once the power scrape was completed, the exposed areas were

shovel scraped and examined by the archeological team to further identify possible features or artifact concentrations. The final step in mitigation was hand excavation of units at these locations. Two relatively
deep sites—an extensive prehistoric shell midden on Cathead Creek
and the Waterfront Site—required a change in methodology. Archeological features and structural remains were exposed in deep profiled
trenches, excavated by using a tracked "excavator" with a one-meter
wide bucket.

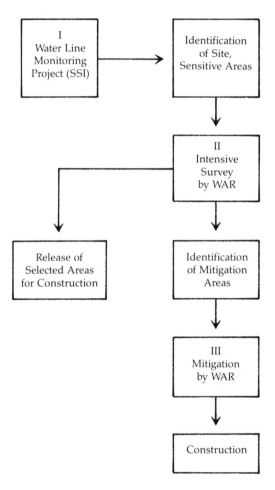

FIGURE 2. **Darien Sewer Project
Phases**

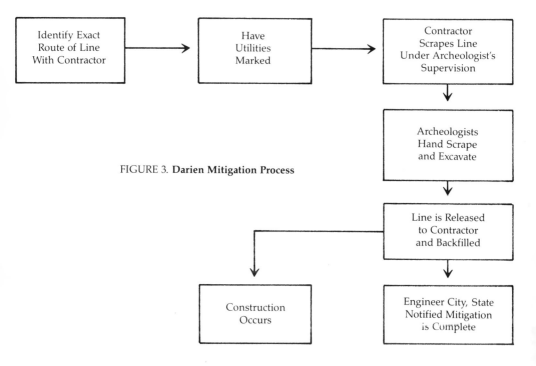

FIGURE 3. **Darien Mitigation Process**

All of the excavated sites are National Register eligible and provide significant information on the cultural history of Darien and the Georgia coast. However, the Waterfront Site is the most sensitive and may have a significant impact on future development in Darien. This site consists of a series of tabby (oyster shell, lime, and sand forming a concrete) ruins, which were once a combination of warehouses, shops, and taverns serving the shipping business. The structural remains date to the early nineteenth century and do not appear to have been rebuilt after the 1863 burning of Darien. Although there has been an extensive amount of surface disturbance or filling, the subsurface remains are largely undisturbed and represent one of the few opportunities to investigate early-nineteenth-century commercial activity associated with a waterfront during a relatively short time period. During the sewer project, close cooperation between the city, the engineers, the contractor, and the archeologists resulted in construction of the sewer lines in an area on the waterfront that would have minimal impact on the existing surface and subsurface structural remains. In addition, the data recovered by the archeological studies will facilitate planning for a proposed waterfront development incorporating the ruins. The artifacts recovered may also be used for exhibits in a museum which is part of the proposed waterfront redevelopment.

Completion of this project has highlighted a number of significant aspects of cultural resource management which can facilitate future public works projects.

1) All major projects would benefit by planning conferences at early stages. All involved parties should be included: engineers, archeologists, contractors, local government officials, and State Historic Preservation Officers. The goal of these meetings is to clarify for all concerned the exact expectations, goals, methodologies, and impacts of a project.

2) A close working relationship with the construction contractor was vital in terms of establishing the exact location of impacts, obtaining satisfactory power equipment operation, avoiding delays in either archeological work or construction, and minimizing resource impacts. The archeologists also learned from the contractor what was feasible from a construction standpoint.

3) Corridor projects have both limitations and benefits. It is often difficult to fully define site extents, and the portion of a site that is sampled may not have the best research potential. On the other hand, the narrow corridors do preserve a significant portion of large sites. Corridors, by the nature of their length, encounter a broad range of sites which can provide a more complete view of the area's cultural history.

4) Public relations play an important part in urban projects. This includes meetings with city personnel, the media, site visits by school students, and conversations with local residents. Effective use of these activities allowed us to avoid objections to working in residents' yards, to avoid delays necessitated by explaining what we were doing, to obtain substantial local historical information, and to provide the public an immediate return on the money being spent on archeology.

5) Public involvement after completion of the fieldwork is also important. The project is not really complete without some form of public presentation of project results. This may take the form of talks or slide shows, public meetings, or laymen's level publications.

In summary, the archeological studies for the sewer project may represent the only opportunity to study most of Darien's cultural resources. We believe this project is a perfect example of a situation for which the federal/state cultural resource legislation and funding was designed.

The Australian Experience: Rescue Archeology Down Under

by Josephine Flood

In Australia it is only over the past fifteen years that formalized cultural resource management has come into being, covering the conservation of archeological sites and artifacts. Government interests and legislation in the protection and control of archeological sites and relics did not materialize until the 1960s and came about through pressure from academics, museums, and concerned citizens groups aware of the alarming deterioration and loss rate of the cultural heritage through natural causes and human impact.

In response to this general concern to conserve our cultural heritage, legislation has been gradually enacted in all states of Australia. The federal/state division of authority in Australia has led to a proliferation of state laws—each one different—applying to archeological sites and artifacts. However, a general principle that has emerged is that all prehistoric relics and the sites containing them should be protected, whereas only selected historic sites should be afforded the same statutory protection.

Detailed discussion of legislation is beyond the scope of this paper, but references to such discussions are available. The state with perhaps the most comprehensive statutory protection for archeological sites is New South Wales, where three acts have relevance:

1) The National Parks and Wildlife Service Act of 1974, which relates to the protection of aboriginal relics, historic sites, and national parks;

2) The Heritage Act of 1977, which was established to "conserve the environmental heritage of the State" and covers "those buildings, works, relics or places, which are of historic, scientific, cultural, social, archeological, architectural, natural or aesthetic significance for the State"; and

3) The Environmental Planning and Assessment Act (1979)—statutory provisions for environmental impact assessment applying to all "activities," which are defined as public works or private works that require the approval of a public authority.

There is also a Federal Act—the Environment Protection (Impact of Proposals) Act (1974). This Act relies for its validity on the powers of Section 51 of the Constitution, which empowers the Commonwealth Government to take action with respect to "matters incidental to the execution of any power rested by the Constitution in the Commonwealth Parliament." The High Court has accepted this "implied power" that enables the Commonwealth Government to engage in enterprises and activities appropriate to the national government. The *National Parks and Wildlife Conservation Act 1975* is a good example of the operation of the Commonwealth's powers.

Environmental impact assessment is a technique used in every state, but only in Victoria and New South Wales is it controlled by legislation. Elsewhere, assessment remains a matter of government policy backed by administrative guidelines for its implementation. The Environment Protection (Impact of Proposals) Act is designed to improve consideration of environmental factors by decision makers through the use of the environmental impact statement and public inquiries.

In deciding to call for an environmental impact statement (EIS), the procedures in the Act require the Minister, or his department, to take into account whether the proposed action may result in

- (a) a substantial environmental effect on a community;
- (b) the transformation of a substantial area;
- (c) a substantial impact on the ecosystems of an area;
- (d) a significant diminution of the esthetic, recreational, scientific, or other environmental quality, or value, of an area;
- (e) an adverse effect upon an area, or structure, that has an esthetic, anthropological, archeological, architectural, cultural, historic, scientific, or social significance or other special value for the present or future generations;
- (f) the endangering, or further endangering, of any species of fauna or flora;
- (g) important long-term effects on the environment;
- (h) the degradation of the quality of the environment;
- (i) the curtailing of the range of beneficial uses of the environment;
- (j) the pollution of the environment;
- (k) environmental problems associated with the disposal of waste; or
- (l) increased demands on natural resources that are, or are likely to be, in short supply.

The past ten years have witnessed the growth of a vigorous conservation movement in all states, and invariably this has been accompanied by the enactment of some sort of environmental impact legislation, usually incorporating an archeological aspect. Environmental assessments have provided archeologists and anthropologists with jobs, and the growth of this aspect of archeology may be likened to a sunrise industry providing hope for employment and a future in the discipline for an increasing pool of young graduate archeologists.

The development of the environmental assessment aspect of archeology/anthropology has nevertheless had its problems. Because developers tend to require archeologists/anthropologists to do the minimum amount of work required in the shortest possible time, the results of environmental assessments often reflect haste and lack of academic context. Although consultant archeologists try to negotiate for more reasonable conditions, they must be prepared to compromise because they "need the job."

In this respect, an encouraging development in recent years has been the emergence of the Australian Association of Consulting Archeologists. This is a self-regulating, professional body, which has established a code of ethics, guidelines for report writing, model brief and contracts, and so forth, all leading to improved professional standards among archeologists.

Another important development has been the increasing need for archeologists to justify their recommendations, particularly when these involve changes in a client's plans and further expenditures for research. This has engendered a vigorous debate on how the significance of sites can best be determined. Early environmental assessments involving archeological sites tended to judge significance purely in terms of potential scientific significance. More recently, this simplistic approach has given way to more complex systems involving assessment of a variety of factors including educational and social aspects. While there can be no doubt that archeologists are the appropriate people to judge the potential research or scientific significance of archeological sites, other aspects must be taken into account.

The importance of environmental impact assessment legislation is that it enables the funding of archeological surveys and rescue archeology as required. However, this does not always happen, because of loopholes in the legislation or less-than-enlightened attitudes by state government officials and others.

The battle to save the archeological sites of Southwest Tasmania from the Franklin Dam is a good example of the need for archeological surveys to be funded by the developer at a very early stage in a project. In this case, the developer was the Hydro-Electric Commission of Tasmania, which spent A$770,000 on an Environmental Impact Assessment but funded no archeological surveys. It was due only to the initiative of archeologists from the Australian National University—Rhys Jones and Jim Allen—that the major ice age caves of the Franklin River were discovered. The belated discoveries of these sites were then denigrated by critics as a convenient "find" by desperate conservationists grasping at straws in order to stall progress. The implication was that the evidence was unimportant and that the archeologists were frauds. This insulting attitude is encountered frequently, but until necessary lead time, skilled personnel, and adequate funds are made available for archeological surveys well ahead of development projects, archeological discoveries will continue to be made inconveniently late, in front of the bulldozers.

Archeological concerns, both prehistoric and historic, should be assigned higher priority than that accorded at present both by government and industry. Archeology emerged as a force in Australia later than community recognition of other conservation issues, such as the National Trust movement or environmental conservation. In most states, archeological sites are commonly the last resource surveyed, and then only after planning decisions have been made by government or industry that ensure that the discoveries cannot alter project planning.

It is vital that the time-consuming processes of site location, recordation, investigation, and evaluation precede developmental projects by a time margin at least equal to that accorded flora and fauna surveys. Those entrusted with the task should be as qualified and as well funded as other scientists. The systematic identification, collation, and data processing of excavated finds, for example, require months more work after the fieldwork has ended.

The story of the lengthy but successful fight to save the World Heritage Area of Southwest Tasmania has been told elsewhere. The dispute was finally resolved in 1983 by a decision of the High Court of Australia that effectively halted the massive hydroelectric power project that would have flooded significant ecological and archeological resources in Southwest Tasmania. The High Court's decision not to allow the flooding of this World Heritage area has been hailed as the greatest environmental victory in Australian history. Whatever one thinks of the decision, it has had important effects on archeology in Australia. For the first time in the history of the discipline, Australian prehistoric archeological sites were thrust into the national and international limelight, thus considerably increasing public awareness of the potential importance of archeological sites.

The Tasmanian dispute also had the effect of underlining the need for survey and identification of archeological sites prior to development proposals. This prior identification of heritage sites is being tackled in several ways. First, there is the establishment of a public inventory of heritage places, the Register of the National Estate being compiled by the Australian Heritage Commission. The Commission came into operation in 1976. Its first priority was the establishment of a Register of the National Estate, defined in the Act as "those places, being components of the natural environment of Australia, or the cultural environment of Australia that have aesthetic, scientific or social significance or other special value for future generations, as well as for the present community."

The aims of compiling the Register are as follows:

1) Identification of the National Estate: We must identify and document what we have as the first step in the conservation of our heritage. The compilation of a Register of the National Estate has provided a strong stimulus to local, state, and national organizations to identify and record our heritage.

2) The Register as a planning tool: The Register lists places of national significance; thus it can be used as a planning tool and early warning system by government and private land managers and developers. A clear identification of the national estate has reduced conflict between conservationists and developers because now the latter can plan around places of heritage value.

3) Education of the public concerning heritage values: The compilation of a Register of the National Estate is increasing public consciousness of the value of our cultural background and natural surroundings. To this end, the Register has been made available to the public in a well-illustrated book form, and editions of the national estate places are now being published within each Australian state. The Register is also available to anyone on microfiche. The Register now includes some 13,000 places (and a huge National Park counts as just one place), but there are still many gaps and unsurveyed regions.

In this situation some of the major Australian developers, such as large mining companies, have found it useful to involve an archeologist from the very beginning of a project. Thus, as soon as an exploitable resource such as coal is located through exploration, an archeologist is engaged by the company as a consultant. The archeologist then works with the developers, identifying archeological sites, assessing their relative significance, and working with the developers to find ways of designing the project to avoid or minimize damage to archeological relics.

Unfortunately, the archeologists often are not brought in until a much later state, for example when much preliminary design work has already been done. Then, if major sites are found, redesign of the facilities to avoid these sites becomes a much more expensive proposition. For example, two uranium projects in the Kakadu National Park area of the Northern Territory were redesigned—after their draft E.I.S. had been published—in light of comments from archeologists, environmentalists, and local aborigines. One project changed from a huge open-cast to an underground mine; the other, a waste rock dump, was redesigned to avoid burying aboriginal sites.

Constantly, of course, sites have to be sacrificed to development. This happens frequently with pipelines, roadworks, railways, and reservoirs. The usual procedure is for the archeologist to make a detailed record of the site *in situ*, then remove the artifacts to the local or state museum. If burials are uncovered by development, the remains are usually removed to a museum for study, then given to the local aboriginal community for reburial in another locality.

Occasionally, a site cannot be salvaged in any way and must be sacrificed. This happened with the Argyle Diamond Project in Western Australia, where the diamond exposure itself was a sacred site of significance to local aborigines. In that instance the aboriginal community agreed to the destruction of the site in return for funding from the company for a variety of community projects.

In other situations, rescue archeology may be carried out to salvage sites that lie in the path of development. A recent notable example of this is the Dampier Archeological Project on the Burrup Peninsula in Western Australia. From a cultural and scientific point of view the Burrup archeological sites are among the most important in the world. This wealth of habitation sites (shell middens and artifact scatters) associated with rock engravings (more than one hundred thousand figures), stone arrangements, and quarries for stone flaking can compare with any of the most famous archeological wonders, such as the European prehistoric painted caves of Lascaux and Altamira, the Egyptian pyramids, or the Maya, Buddhist, or Greek temples of America, Asia, and the Mediterranean.

Moreover, the Burrup Sites have links to a still-living culture. The discovery of natural gas on the Northwest Shelf in 1971 stimulated a strong interest in the commercial development of the Burrup Peninsula. Prior to submitting an environmental review and management program to the W.A. Government, Woodside Offshore Petroleum commissioned the assistance of the W.A. Museum, and several preliminary surveys were undertaken. The Department of Aboriginal Sites was subsequently contracted by Woodside Offshore Petroleum to (1) assess the archeological sites occurring in a number of areas where the project's shore facilities and communication network might be established; (2) advise on the cultural importance of archeological features there; and (3) suggest the procedures whereby information pertaining to sites that may be disturbed could be catalogued and preserved. Reports of these investigations established the basis upon which Woodside commissioned the Museum to undertake the Dampier Archeological Project.

The Dampier salvage project was the largest ever carried out on archeological sites in Australia, and it was funded by the developer, Woodside Offshore Petroleum at a cost of about $750,000. The Australian Heritage Commission funded additional site survey and recording in the areas outside but adjacent to the area of direct impact. A full report is now being produced and will be available from the Western Australian Museum, Perth.

Australia has much to learn from the rest of the world with regard to rescue archeology but also, I hope, much to contribute to the international cause of heritage conservation.

Contributors

George A. Aarons is Technical Director of Archeology, Jamaica National Trust Commission, Kingston, Jamaica.

Steve Baker is Archeologist, Centuries Research, Inc., Montrose, Colorado.

Larry D. Banks is Southwestern Division Archeologist, U.S. Army Corps of Engineers, Dallas, Texas.

Ray Barnhart is Administrator, Federal Highway Administration, U.S. Department of Transportation, Washington, D.C.

Leopoldo José Bartolomé is Anthropologist, Entidad Binacional Yacyretá, Misiones, Argentina.

Eduardo D. Brenes is Jefe de la Dirección de Desarrollo Humano, Servicio Nacional de Riego y Avenimiento, San José, Costa Rica.

Robert J. Burton is District Archeologist, Fort Worth District, U.S. Army Corps of Engineers, Fort Worth, Texas.

Carl Chapman is Professor, Department of Anthropology, University of Missouri, Columbia, Missouri.

Igor Chmyz is Chefe de Departamento Psicología e Antropología, Universidade Federal de Paraná, Brazil.

Jacques Cinq-Mars is Chief, Rescue Archaeology Programme, Archaeological Survey of Canada, National Museum of Man, Ottawa, Canada.

Henry Cleere is Director, Council for British Archaeology, London, England.

Michael Collins is Professor, Department of Engineering, Southern Methodist University, Dallas, Texas.

María José Con is Coordinadora de Centros Regionales y Delegaciones del

227

Instituto Nacional de Antropología e Historia (INAH), Mexico City, Mexico.

Robert J. Dacey, Brigadier General, is Southwestern Division Engineer, U.S. Army Corps of Engineers, Dallas, Texas.

Martin F. Dickinson is with Water and Air Research, Inc., Gainesville, Florida.

Paul F. Donahue is Director, Alberta Culture Archaeological Survey, Old St. Stephen's College, Edmonton, Alberta, Canada.

John Driskill, Colonel (ret.), is Senior Vice President, Land Development, Las Colinas Corporation, Irving, Texas.

Bruce A. Eberle is Archeologist, Federal Highway Administration, Office of Environmental Policy, Washington, D.C.

Josephine Flood is Archeologist, Australian Heritage Commission, Canberra, Australia.

William L. Fullen is Program Director, The Wallisville Heritage Park, Wallisville, Texas.

Alberto Rex González is Director Nacional de Antropología y Folklore, Ministerio de Educación y Justicia, Buenos Aires, Argentina.

Sally Greiser is Research Archeologist, Historical Research Associates, Missoula, Montana.

George Gumerman is Professor, Department of Anthropology, Southern Illinois University, Carbondale, Illinois.

Ann Guthrie is Executive Director, Cultural Properties Advisory Committee, U.S. Information Agency, Washington, D.C.

George Hasseman is Archeologist, Instituto Hondureno de Antropología e Historia, Tegucigalpa, Honduras.

James J. Hester is Professor of Anthropology, Department of Anthropology, University of Colorado, Boulder, Colorado.

Harry Hutchens is Senior Vice President, Brown-Root Construction Company, Houston, Texas.

Bennie C. Keel is Assistant Director, National Park Service, Washington, D.C.

Ronald Kelsey, Lieutenant Colonel, is Chief of Engineers' Environmental Officer, U.S. Army Corps of Engineers, Washington, D.C.

Thomas F. King is Director, Office of Cultural Resource Preservation, Advisory Council on Historic Preservation, Washington, D.C.

Esther Kirkland is Assistant to the Minister of Public Works, Panama, Republic of Panama.

Ruthann Knudson is Director, Cultural Resource Services, Woodward-Clyde Consultants, Walnut Creek, California.

Leonard Lardavera is Consulting Archeologist, North American Coal Corporation, Dallas, Texas.

Donald Lathrap is Professor, Department of Anthropology, University of Illinois, Champaign-Urbana, Illinois.

James A. Lee is Director, Environmental & Scientific Affairs, The World Bank, Washington, D.C.

José Luis Lorenzo is Research Archeologist, Consejo de Arqueología, Instituto Nacional de Antropología e Historia (INAH), Mexico City, Mexico.

Gloria Loyola-Black is Chief, Technical Unit of Interdisciplinary Research, Department of Cultural Affairs, Organization of American States, Washington, D.C.

Hugo Ludeña is Director de Conservación del Patrimonio Cultural, Instituto Nacional de Cultura, Lima, Peru.

Darrell Mach is Chief of Planning, Bureau of Reclamation, U.S. Department of the Interior, Washington, D.C.

Jorge G. Marcos is Director, Escuela Superior Politécnica del Litoral (ESPOL), Guayaquil, Ecuador.

Betty J. Meggers is Research Associate, National Museum of Natural History, Smithsonian Institution, Washington, D.C.

Gary L. Melvin is Senior Manager, Environmental Group, Peabody Coal Co.—Arizona Division, Flagstaff, Arizona.

Michael Moseley is Professor, Department of Anthropology, University of Florida, Gainesville, Florida.

Presley Norton is Director Ejecutivo, Programa de Antropología para el Ecuador, Quito, Ecuador.

Lautaro Núñez is Professor, Departamento Arqueologío, Universidad del Norte, Antofagasta, Chile.

Víctor A. Núñez is Research Archeologist, Asociación Venezolana de Arqueologío, Maracaibo, Venezuela.

Miguel Orrego is Professor, Instituto de Antropología e Historia, Guatemala, Guatemala.

Lee Patterson is Manager, Environmental Affairs—Engineering, Tenneco, Inc., Houston, Texas.

Peter Patton is Associate Professor of Earth Sciences, Department of Earth and Environmental Sciences, Wesleyan University, Middletown, Connecticut.

Galo Plaza is Former President of Ecuador and Former Secretary General, Organization of American States, Quito, Ecuador.

L. Mark Raab is Assistant Professor, Department of Anthropology, California State University, Northridge, California.

Sapolo Artur Ramea is a social anthropologist in Argentina.

Jerry L. Rogers is Associate Director, National Park Service, U.S. Department of the Interior, Washington, D.C.

Barry G. Rought is Chief of Planning, Southwestern Division, U.S. Army Corps of Engineers, Dallas, Texas.

Mario Sanoja is Professor, Departamento de Arqueologío y Etnografía, Universidad Central de Venezuela, Caracas, Venezuela.

Donald Shields is President, Southern Methodist University, Dallas, Texas.

Victor Smirnoff is an architect in Lima, Peru.

Michael J. Snarskis is Director Ejecutivo, Asociación Aiqueologío de Costa Rica, San Pedro, Montes de Oca, Costa Rica.

Theodore Stroup, Colonel, is Fort Worth District Engineer, U.S. Army Corps of Engineers, Fort Worth, Texas.

Raymond H. Thompson is Director, Arizona State Museum, University of Arizona, Tucson, Arizona.

Harold Tso is with the Division of Natural Resources, Navajo Tribe, Window Rock, Arizona.

Iraida Vargas is Professor, Departamento de Arqueología y Etnografía, Universidad Central de Venezuela, Caracas, Venezuela.

Lucy B. Wayne is with Water and Air Research, Inc., Gainesville, Florida.

Ward F. Weakly (dec.) served as Archeologist, Engineering and Research Center, U.S. Bureau of Reclamation, Denver, Colorado.

Fred Wendorf is Henderson-Morrison Professor of Prehistory, Department of Anthropology, Southern Methodist University, Dallas, Texas.

Daniel Wolfman is Archeologist, Arkansas Archeological Survey, Arkansas Tech University, Russellville, Arkansas.

Carlos G. Zea-Flores.